Dear you...

With admiration,
love, and gratitude
for our long
friendship.

Don't feel you
have to read it
all!

XO

Rick

New Formalist Criticism

New Formalist Criticism

Theory and Practice

Fredric V. Bogel

Professor of English, Cornell University, USA

First published 2013 by
PALGRAVE MACMILLAN

Palgrave Macmillan in the UK is an imprint of Macmillan Publishers Limited, registered in England, company number 785998, of Houndmills, Basingstoke, Hampshire RG21 6XS.

Palgrave Macmillan in the US is a division of St Martin's Press LLC, 175 Fifth Avenue, New York, NY 10010.

Palgrave Macmillan is the global academic imprint of the above companies and has companies and representatives throughout the world.

Palgrave® and Macmillan® are registered trademarks in the United States, the United Kingdom, Europe and other countries.

ISBN 978–1–137–36258–2

This book is printed on paper suitable for recycling and made from fully managed and sustained forest sources. Logging, pulping and manufacturing processes are expected to conform to the environmental regulations of the country of origin.

A catalogue record for this book is available from the British Library.

A catalog record for this book is available from the Library of Congress.

Contents

Acknowledgments

This study has been a long time in the making. Its distant origins lie in an undergraduate seminar on modern critical theory taught at Dartmouth College by the late Frank Brady, and in a graduate seminar, Theories of Poetry, taught at Yale University by the late William K. Wimsatt. Between that time and the present, I have profited from generous conversations and written exchanges with a variety of colleagues and friends at Yale University, Connecticut College, The University of Washington, Cornell University, and elsewhere, including: M. H. Abrams, Charles Altieri, G. Thomas Couser, Jonathan Culler, Heather Dubrow, Michel Ferber, Debra Fried, John M. Fyler, Janet Gezari, H. Marshall Leicester, Marjorie Levinson, Douglas Mao, Neil Saccamano, Susan Sandman, the late Raman Selden, Mark Seltzer, James Simpson, J. Mark Speyer, and Susan Wolfson.

Over many years, I have also enjoyed the extraordinary stimulation of conversations in and out of the classroom with a remarkable group of undergraduate and graduate students, among whom I will single out for special thanks: Michael Barany, Mark Blackwell, Lauren Boehm, Colin Dewey, Ryan Dirks, Andrew Dreyfus, Sarah Ensor, Reed Flaschen, Richard Halpern, Elisa Jillson, Suvir Kaul, Jess Keiser, Sarah Senk, and Marty Wechselblatt.

My children have sustained and encouraged me throughout, in ways impossible to describe or count. In addition to their love and support, Alexander has provided an example of inspired teaching and literary analysis, including a timely and dazzling discussion of Raymond Carver's "Cathedral"; Liz has set the bar for lucid and eloquent prose dauntingly high; and Nicholas has shared his wonderful formalist reading of the conclusion of Thoreau's *Walden*.

Catherine has read everything, edited everything, improved everything. Far beyond this, she has been a continuing source of strength, joy, and love.

Ben Doyle, Commissioning Editor, and Sophie Ainscough, Editorial Assistant, at Palgrave Macmillan and Rajeswari Balasubramanian, Project Manager at Integra, have been swift, shrewd, supportive, and encouraging; I am very grateful to have worked with them. I also want to thank the anonymous reader of the manuscript for a thoughtful, detailed, informed, and encouraging report. Finally, this book adapts portions of an essay published in a collection edited by Verena Theile and Linda Tredennick, *New Formalisms and Literary Theory*, 2013, Basingstoke, UK: Palgrave Macmillan. The full published version of this publication is available from: http://www.palgrave.com/products/title. aspx?pid=579198 and http://www.palgraveconnect.com/pc/doifinder/ 10.1057/9781137010490

Introduction

Writing in the early 1970s, Paul de Man remarked:

> To judge from various recent publications, the spirit of the times is not blowing in the direction of formalist and intrinsic criticism. We may no longer be hearing too much about relevance but we keep hearing a great deal about reference, about the nonverbal "outside" to which language refers, by which it is conditioned and upon which it acts.[1]

In the roughly 40 years since de Man's comments, the spirit of the times has not changed direction sharply. From early feminism and Marxism to variations on historicist, ideological, and political criticism (stressing race, class, gender, and sexuality), to postcolonial studies, to New Historicism and cultural studies, and on to queer theory, cognitive science, and ecocriticism, the main tendencies of literary studies have remained historicist, referential, contextual. Although de Man sidesteps that now quaint motto of the 1960s, "relevance," it is clear that the pertinence of literary works to social, cultural, and historical contexts, and of those contexts to literary works, continues to be a central preoccupation of criticism and theory.

W. J. T. Mitchell acknowledges this, yet tells a counter-story as well. There are, he concedes, "reasons for thinking that literary scholars have, in the half century since the New Criticism was dominant, thought of themselves as moving beyond formalism into more capacious arenas like history, culture, and politics" yet "I think most people will recognize that the contrary story could be told as well, the one in which formalism keeps returning,... continues to rear its head, even when most fervently disavowed."[2] And in truth, a never-dormant array of formalist analyses and assumptions has acquired significant range, rigor, and complexity since those words were written, such that a critic could express in 2006 "the exciting feeling that formalism is really coming back, and not in its old, tired guises but in a whole range of reinvigorated and reinvigorating ways."[3] More recently still, Heather Dubrow – in her Foreword to *New Formalisms and Literary Theory*, a 2013 collection of contemporary essays – sketches this brief, recent genealogy of what she calls "the New Formalist turn":

> [C]alls for a New Formalism were issued as early as the 1990s. But that turn came into its own at the turn of the century and the decade that succeeded it, heralded and advanced by an issue of *Modern Language Quarterly*, by the volume that expanded that issue entitled *Reading for Form*, and by collections such as Mark David Rasmussen's *Renaissance Literature and its Formal Engagements* and Stephen Cohen's *Shakespeare and Historical Formalism*. Books published in that decade, notably Susan Wolfson's *Formal Charges*, by precept and example, advanced the development of New Formalism.[4]

One significant spur to the recent growth of New Formalist criticism, of course, is precisely distress that the formal and linguistic dimensions of texts have been glossed over in favor of content, reference, themes, ideas, and political or other "positions." To many, this preoccupation has seemed to sacrifice the category of form to a more fluent and facile discourse resting on paraphrase, content analysis, and ideological and political thematics. "Triumphant antiformalism," charges Herbert F. Tucker, has helped bring about a "serious dereliction: the enervation of literary close reading in critical practice." Tucker sees "widespread atrophy of a disused set of critical skills in whose revival – I almost said survival – a self-interested literary studies would do well to get actively involved."[5] Another prominent student of form, Ellen Rooney, complains that "reading has been displaced by a project of sorting by theme"; the work of formalism, she clarifies, is not a matter "of barring thematizations but of refusing to reduce reading entirely to the elucidation, essentially the paraphrase, of themes – theoretical, ideological, or humanistic."[6] Critics like Rooney worry, in Marjorie Levinson's words, that "we have come to treat artworks as 'bundles of historical and cultural content,' a simpleminded mimesis replacing the dynamic formalism that characterized early new historicism."[7] Or as Richard Strier puts it,

> The relation between formalism of any sort and new historicism in literary studies might be captured by the "use-mention" distinction familiar in the work of Quine and other analytic philosophers. Formalists are concerned with the uses to which details in literary (and other) texts are put.... New Historicism, like very old historicism, is concerned with mentions.[8]

As this comment suggests, moreover, the damage that inattention to form can inflict goes beyond the discipline of literary criticism. "The loss of the *work* of form should be the focus of our concern," writes Rooney, because "the extinction of an entire range of modes of formal analysis has eroded our ability to read *every genre of text* – literary texts, nonliterary texts, aural and visual texts, and the social text itself."[9]

Of course, formalism as a technique of textual analysis – "close reading," as it is often called – has never disappeared but continues to function in a variety of modes and contexts even apart from those we might term formalist. It remains a staple of many classroom introductions to literary study, and of some advanced courses as well. It is called upon to supply exactness, depth, and nuance to critical studies that are not mainly formalist but seek, nonetheless, to escape reliance on paraphrase and abstract thematics alone. Somewhat more problematically, close reading has become an analytic tool for certain scholars who are distrustful of critical theory and who seek to restore literature to what they take to be its proper position in the academy and in literate culture. Most significantly for this study, formalist analysis has been developed, theorized, and adapted to a variety of interpretive projects by critics who seek to advance its theory and practice in our time but who also have long considered themselves significantly or principally advocates of formalism. In consequence, anyone who seeks to apply terms such as "New Formalism" or "New Formalist" to certain contemporary critical practices, as I do here, must recognize that, for a significant number of scholars and critics with a range of interpretive interests and agendas, formalism has never been allowed to grow old.[10] It would be a mistake, moreover, as Samuel Otter has remarked, to suppose that "New Formalism" names a new and fully unified system of thought or a single "sustained method" rather than a multiplicity of related forms of attention to the verbal status of texts.[11]

Nonetheless, the complaints of Rooney and others are real and cogent, and point to an undeniable diminishment of formal analysis in the wake of developments in historicist, contextual, and political modes of criticism. While the general aim of formalism, old and new, has always been to liberate textual meanings – and kinds of meaning – unavailable to non-formalist strategies of interpretation, a strong secondary aim of contemporary formalism is indeed to insist on the linguistic dimension of works of verbal art. This book argues that New Formalist criticism is necessary to maintain and foster concern with the literary specificity – the linguistic or verbal character – of literary works, and that this concern is generated not by the inherent character of textuality but by questions of aim, method, and disciplinarity. Challenging claims that the nature of the object studied determines the mode of analysis – claims that misrepresent the actual generation of methods, modes of analysis, and objects – it contends that exactly the reverse is true. Just as Kant argued that we do not know the world in itself but only the world as the forms of human consciousness allow it to be apprehended, so critical methods actually determine the nature of the object they study by conceptualizing it in particular ways. Thus, a choice of method based on what a text is rests on an earlier, sometimes tacit or unconscious, choice of what we most wish or need a text to be – in a particular instance or in general. The choice of a critical method, that is, precedes the constitution of a literary text, and the need for a text to be a certain kind of text precedes the choice of critical method.

That the text is first and foremost a linguistic object is a founding assumption of contemporary formalisms. Whatever else the text is – a play of themes, a historical document, a production of a particular author or era, a real-world political manifesto – it is fundamentally a structure of language. A proper contemporary formalist analysis, as a result, must show how the text's language is what makes it any of those other things. If a given text, for example, is understood as a representation or imitation of a real-world event or situation, formalist criticism and theory make it possible to understand the concept of mimesis as a textually produced phenomenon and, in consequence, to rethink the text's relation to readerly or human experience. To understand the literary object in this way, of course, is inevitably to reopen the debate between proponents of formalism and proponents of reference and historicism – of what de Man terms "the nonverbal 'outside' to which language refers." And doing that, in turn, requires addressing historicist critiques of formalism that condemn it as history-denying, idealizing, universalizing, aestheticizing, and so on, as in Walter Benjamin,

Fredric Jameson, Terry Eagleton, and others; there is no way around that discussion. If historicist arguments too often minimize or dilute formalist assumptions and achievements, contemporary formalism must not replay that bias in another key.

One difficulty in clarifying the relation of formalist to historicist analysis is that this relation is too often understood in oversimplified and tendentious ways when it is, in fact, quite complex. As Geoffrey Hartman remarks, gesturing toward some of that complexity, "Interpretation is bringing the poem forward into the present, which is acknowledging its historicity, which is grounding our terms in history."[12] Northrop Frye conceptualizes the relationship of past to present in a different but related way. Drawing on Kierkegaard's notion of repetition, Frye sees the historicist imperative as "not the simple repeating of an experience, but the recreating of it which redeems or awakens it to life." He elaborates:

> [T]he goal of historical criticism, as our metaphors about it often indicate, is a kind of self-resurrection, the vision of a valley of dry bones that takes on the flesh and blood of our own vision. The culture of the past is not only the memory of mankind, but our own buried life, and study of it leads to a recognition scene, a discovery in which we see, not our past lives, but the total cultural form of our present life.... Without this sense of "repetition," historical criticism tends to remove the products of culture from our own sphere of interest. It must be counterpoised, as it is in all genuine historical critics, by a sense of the contemporary relevance of past art.[13]

This passage is remarkable for its flickering movement between historical and contemporary investments in the work of art, and for its refusal of more traditional accounts of the relationship between present readers and older texts.

In Frye's formulation, we do not attempt to recreate or join the historical audience of Homer or Shakespeare, allegedly leaving behind our own contemporaneity. But neither do we simply "breathe new life" into older works, turning the dead letter into living meaning by an act of sympathetic understanding that may also be an unexamined ascription of contemporary relevance. Older texts are indeed afforded a "recreation of function in a new context," but what gets resurrected is not, as in traditional humanistic accounts, a previously moribund text but rather our contemporary selves. Current life and cultural identity are themselves reborn, made new, by being seen in a context that now includes the dimensions of the past represented by the texts we read. Therefore, early portions of the present study undertake a critique of the historicist critique of formalism, propose a modified sense of the historical, and explore the limitations of understanding literary studies as principally a historicized prelude to social action – or indeed a purely historicizing discipline. Among the goals is to explore the possibility of non-universalizing formalisms, and of texts, beliefs, and actions not reducible to historicist etiology.

Once criticism moves beyond the unpromising choice between a formalism that naively appropriates the text for present needs and a historicism cannily reinserting the text into a history both distant and unusable, text–reader relations emerge as a complex play of distance and nearness, detachment and immersion. Such relations display what Hans Vaihinger called an "as if" character: a provisionality of identification, a rehearsal of attitudes, a trying-on of roles and situations that is more subtle, more tentative, and more amenable to readerly "use" than the coziness of simple identification or the chilly distance of simple historicizing.[14] Charles Altieri, for example, re-envisions the reader–text relation as a poetic modification of rhetorical strategies and expectations, a modification that brings literary experience to bear on the everyday life of readers in a particular way:

> Rhetoric is the art of exemplification. Rhetors typically ask audiences to identify with the ethos they demonstrate in order to establish ways of thinking through problems or performing the work of praising or blaming. Poetry is that aspect of rhetorical practice that invites us to "see in" to the minute particulars of expressive activity: the language used becomes at least as significant a source of identifications as the thoughts presented or character demonstrated. This "seeing-in" then offers the capacity of trying on particular modes of feeling, thinking, and speaking that provide a possible repertoire of responses to various kinds of situations. Therefore taking up a rhetorical perspective toward what poems offer affords the possibility of making more supple, more intricate, and more intense our repertories for engaging, understanding, and shaping experience in the world beyond the text. Education into "seeing-in" enriches our possibilities for "seeing-as," and thus for sorting what matters to us in the circumstances we deem relevant.[15]

Rethinking the formalist/historicist opposition and the relation of readers to texts in this way also enables – indeed, requires – a revision of the concept of the intrinsic: of the New Critical language of intrinsic literariness or poeticalness, of Roman Jakobson's "poetic function," and of other attempts to define literary meaning and other features as inherent properties of texts even prior to their interpretation. Rather than inhering in literary works, poetic or literary meaning emerges from the meeting of readers who employ particular interpretive assumptions or frameworks and texts realized in accordance with those assumptions and frameworks. Thus, for contemporary formalists, literary criticism is neither a projection onto the text of readerly needs and desires nor an extraction from the text of meanings inherent in it. Rather, it is the construction of a revisable interpretive structure – a heuristic and, in a special sense, even a fictional structure that brings the text to realization; scrupulous attention to form is what enables this realization and thereby establishes the particular contribution of formalism.

ii

Historically, the term "formalism," in criticism and theory as in aesthetics, usually signifies a concern with an artwork's formal features, not just its thematic or representational elements. As Cleanth Brooks puts it, "A good poem is an object in which form and content can be distinguished but cannot really be separated."[16] In the extreme formalism of the artist and critic Roger Fry, attention to form was sharply separated from issues of content and meaning and at times displaced them entirely. Indeed, the painter J. A. M. Whistler seemed to anticipate Fry's thinking when he gave to his 1871 portrait of his mother the coolly abstract title, "Arrangement in Grey and Black."[17] But for most formalist critics, the isolation of formal properties is only a necessary first step; the second is to interpret those properties so as to connect their signifying power with the meanings produced by semantic and thematic elements. One reason a work's form cannot finally be separated from its meaning is that form itself, when interpreted, is an essential source of meaning.[18]

Not confined to a single critical school, modern formalism is most often associated with the linguistically oriented Russian Formalists and their efforts to define features and effects of poetic language, with Anglo-American New Critics' concern to eschew paraphrase and disclose the distinctive language, structure, and organic unity of poems, and with the French pedagogical tradition of *explication de texte*. Formalism's technique of detailed textual attention – "close reading" – links it, as well, with the philologically based criticism of E. R. Curtius and especially Erich Auerbach and Leo Spitzer, and with the tradition of

European stylistics exemplified by Karl Vossler, Emil Staiger, and others. More recently, close reading has also been a feature of deconstructive criticism – which attempts to read with singular closeness and patience, but rejects (among other things) the New Critics' quest for textual unity in favor of what Barbara Johnson calls "the careful teasing out of warring forces of signification" – and, to some extent, of New Historicism, which at times applies close reading to literary texts as well as non-literary documents, and to cultural beliefs, practices, and material objects.[19] While most of these modes of analysis employ techniques of close reading, however, it was Anglo-American New Criticism that focused most intently on the language and meaning of texts understood as formally unified wholes, complex organizations of meaning.

The link between form and meaning, however formulated or understood, is essential to formalist undertakings. Geoffrey Hartman has succinctly defined formalism as "a method: that of revealing the human content of art by a study of its formal properties."[20] In seeking to discover that human content, formalist critics attend to virtually all features of language: semantics, grammar and syntax, figures of speech, diction and vocabulary, etymology, aural and visual patterns. They also identify literary forms – not simply to classify them, or from faith in their a priori valence, but to disclose the signifying power of form in the individual instance: the hovering presence, for example, of the traditionally male-voiced Petrarchan sonnet in Edna St. Vincent Millay's female-voiced and anti-Petrarchan "I, Being Born a Woman and Distressed"; or the way fixity of goal and obliquity of access define not only the "rigid house" and "winding pathway" in Elizabeth Bishop's "Sestina" but also the performance of the sestina form itself, which requires that the poet follow an elaborate formal route to a goal at once predetermined in the abstract yet defined concretely by the particulars of the route chosen. Beyond such concerns with traditional forms, a number of contemporary formalists focus on what Denis Donoghue calls "the particularity of form in every work of art" – the way each work discloses a formal identity of its own even as it may also be an instance of terza rima or the heroic couplet, epyllion or novella. "Form," Donoghue elaborates, "is the distinguishing characteristic of art; there is no reason to assume that it is unproblematically given, like the counting of syllables in an iambic pentameter."[21] To contemporary formalisms, that is to say, form is "the effect of reading."[22] Or, as Angela Leighton paraphrases Henri Focillon, "The life of forms is simply the innumerable ways in which the artwork comes to life through interpretation."[23] Thus, by demonstrating the way critical activity generates particular forms, and by exploring their significance for criticism, this book seeks to replace the givenness of form with the interpretive production of form.

Historically, New Formalism grows out of the New Criticism of the 1920s, 1930s, and after, a "school" to which later formalisms are profoundly indebted and toward which they also adopt an inescapably revisionist posture.[24] This study both narrates a version of that historical, critical, and theoretical trajectory and investigates key elements of New Formalist revisionism. In different ways, and working from different premises, figures such as T. S. Eliot, I. A. Richards, William Empson, Cleanth Brooks, and Robert Penn Warren (among others) sought to understand formal elements of texts not as containers or ornaments but as essential constituents of signification – conveying, performing, and shaping meaning both on their own and in concert with semantic elements. This effort, that is, aimed not just to read more closely but to find what had been taken to be decorative or inert elements of texts newly significative, newly readable. As noted, however, New Formalisms inevitably critique and revise many of the theoretical assumptions of New Criticism, including its conceptions of form and meaning, the ideas of intrinsic meaning and intrinsic literariness, "organic" and other kinds of unity, the fiction of an "ideal reader," the operations of naïve empiricism, "meaning" versus "use" of texts, questions of artistic value and evaluation, and more. That critique is part of an effort to work out and disseminate New Formalist principles and practices.

But New Formalism goes well beyond the activity of differentiating itself from the New Criticism. For one thing, it rethinks the nature and significance of textual tensions, contradictions, and disharmonies; it displays a new concern with issues of power and politics; and it focuses energetically on cultural and political significances of form. Another version of New Formalism develops contemporary trends in aesthetics, including revisions of Kant, and does so with considerable range and variety. This aesthetic strand of formalism explores links between aesthetics and questions of form, rethinking the form/meaning relation in a number of ways, and argues for form as the product of interpretation – thus developing the notion (linked above to Donoghue) that New Formalisms must shift focus to analyses of the particularity of form as opposed to conventional generic and formal classification. Extending this aesthetic exploration of the category of form, theorists like Robert Kaufman contend that "aesthetic thought-experience in some way *precedes* objective, content-and-use-oriented thought; in that sense, aesthetic experience is 'formal' because it provides *the form for* conceptual, 'objective' thought or cognition." Indeed, "aesthetic form" contributes to "the possibilities of critical thought and agency."[25] In a related effort, this study's version of New Formalism works to revise central aesthetic (and New Critical) concepts of textuality in such a way that intention, speaker, audience, context, and reference are shown to be textually generated by a mechanism comparable to linguistic back-formation. That is, if interpretation produces form, it also produces the peculiar ability of literary texts to generate the reality they seem merely to describe after the fact. Thus, any literary text can display either a referential relation to an anterior reality or a rhetorical relation to the reality-effect it creates. Frequently, the tension between these two modalities of textual performance is itself a central locus of meaning.

iii

This relation between the referential and the rhetorical (or the mimetic and the textual) dimensions of a text is an important focus of New Formalist exploration, both on a theoretical level and in the highly particularized minuteness of individual interpretations. For that reason, among others, the present study offers illustrative analyses, some brief and some quite extensive, in order to demonstrate both the characteristic interpretive procedures of contemporary formalism and something of their variety. It first explores the varying relations of rhetoric and reference in literary texts such as Keats's "Bright Star," Williams' "This Is Just to Say," Milton's "When I Consider," and Browning's "My Last Duchess." Another group of readings develops the notion of interpretive patience. Drawing on Theodor Adorno's discussion of "the tempo, the patience and perseverance of lingering with the particular," I address two poems that have generated different kinds of critical impasse: Jonson's "To Celia" and P. B. Shelley's "England in 1819."[26] This discussion also attempts to clarify further the traditionally vexed relations between the concept of form and questions of politics and culture. It builds, in part, on Susan Wolfson's contention that "choices of form and the way it is managed often signify as much as, and as part of, words themselves," and that an era's "involvement with poetic form ... participates in central discussions of its historical moment."[27] In this context, the book offers a critique of ideas of "the politics of form" in Antony Easthope, Terry Eagleton, and J. Paul Hunter, and develops extended New Formalist analyses of couplet rhetoric in Pope's *The Rape of the Lock* and *The Dunciad*, and of syntax and the thematics of race in Wheatley's "On being brought from AFRICA to AMERICA."[28]

Contending that New Formalist interpretation need not confine itself to the study of literature, the book then develops analyses bringing out important but otherwise inaccessible dimensions of meaning in non-literary texts. Examples are taken from political oratory (Mario Cuomo, 1984 DNC Keynote Address); medicine-physiology-semiotics-cultural studies (Jonathan Miller, *The Body in Question*); popular history (Barbara Tuchman, *A Distant Mirror: The Calamitous 14th Century*); and economics-sociology-satire (Thorstein Veblen, *The Theory of the Leisure Class*). These texts and analyses suggest the pertinence of formalist analysis to the varied disciplines of the humanities and the social sciences and its role in furthering textual and conceptual understanding in those disciplines. The goal is not to add a "literary dimension" to texts in non-literary fields but to perform a kind of analysis that expands a field's own understanding of its texts. In this mode, New Formalism becomes part of the analytic apparatus of a wide range of disciplines, liberating dimensions of meaning unavailable to traditionally non-textual conceptual analysis. Beyond the humanities and social sciences, contemporary formalism is also capable of illuminating such limiting cases as the rhetoric of science and the discourse of mathematics – usually not considered textual at all – as well as the cultural assumptions and ideologies on which those disciplines rely. In exploring these issues, I make use of recent theoretical studies such as Michael Barany's "Mathematical Ideality and the Practice of Translation," and other essays.[29] If the larger discussion in this portion of the book assumes that there is no discourse – whether politics, history, social science, physiology, semiotics of culture, or others – without a rhetoric of *some* sort, the discussion of mathematics seeks to extend that discursive given to symbol systems not obviously poetic, literary, or even principally linguistic.

iv

The final chapter of the book – "Textual Infatuation, True Infatuation" – attempts to bridge the gap between the analysis of texts and the conduct of our affective, passional, and romantic experience – in particular, the ways we know the persons we admire, love, and desire. This attempt rests on the assumptions that, in order to know a literary text intimately and profoundly, one must risk a sustained raptness of attention that transgresses the boundaries of moderation and seemliness, and that such attention finds a non-textual parallel in the immoderate scrutiny and heedfulness that characterize the phenomenon of romantic infatuation. The chapter has two principal and interconnected aims. The first is to rethink and rehabilitate two forms of intensive scrutiny that regularly draw skepticism and even scorn: what is called "overreading" in literary criticism, and what is termed "infatuation" in romantic and affectional life. In both spheres, I argue, a particular kind of attention, even hyper-attentiveness, generates forms of knowing both singularly valuable and entirely legitimate and objective. The second aim is to question traditional allegiance to the concepts of wholeness and unity in literary criticism – not in order to reject them, but to liberate the minute attention to parts that is inhibited and overshadowed by what Adorno calls "this passing-on and being unable to linger, this tacit assent to the primacy of the general over the particular."[30] To this end, I theorize and advocate a conscious, New Formalist fetishizing of parts – of textual elements – to a point at which the whole they constitute recedes almost to vanishing, or is bracketed almost to the point of annihilation. Such an effort does not represent an ultimate denigration of textual or other artistic wholes; instead, it enables a realization of individual elements that would otherwise be impossible – a realization that can redeem both the charge of critical overreading and that of romantic infatuation.

Literary criticism since Aristotle – and particularly since Coleridge – has paid energetic allegiance to connections among the concepts of identity, wholeness, unity, and generality. This chapter offers a concise critique of the valorization of these concepts in literary criticism and elsewhere, briefly surveying the Western elevation of "whole" over "part" in aesthetics, epistemology, discourses of truth, apothegms, normative versus "perverse" conceptions of eros, and so on. The insistence on wholeness and unity also appears, of course, in the New Critical idea of organic unity, especially as articulated by Eliot and developed by Brooks and Warren, among others. While that concept helpfully shifted focus away from isolated quotations, *sententiae*, and "gems" to texts understood as meaningful wholes, it has also stifled rethinkings of part–whole relations and unintentionally misrepresented much of the actual work of formalist criticism. But countercurrents and contrary precedents can be found, even within New Criticism itself. John Crowe Ransom's conceptualization of structure and texture, for example – in contrast to Brooks' "pattern of resolved stresses" – gives us a verbal object fundamentally at odds with itself. For Ransom, the divided and heterogeneous character of a poem's mode of existence offers "a kind of knowledge which is radically or ontologically distinct" from scientific knowledge – a knowledge that can "recover the denser and more refractory original world which we know loosely through our perceptions and memories."[31] This knowledge is the product not of poetic unity but, on the contrary, of textual particulars that refuse to be subdued to an encompassing whole. (Wimsatt makes a different but related argument in his critique of Crocean ideas of the assimilation of parts to wholes in artworks.)[32]

Somewhat surprisingly, such arguments link Ransom (as well as Allen Tate) with the cultural critique of the Marxist-influenced Frankfurt School. While Tate and Ransom do not employ Adorno and Horkheimer's economic and political vocabulary, or their post-Hegelian and Marxist conceptual apparatus, all share distress at the felt ontological fragility of the world's particulars – including the self – under the dominion of science and industrialism. Ransom's "fundamental interest," in the words of Douglas Mao, lies "in protecting the concrete particular from the onslaught of abstracting generalization." Natural particulars, threatened by "science's violence" and "will to mastery," are defended by art, "which counters the will to mastery by promoting contemplation of the particular for its own sake."[33] With the help of Ransom, and especially of Adorno's rethinking of part–whole relations, I argue that, despite the Western enshrinement of wholeness and generality in aesthetics, ontology, and even ethics, there is an actual centrality of attention to parts in much of the practical business of literary criticism and analysis, in and out of the classroom. Most of the time, in fact, the critic's construing of a text into meaningful wholeness is not even thinkable without the minute and recursive attention to parts that constitutes the majority of the work of interpretation.

Simon Jarvis argues that Adorno "offers to give a philosophically stringent account of art and of aesthetic judgment... without losing its immersion in the minutest details of works of art themselves. Indeed, on Adorno's account it can only do this if it does not sacrifice such immersion."[34] My argument develops a similar program within the sphere of formalist criticism and theory – a partiality toward the partial that is, finally, designed to serve interpretive justness. Similarly, I develop a parallel between Adorno's canny and skeptical valorization of the partial and particular and a revised understanding of the human experience and human value of romantic infatuation in order to re-evaluate and in some sense redeem the latter. The argument about infatuation enlists Troy Jollimore's recent philosophical study of *Love's Vision*, which focuses on epistemology, ethics, the singularity and non-comparability of the object of "love's vision," and the lover's "realization" of the love-object.[35]

My aim is to reconceptualize and rehabilitate the analogous phenomena characteristically termed "overreading" and "infatuation," and
to tie a revised understanding of the part–whole relation to the ideas
of discovery and "surprise" – surprise not as an affective experience,
but as a methodological, epistemic, and hermeneutic possibility aris-
ing from investigation of specifically formal features of a text. Thus,
both the argument about parts and wholes and the parallel between
romantic "infatuation" and critical "overreading" ultimately serve the
development and exposition of a New Formalist methodology. The
book terms this sort of hyperattentive realization, whether of persons
or of texts, "true infatuation" – a phrase that attempts to cross the
divide between the conventionally opposed categories of "true love"
and "mere infatuation." Like Adorno's at times dizzying revisions of
conventional relations between general and particular, "true infatuation" calls attention at once to the limitations of the conventionally
privileged concept and to the hidden powers of the conventionally
inferior one, troubling the tidiness and the hierarchical character of
the opposition between them. As a kind of solecism, the phrase "true
infatuation" detaches itself from both common usage and a normative
hierarchy of value and attempts to name an as-yet-emergent category –
a category pertinent to the development of a contemporary formalist
analysis and, secondarily, to a contemporary erotics. In both the textual and the romantic forms of infatuation, a mode of hypertrophied
attention enables a fuller and truer realization of the "object" than
would otherwise be possible. In a sense, my argument works to rehabilitate two parallel modes of unseemly attentiveness and absorption by
dividing each internally into a fantasmatic or ungrounded and a realistic or grounded ("true") form of interpretation. This means situating
formalist critical scrutiny as well as romantic hyperattentiveness in a
larger interpretive, epistemological, and ethical context concerned not
with comparisons and evaluative hierarchies but with an apprehension
of otherness patient enough and inventive enough to be adequate to
its object.

From a different angle, Jonathan Culler offers an argument pertinent
to the idea of textual infatuation in his contribution to the volume
Interpretation and Overinterpretation. There, humorously but also quite
seriously, he contends that "a little paranoia is essential to the just appreciation of things" – "paranoia" here evoking not the fear of persecution
but the compulsion to ascribe meaning and meaningfulness to virtually
everything, as in some of the fiction of Pynchon or Nabokov.[36] Respect-
fully disagreeing with Umberto Eco's attempts to delimit interpretive

freedom in light of Eco's belief that "the rights of the interpreters have been overstressed," Culler offers this formulation:

> Eco linked overinterpretation to what he called an "excess of won-der," an excessive propensity to treat as significant elements which might be simply fortuitous. This *déformation professionale*, as he sees it, which inclines critics to puzzle over elements in a text, seems to me, on the contrary, the best source of the insights into language and literature that we seek, *a quality to be cultivated rather than shunned.* It would be sad indeed if fear of "overinterpretation" should lead us to avoid or repress the state of wonder at the play of texts and interpretation, which seems to me all too rare today.[37]

Culler's defense of "overinterpretation" is directly relevant to the inten-sity of focus and energy of realization that I am linking to New Formalist interpretation, and the interpretive caution that troubles him becomes clearer when we recall that charges of overinterpretation vastly outnum-ber charges of underinterpretation and imply a degree of recklessness and folly that rarely attaches to the latter. Frye sees a similar sort of cau-tion when he remarks that "so much criticism is produced with so little intellectual energy that it has all to be done over again."[38]

My discussion returns to the part–whole discussion by conceding a real – though diminished – place for active concern with the total, the general, the paraphrasable, the defined and labelled. It explores the idea of the "whole text" as a regulative fiction – something that can inau-gurate and initially propel analysis but that is held in abeyance and subordinated to the multiform realization of the parts that constitute it. Of course, the textual whole must be reinvoked at some point, or allowed to remain, penumbrally and almost invisibly, at the margins of the focused analysis from which it has been all but banished. But, as Adorno puts it,

> truth itself depends on the tempo, the patience and perseverance of lingering with the particular: what passes beyond it [the particular] without having first entirely lost itself, what proceeds to judge with-out having first been guilty of the injustice of contemplation, loses itself at last in emptiness.[39]

How that wholeness or unity is to be approached is thus a central interpretive question that will differ with specific acts of interpreta-tion. Nonetheless, the work of fully realizing the elements of those wholes – whether texts or persons – is a mode of "textual infatuation" or of "true infatuation," and it is an essential feature of the New Formalism that I try to describe, theorize, illustrate, and advocate.

V

This study, then, attempts to ground formalist criticism in contemporary theory and contemporary critical practice – to define and theorize a mode of formalist criticism that is conceptually compatible with current thinking about literature and theory; to make a fuller case than has been made for the theoretical grounding of New Formalism; to argue for the singularity and value of such a formalism; to discuss its role in non-formalist modes of literary criticism and also in other, non-literary, disciplines; to illustrate New Formalist criticism through sample analyses of texts; to argue the case for the linguistic centrality of the text, and for a revised conception of non-historicist criticism; to explore the pertinence of both theory and context to the interpretive enterprise; and to envision the reading of literature as a provisional rehearsal of existential postures and attitudes in the inevitably historical "present" of the reader.[40]

Beyond its central arguments, I hope that readers will find useful the fullness with which the book establishes the theoretical groundings available to New Formalisms, the range, detail, and concreteness of the "sample analyses," the effort to rethink inescapable critical concepts such as intention, reference, unity, and part–whole relations, and the attempt to write criticism and theory in as lucid a fashion as the topics permit. While not a textbook, *New Formalist Criticism: Theory and Practice* is decidedly pedagogical in emphasis. Its primary audience consists of professional literary critics and theorists and graduate students, but I believe it will also be of considerable use to undergraduates interested in critical method and the study of literature. I have, in fact, assigned portions of it in both graduate and undergraduate classes, with gratifying success.

1
Method, Meaning, New Formalism

i Critical method and the production of literary texts

It is a commonplace of contemporary ideas of knowledge, deriving most directly from Kantian epistemology in the eighteenth century, that what we see or observe or know depends powerfully upon the point of view from which we know it. As one philosopher summarizes Kant's central insight,

> we know about the world insofar as we experience it according to the unchanging and universally shared structure of mind. All rational beings think the world in terms of space, time, and categories such as cause and effect, substance, unity, plurality, necessity, possibility, and reality. That is, whenever we think about anything, we have to think about it in certain ways (for example, as having causes, as existing or not existing, as being one thing or many things, as being real or imaginary, as being something that has to exist or doesn't have to exist), not because that is the way the world is, but rather because that is the way that our minds order experience. We can be said to know things about the world, then, not because we somehow step outside of our minds to compare what we experience with some reality outside of it, but rather because the world we know is always already organized according to a certain fixed (innate) pattern that is the mind.[1]

In our time, Kant's fundamental argument about human cognition has been metaphorically extended from the mind as such to the structure of various disciplines and subdisciplines. Nelson Goodman describes a trajectory of influence that "began when Kant exchanged the structure of the world for the structure of the mind...and now proceeds to exchange the structure of concepts for the structure of the several symbol systems of the sciences, philosophy, the arts, perception, and everyday discourse." As he tersely summarizes, "The movement is from unique truth and a world fixed and found to a diversity of right and even conflicting versions or worlds in the making."[2]

Each discipline, then, asks different sorts of questions, is structured by different conceptual conventions and assumptions, and construes its objects of study in different ways. Thus an anthropologist will understand a particular society in a different way than an epidemiologist will; a chemist will have a different understanding of cyanide than a poisoner, and physicians know our bodies in a different fashion than lovers. There may, of course, be overlaps of perspective, or one person may adopt more than a single perspective. An epidemic of infectious disease may alter social organization and thus also count as an anthropological fact. A would-be poisoner may find a chemical understanding of the toxicity of cyanide useful in planning a crime. And a doctor and patient may discover – even act upon – an erotic attraction.

This alertness to disciplinary conventions can take a variety of forms. Most modestly and least disruptively, the shaping power of such conventions is understood on the model of a lens or perspective. To look at an object from a chemical or psychological or neurological perspective is to see the same object from a different angle or with a different emphasis; a single instance of human behavior – say, an act of aggression – would thus display a chemical dimension, or a psychological dimension, or a neurological dimension. To this way of thinking, often understood on a visual model, the world and its objects remain constant; only our viewpoint or perspective changes. In a more radical understanding, however, disciplinary conventions and expectations actually generate one object or kind of object rather than another. Identity here is not stable across disciplines but produced by the very nature of the disciplines themselves.

In literary criticism, to narrow our focus sharply, this is the position of Stanley Fish. After arguing that the meanings of a poem are not stable and intrinsic to the text but the product of "interpretive communities that are responsible both for the shape of a reader's activities and for the texts those activities produce," Fish goes on to explain "How to Recognize a Poem When You See One." Here, he extends his argument that the meanings of a poem are produced by interpretive communities to claim that the very establishment of a written text as a poem (or "work of literature") is also the product not of the text's intrinsic features but of a set of interpretive conventions and expectations.[3] Thus, we do not "recognize a poem" – recognize that something *is* a poem – by observing certain distinguishing linguistic features shared by literary but not non-literary texts. Rather, we *produce* a poetic or literary text by paying a certain kind of attention, bringing certain expectations, to a text so as to make that text function as a poem – indeed, be a poem: "It is not that the presence of poetic qualities compels a certain kind of attention but that the paying of a certain kind of attention results in the emergence of poetic qualities."[4] This is a far cry from a merely perspectival understanding of differing points of view on an allegedly unchanging object.

Having moved from Kant on human consciousness to the array of investigative disciplines, and then to a single one of those disciplines, literary criticism, we can go a step further within the field of criticism itself: to the notion that our particular critical orientations are also forms of attention that generate particular kinds of textual features, different kinds of literary text. Though, again, there can be overlaps of assumption and attention, it is obvious that a psychoanalytic reading of a literary text produces a different kind of textual object than a formalist reading produces, or a prosodic reading, or a postcolonial reading, and so on. Moreover, unlike the forms of consciousness as described by Kant – "the unchanging and universally shared structure of mind," as Daniel puts it – the conventions and procedures of various disciplines (history, psychology, linguistics) and subdisciplines (deconstructive criticism, New Historicism, feminist and gender criticism), though defined and legitimized by what Fish terms "interpretive communities," can change in the course of time, and can be to some extent both freely chosen and freely modified by practitioners. Too great a modification, of course, may not count as a legitimate move in the particular disciplinary game being played and may be marginalized or rejected as wayward. But if the new interpretive strategy proves productive and compelling enough, it will gradually and quietly enter – and thus expand – the repertoire of that discipline's canonical procedures, what Thomas Kuhn calls its "normal science."[5]

While it may be difficult, then, for an individual critic to alter an established practice, just as it is difficult for an individual speaker to alter a given language, it is not difficult to choose a critical practice or mode or school based on what it makes of the texts it takes up for analysis – the kind of thing that the analysis, and we, want those texts to be. Do we want them to tell us about their authors' lives and thus count as biographical documents, or about the society in which they were produced and thus serve as cultural and historical documents? Do we want them to disclose a system of gender relations and gender politics, whether biographical, historical, or fictional – one thematic element in relation to other elements of the texts? Do we want texts to be unified wholes, in which every element is expected to (and thus does) connect meaningfully with the other elements, and in which tensions and dramatic conflicts finally compose into "a pattern of resolved stresses"?[6] Do we want the poem to be the fully realized intention of its author? Or do we want the text to differ from itself, harboring a discourse that counters or subverts its ostensible thrust? Do we want texts to tell or show us how to live, or how things are, or how they should be? Do we want them to offer historically specific representations of reality, or general truths adaptable to particular circumstances? Or do we want texts to supply occasions for us to note their limitations, mystifications, and blindnesses?

Whenever we give an answer to questions like these, we are also implicitly designating a mode of analysis. While choices of critical method, then, are frequently thought to be determined by ideas about how language works, about what literature intrinsically is, about what we conceive authors' intentions to be, and so on, these considerations are finally subordinate to the question of what we want the texts we interpret to emerge as, to do for us, to be. We may say – and say truthfully – that we find a Marxist approach most satisfying because literary texts are inescapably products of material and political forces that shape their form and meaning. But this choice of method based on what a text is rests on a prior, perhaps tacit or unconscious, choice of what we most need a text to be – in general, or in a given instance. It is in this sense that the choice of a critical method is prior to the constitution of a literary text, and the need for a text to be a certain kind of text is prior to the choice of critical method. We denominate the text a certain kind of text in order to get from it a certain something in preference to other somethings.[7]

ii   The text as language (1)

New Formalism, the array of critical practices that I want to describe and argue for in this essay, derives from the need – mine, but certainly not mine alone – for a text to be principally a linguistic object, a piece of language: language that is rewardingly susceptible to various strategies of detailed formalist analysis or interpretation – what is often called "close reading." Whatever else the text is – a play of themes, a historical document or symptom, a certain kind of readerly experience, a meditation on or transformation of a genre, a production of a particular author or school or era, a real-world political manifesto or tract – it is also a linguistic construct. Further, the text is those other things only as they are embodied in or performed by the text's language. In consequence, a properly formalist analysis must engage with that language no matter what it also takes the text to be – must show how it is the text's language that makes it any of those other things. To do otherwise is to stray into a kind of logocentric fallacy in which a text's content or meaning or identity is fantasized to be separable from its medium. As David Lodge puts it in discussing elements of fictional narrative:

> All good criticism is ... necessarily a response to the creative use of language, whether it is talking explicitly of "plot" or "character" or any other of the categories of narrative literature. These terms are useful – indeed essential – but the closer we get to defining the unique identity and interest of *this* plot, of *that* character, the closer we are brought to a consideration of the language in which we encounter these things.[8]

The early formalism of the New Criticism, in the 1930s and 1940s, assumed that the aspects of a text emphasized by New Critical techniques – paradox, irony, a unity composed of "resolved stresses," to name only a prominent few – were by and large peculiar to literary texts – indeed, intrinsic to them. My representation of formalist criticism and the attendant techniques of close reading assumes no such thing: neither the distinctiveness of literary language nor the intrinsic character of the textual features disclosed by formalist analysis.[9] Instead, my advocacy of formalism and close reading is tied to a particular idea of the meaning, significance, and purposes of literary criticism. Nor am I advocating formalist criticism exclusively. What I am contending is, first, that formalist analysis should be a vital part of any interpretive method that cares to be called "literary critical," and, second, that it produces or discovers or discloses dimensions of textual meaning and textual performance that are of the greatest readerly, cultural, and social significance. Such a formalist commitment is in part an attempt to recover the specificity of the literary obscured by a number of contemporary modes of reading and interpretation, not by insisting on an allegedly literary or poetic language specific to what we designate as literary artworks but by attempting to counter a prevalent surrender of attention to the verbal and textual as such. This emphasis recalls, in certain ways, Susan Sontag's 1961 affirmation of formal analysis in "Against Interpretation":

> What is needed, first, is more attention to form in art. If excessive stress on *content* provokes the arrogance of interpretation, more extended and more thorough descriptions of *form* would silence. What is needed is a vocabulary – a descriptive, rather than prescriptive, vocabulary – for forms.[10]

This effort to recover the verbal specificity of texts is not simply a matter of using close reading to support or supply evidence for points made discursively – as if one were to claim in a critical essay that "Charles regularly infantilizes Susan," and then cite a bit of Charles's dialogue: "You're a child, Susan." Such citational use of the text's language is important in an evidentiary way but it is often interpretively trivial. Rather, I am speaking of the possibility of taking the work with adequate seriousness, regarding every feature of it as potentially meaningful, and of attending to what its language is and does – not just what it "says" – in order to move beyond the twilit half-knowing of paraphrase and other crude (if at times necessary or useful) reductions toward something like the reality of the text itself. Close reading, that is to say, is not simply the marshaling of verbal evidence; it's what allows us to pass beyond superficial acquaintance, paraphrase, a fixation on theme, content, and semantic import in order to discover dimensions of meaning that inflect, complicate, exceed, perhaps even contradict what attention to content tells us.

To attempt to read this way is somewhat like attempting to move beyond the point at which we think of an acquaintance as a middle-aged Catholic female who enjoys softball, learns languages easily, has a good sense of humor, is fascinated by Chomskyan linguistics, and is lactose intolerant – to move beyond the accurate yet estranging generality of such categories and approach more closely to an actual understanding of the particularity, the thisness, the complexity and meaningfulness enacted by this person's way of being in the world. The comparison may seem fanciful, but, as Walter J. Ong says in the course of making a very different argument, "Anything that bids for attention in an act of contemplation is a surrogate for a person. In proportion as the work of art is capable of being taken in full seriousness, it moves further and further along an asymptote to the curve of personality."[11] Jane Gallop draws out the ethical implications of this position:

> I believe it is ethical to respect other people, by which I mean: listen to them, try and understand what they are actually saying, rather than just confirming our preconceptions about them, our prejudices. I believe it is our ethical obligation to fight against our tendency to project our preconceptions, that it is our ethical duty to attempt to hear what someone else is really saying. Ultimately, close reading is not just a way of reading but a way of listening. It can help us not just to read what is on the page, but to hear what a person really said. Close reading can train us to hear other people.[12]

As I see it, close reading – patient, inventive, detailed attention to how language works in a text – represents our best hope of getting beyond the clichés of superficial acquaintance, taking responsibility for the being and interpretation of the full text, and allowing ourselves to be surprised both by what it is and by how much it differs from what we had thought it was. I'll add that I take this to be as much an ethical as a hermeneutic and intellectual imperative.

One of the things implied by that perhaps ponderous-sounding claim is that close reading is not just a skill or tool or interpretive implement – the hermeneutic equivalent of a high-powered microscope – though even at that instrumental level, close reading has been recognized as a central and powerful technique: even "the single defining skill of our discipline."[13] Beyond that, close reading has been recognized as a technique for mounting a regular and salutary resistance to the surmises and projections of the interpreter and the more or less fantasmatic coalescences of meaning that can obscure the text's linguistic actuality. "The authority of language," as Geoffrey Hartman has said,

> can only be tested by close reading and resides in language itself as used and used again. Explanation gives way to explication, and explication becomes a genre that *maintains the art work itself, the peculiar authority of its diction*, amid the figuration or the chaos of suppositions coming from the combined forestructure of language and the interpretive mind.[14]

More reductively put, close reading is what rescues texts – and readers – from the easy distortions of paraphrase. "The crux," Theodor Adorno once said of a philosophical text, "is what happened in it, not a thesis or a position, the texture, not the deductive or inductive course of one-track minds."[15] For Paul Valéry, "A bad poem is one that vanishes into meaning."[16]

Why is it so important to insist that a poem is made of language? Isn't a poem also "made of" many other things? An author's sentiments or beliefs or assumed attitudes? Contemporary cultural and ideological assumptions? Generic and formal conventions? Various allusions and kinds of allusion? A temporally unfolding narrative or argument or sequence of episodes, ideas, images? And more? Why single out the linguistic dimension of the poem for special scrutiny and identify it so closely with the principal object of New Formalist analysis? Perhaps a non-verbal example can help answer these questions. Imagine a museum gallery devoted to contemporary clothing and accessories, and imagine one particular exhibit in this gallery, a woman's shoe. Following the list immediately above, we could contend that the shoe embodies some of its creator's attitudes toward fashion, or gender, or footwear; that it carries within it contemporary ideas of sartorial appropriateness, or contests such ideas; that it evokes conventional features of the sandal, or the slingback pump, or the running shoe; that its coloring or construction alludes to certain earlier shoes, or certain kinds of social context, or certain designers, or to the story of Achilles' heel; that its shape or line – moving from heel to toe, say – constitutes a meaningful arc or spatial trajectory, perhaps a mini-narrative of stylistic evolution. Like a poem, then, the shoe exhibited in the gallery is "made of" intentions and attitudes, cultural values, generic conventions, allusions, narrative or aesthetic or semiotic sequences, and more. All of this is undeniable.

Now, would it matter to the meaning or significance of the shoe if instead of just one, there were seven visually identical shoes, the first made of calfskin, say; the second of ivory-billed woodpecker skin; the third of human skin; the fourth of blank paper; the fifth of papiermâché; the sixth of painted zinc; and the seventh of light beams, since it is a *virtual* shoe – a holographic projection? For a resolutely thematic or ideological analysis that pays attention to meaning but not to medium, each of these shoes carries the same array of meaning and significance. Yet surely a great deal is lost in such an interpretive procedure. If we read in terms of cultural ideas of fashion, for instance, the ivory-bill shoe may glance toward notions of reckless despoliation and exploitation, and a subordination of natural rarity to commerce and bodily adornment. The shoe constructed of human skin may go further, carrying a grim sense of exploitation that evokes sweat shops, child labor, and related brutal instrumentalizings of human beings, including the Holocaust. The holographic projection, in turn, may implicitly define the high-fashion shoe (and similar items) as unreal, substanceless in several senses – an emblem of vacuous devotion to the merely visible. Since the shoes are merely hypothetical, of course, so are these interpretive possibilities. But it is clear that the medium is central to – that it constitutes – the meaning and significance of the interpreted object. Form, Focillon contends, "does not behave as some superior principle modeling a positive mass, for it is plainly observable how matter imposes its own form upon form" in what he terms "this magnificent, this unequivocal bondage."[17] If the object is a literary text, that medium is language. Thus, in the case of literary criticism, to focus on theme, or content, or ideology, or whatever – to the exclusion of attention to language – is, in effect, to equate one shoe with another, or with the others. It is to abstract meaning or content from form so ruthlessly or thoughtlessly that the shoe of human skin and the shoe of light waves are, in effect, interchangeable. This can't be a good idea. Whatever else the literary text may be, language is what it always is.

iii   The mute text

In what is only an apparent paradox, both Hartman and Adorno seem to say that the text requires the labor of interpretation if it is to have any chance of disclosing its plenary identity; that it needs to be mediated to readers by intensive critical performance if it is to show forth what it is, does, and means. The model of knowing presupposed here is clearly different from what might be called textual versions of naive empiricism: "originalist" or "strict constructionist" ideas of legal interpretation, for example, which verge as far as good sense allows (and frequently further) on an ideal of textual meaning as "in" the text, simply readable without efforts of interpretation, and needing only to be permitted to appear. Interpretive activity is here only a perverse obstacle to a sure, direct grasp of the text's plain sense. This model presupposes not only the efficacy of an ideally unobtrusive and receptive reading posture but also full expressive agency on the part of the text. If readers will "only stand and wait," like Miltonic angels, the text will fully and reliably speak itself.

The alternative model, in dramatic contrast, conceives of reading not as self-negation or "wise passiveness" but as the active production of meaning through interpretation. Perhaps more surprisingly, it conceives of the text not as ideally and independently expressive but as in need of interpretive activity for its own production of meaning. Indeed, in a highly particular way, this model conceives of the text as mute – a notion that can take many forms, and entail small or large claims. In the course of a critique of George Poulet's intuitive if often compelling "criticism of consciousness," for example, Geoffrey Hartman reflects on Poulet's persistent lack of attention to form:

> By looking through form, as Blake claims to look through rather than with the eye, Poulet gains his unusually intimate access to the writer's mind. It does not matter to him whether he enters that mind by door or window or through the chimney: he tells us what he finds there without telling us how he got in. Yet one thing he cannot properly describe – *the essential latency of what he finds, the quality of art's resistance to intimacy.*[18]

Such latency or resistance is not simple muteness, but it is a step away from plenary expressivity, from the idea of a text speaking itself forth to a receptive auditor or reader. As with Keats' Grecian urn, a "silent form" that can "tease us out of thought," Hartman's conception of the text attributes to it both the delights of intimate knowledge or enjoyment and the distance of what is not quite possessed: the urn is "still unravish'd" – "still" meaning "as yet" but also "silent" – yet its "resistance to intimacy" speaks volumes.[19]

But there are more radical forms of muteness that bear on the New Formalist project. In a stimulating essay on "The New Critics and the Text-Object," Douglas Mao first notes that for the New Critics, "the poem as found object was precious above all by virtue of its reticence."[20] This is not very far from Hartman's "resistance to intimacy." Somewhat later, speaking in larger methodological terms, Mao notes that "the notion of the text-object provides one of the conceptual foundations for the kinds of reading procedures currently employed by a wide range of literary critics." This notion, he adds, "serves as the major alternative – or better, complement – to the only other such foundation currently in play, the idea of the unconscious."[21] If we combine the New Critical text-object model – and its "governing assumption that the meaning of the text is not remotely exhausted by what the text explicitly seems to 'say'"[22] – with a critical model based on the unconscious, we can generate a different and perhaps more far-reaching idea of textual muteness. A particular logic links these two models, for the difference between what a text seems to say directly and what a critic discovers in it is much like the difference between what an analysand explicitly says in a psychoanalytic session and what the analyst discovers in the analysand's language. The young analysand hears himself saying how pleasant Thanksgiving at home with his parents had been; the analyst hears that, but also hears that the analysand only refers to his parents as "they" or "them," only uses the present tense ("So, they're having cocktails, when …"), assigns active verbs only to his parents, not himself or other persons – and a host of other details. In each case, different though they are, the text's un-uttered features and its modes of enactment are at least as significant as its paraphrasable or explicit content.

It is not that those features or enactments express the literary text's unconscious, whatever that might mean, but that – like the contents of the unconscious – they are what the text as explicit utterance cannot articulate even though they may be of far greater significance within a particular interpretive framework. Yeats translates this necessary muteness to an existential context in one of his last letters when he says that "Man can embody truth but he cannot know it."[23] And Northrop Frye makes such muteness one of the founding assumptions of his effort to reconstruct the discipline of literary studies in *Anatomy of Criticism*. First alluding to J. S. Mill's famous remark, "eloquence is *heard*; poetry is *over*heard,"[24] Frye comments: "The axiom of criticism must be, not that the poet [a formalist would say 'the poem'] does not know what he is talking about, but that he cannot talk about what he knows."[25] A little later, he generalizes more fully: "Criticism … is to art what history is to action and philosophy to wisdom: a verbal imitation of a human productive power which in itself does not speak."[26] Such formulations recall lines from Archibald MacLeish's 1926 poem, "Ars Poetica":

> A poem should be palpable and mute
> As a globed fruit,
> Dumb
> As old medallions to the thumb,
> Silent as the sleeve-worn stone
> Of casement ledges where the moss has grown –
> A poem should be wordless
> As the flight of birds ….
> A poem should not mean
> But be.[27]

Mute, dumb, silent, wordless – MacLeish takes a poem, at least a good or proper poem, to be less a statement about something than a thing in itself, a matter not so much of meaning as of being. Using this poem's proliferation of material images (fruits, medallions, stones, leaves, etc.) to extend Frye's analogies in the direction of thingness, one could venture that criticism is to literature as botany is to plants: the articulator of an identity that the object of study perfectly embodies but cannot know or speak.

Such a focus on what a poem is rather than what it says is of course, as Frye notes, no denigration of poets, nor even a suggestion that poetry is conceived in a mysterious state of vatic sublimity. Rather, it designates a place for literary criticism by underscoring that the poem can say little or nothing of itself, of its own being. That's not quite right, of course, because there are many poems that comment – sometimes slyly and implicitly, sometimes directly – on their own procedures. In what sense are such poems also "mute?" Let's invent two examples, poems A and B:

> A
> "I wish he would explain his Explanation"–
> I'm quoting Byron here, with admiration.
> B
> Clouds hang like gauze over the bright wound of sunset.
> Is it possible to *admire* an image like that one?

Example poem A comments in line two on its borrowing from *Don Juan* in line one. Poem B begins with a figurative description the merit of which its second line goes on to question. In some sense, each poem comments on itself rather than remaining mute. But the second line is part of each poem too. What neither poem – necessarily – can do is comment on the relation between line one and line two, the meaning or significance of these pairings of poetic and metapoetic utterances. Of course, one can get around that claim too, for a moment:

> C
> Clouds hang like gauze over the bright wound of sunset.
> Is it possible to *admire* an image like that one?
> (The second line takes the wind out of the first.)

Here, line three does indeed comment on the relation between lines one and two – but it cannot comment on its *own* relation to them. We are left then with a situation of potentially infinite regress, in which the text tries hopelessly to encompass or stand outside itself but simply ends up gesturing toward a limitless verbal hypertrophy. An example like this reminds us that, to put it crudely, while a poem may express something about something, we need literary criticism to express something about the poem.[28]

iv The text as language (2)

If "A poem should not mean/But be," then – though only in a highly particular sense – what sort of thing should it be? Many sorts of thing, of course, but to most formalist or neoformalist critics, a poem is first and foremost a linguistic object, a piece of language, a structure whose "material cause," in Aristotelian terms, is the language in which it is written. There have been many claims for the centrality of language in treating poetry, or literature in general, and they are far from being always versions of the same claim. For a poet-critic like W. H. Auden, the insistence on language expresses a foregounding of craft, an elevation of technical competence over expressiveness or theme or sensibility, and a view of the linguistic medium as something possessing its own agency and not just instrumentality. Language, in Auden's image, is something that the poet is engaged to – is courting, even. Here is part of his discussion:

> A poet is, before anything else, a person who is passionately in love with language. Whether this love is a sign of his poetic gift or the gift itself – for falling in love is given not chosen – I don't know, but it is certainly the sign by which one recognises whether a young man is potentially a poet or not.
>
> "Why do you want to write poetry?" If the young man answers: "I have important things I want to say," then he is not a poet. If he answers: "I like hanging around words listening to what they say," then maybe he is going to be a poet.[29]

The primacy accorded to language here is, one might say, a working poet's implicit corrective to notions of poetry that emphasize imagination, or inspiration, or the author's experience, or the truths and insights poems are taken to offer. Like the phenomenological rallying cry "Zu den Sachen selbst" ("To the things themselves"), Auden's account of the poet calls for a return to the fundamental elements of the discipline: in this case, words, language.

The New Critic Cleanth Brooks provides a different view of the foundational character of language in literary art. He cites with approval this excerpt from the linguistic philosopher W. M. Urban's *Language and Reality*: "The artist does not first intuit his object and then find the appropriate medium. It is rather in and through his medium that he intuits the object."[30] Language is here more than the object of interest, love, and craftsmanship that it is for Auden. In Urban's account, language – artistic language, at least – is inseparable from the object it realizes: it is at once a means to and the singular form of the intuition or representation that is the work of art. Refusing, like Auden, to subordinate language to the subject or idea or emotion of the poem, Urban goes further to make that subject or idea or emotion inaccessible except through the poem's language and inseparable from it. Brooks puts it another way when he explains why any paraphrase of a poem must misrepresent it. The poem, he writes,

> is not only the linguistic vehicle which conveys the thing communicated most "poetically," but…it is also the sole linguistic vehicle which conveys the things communicated accurately. In fact, if we are to speak exactly, the poem itself is the *only* medium that communicates the particular "what" that is communicated.[31]

Where Urban argues that the object is intuitable only through the artistic medium, Mao's paraphrase of Brooks radicalizes this claim to suggest that the poet's work in the artistic medium of language is what *creates* the object. For Brooks, "the object simply does not exist, as such, prior to the form."[32] This is what Lodge terms "a profound paradox at the heart of literary language,…that the imaginative writer creates what he describes. It follows from this that every imaginative utterance is an 'appropriate' symbolization of the experience it conveys, since there is no possible alternative symbolization of 'the same' experience."[33] Here we arrive at the large, post-mimetic claim about the centrality of language to the idea of a poem or other literary text: that language is what creates the object it is often taken merely to describe or render or represent. In the formulation of R. P. Blackmur, a critic contemporary with the principal voices of the New Criticism though not exactly a card-carrying member of that loosely united group, "The art of poetry is amply distinguished from the manufacture of verse by the animating presence in the poetry of a fresh idiom: language so twisted and posed in a form that it not only expresses the matter at hand but *adds to the stock of available reality*."[34] With these last few pronouncements, it becomes clear that the formalist concern with language is not merely an effort to license the practice of close reading, or to sidestep the incoherences of referentiality, though it is these and much more. What Urban and especially Brooks, Lodge, and Blackmur make clear is that for formalists, whatever subject a poem is "about," whatever is "in" a poem, the precondition of that subject's being and of its meaning – of its entire mode of existence – is the linguistic possibility that produces and embodies it.

There is a striking correspondence between such notions of the literary text and certain twentieth-century philosophical speculations about the roles of language and symbol in the production of human knowledge and the construction of reality. In the three volumes of his *Philosophy of Symbolic Forms*, published in the 1920s, and in his roughly contemporary *Language and Myth,* later published in 1946 in Susanne Langer's translation, Ernst Cassirer seeks to disclose the degree to which language, far from mirroring or representing the world, actively produces it.[35] The implications, and the neo-Kantian and even Romantic character, of Cassirer's central argument are caught in an early passage of *Language and Myth*.[36] There, rejecting the conventional mimetic notion that the truth of intellectual forms is to be determined by the fidelity with which they represent a reality distinct from and external to themselves, Cassirer argues that

> we must find in these forms themselves the measure and criterion for their truth and intrinsic meaning. Instead of taking them as mere copies of something else, we must see in each of these spiritual forms a spontaneous law of generation...From this point of view, myth, art, language and science appear as symbols; not in the sense of mere figures which refer to some given reality by means of suggestion and allegorical renderings, but in the sense of *forces each of which produces and posits a world of its own*. In these realms the spirit exhibits itself in that inwardly determined dialectic by virtue of which alone there is any reality, any organized and definite Being at all. Thus the special symbolic forms are not imitations but *organs* of reality, since it is solely by their agency that anything real becomes an object for intellectual apprehension, and as such is made visible to us.[37]

The point of invoking Cassirer on symbolic forms is not to suggest that he is writing as a literary theorist, nor to claim for Brooks or Lodge or Blackmur a general theory of language or symbolism or cultural construction. It is simply to designate an historical and intellectual context for what might be called the constructivist dimension of the New Critical and related formalist projects, and to highlight a particular twentieth-century interest in moving beyond mimetic or representationalist epistemologies and aesthetics: an interest that saw something of a resurgence in the second half of that century, in critical theory as in other fields. In a 1978 essay, to take just one example, Walter Benn Michaels provides a counterpart in the realm of belief and ideology to Cassirer's substitution of an instrumentalist ("organs") for a representationalist ("imitations") model of the relation between symbolic forms and reality. "Our beliefs," Michaels writes, "are not obstacles between us and meaning, they are what makes meaning possible in the first place. Meaning is not filtered through what we believe, it is constituted by what we believe."[38] This is, in effect, Lodge's "profound paradox... that the imaginative writer creates what he describes" rewritten in the key of ideology and general epistemology.

And though, as I have remarked, Cassirer is not writing as a literary critic or theorist, or even as a general aesthetician, he does venture very close to one of the assumptions that undergird the kind of formalist project I am attempting to describe. In the second volume of *The Philosophy of Symbolic Forms*, he details the conceptual movement from mythological to linguistic to artistic modes of symbolization, saying of the latter:

> Here for the first time the image world acquires a purely *immanent* validity and truth [i.e., neither fusing magically and mythically with external reality nor linguistically designating it from a distance]. It does not aim at something else or refer to something else; it simply "is" and consists in itself.... Thus for the first time the world of the image becomes a self-contained cosmos with its own center of gravity.[39]

Just as, in the realm of general epistemology, each of the symbolic forms "produces and posits a world of its own," so in the more restricted sphere of art (which Cassirer also refers to as "the image world," "creative art," "the aesthetic world," etc.), the artwork constitutes a correspondingly independent and meaningful whole, a metaphoric "cosmos." More particularly still, and extrapolating from Cassirer's text, we can say that the *linguistic* artwork ("poem" or "literary text"), though constructed of the same elements as texts and utterances serving other purposes – magic spells, scientific observations, road signs, warning labels, everyday conversation – uses those elements in a different way. More accurately, contemporary formalists use literary texts and their elements in a singular and characteristic way, *as though* each were "a self-contained cosmos with its own center of gravity." Such use is part of what makes the text under scrutiny into a literary text.

Like the term "symbolic" in Cassirer's discourse, then, the term "literary" in the language of formalism seems to entail certain assumptions. These include the primacy of the linguistic identity of the text; the text's inability to interpret itself (with the consequent need for critical analysis); and its performance of a creative or constructivist rather than a mimetic relation to reality (producing and positing a world of its own, to adapt Cassirer's formulation). In part because of its freedom from mimesis or referentiality, that is, the text is to a great extent an independent structure of discourse. The next question is, how do these (and other) assumptions about the literary text enable New Formalist analysis, and what is unique and significant about that analysis?

v The text, experience, history

Whatever ideas or themes or messages texts "carry," then, in the sense of "allow us to abstract from them," must be understood in terms of the shaping and transformative powers of the linguistic medium – indeed, understood as inseparable from that medium. This sounds as though I am urging close reading as an inescapable part of formalist critical analysis, and I am, but that is not all that I am urging, or all that a New Formalist approach entails. For close reading can function as a powerful and integral part of any sort of critical analysis, including those contextual or ideological or political modes of criticism that eschew close reading as a decadent, aestheticizing distraction from power and Realpolitik. In Caroline Levine's view, "formalism is precisely what gives value – and analytic and political power – to literary and cultural studies."[40] Often, as Brooks himself contends, "the details and nuances of a work reveal the special nature of its cultural matrix."[41] In a more contemporary idiom, Frank Lentricchia says something similar: "the nonformalists who have dominated literary criticism and theory over the last decades of the twentieth century do their most persuasive work by attending closely to the artistic character of the text before them."[42] If you want to discover covert colonial bias in a professedly anticolonial novel, why rely on the flimsiness of paraphrase, refusing the aid of an analytic strategy that can disclose and minutely anatomize such bias at the level of grammar and syntax, vocabulary, and figures of speech? If you are working out a psychoanalytic reading of a poem or story or private correspondence, aren't details of language the place where the mysteries of the psyche get most intricately and profoundly performed? And even if, in a more historical and sociological vein, you are exploring the socially educative or socially coercive ways didactic novels attempted to shape a female readership in the seventeenth or eighteenth centuries, aren't the overt rules, maxims, and exemplary scenes in such novels only a starting point for analysis? For it is surely the "minute particulars," in Blake's phrase, that constitute the most powerful and potentially insidious mechanisms for readerly control and fashioning: particulars such as narrative voice, the construction or interpellation of audience, detailed modes of address, figurative shapings of attitude and interpretation, the metaphorics of authority and instruction, and so on.

But if close reading can function powerfully in any mode of literary and cultural analysis, and perhaps in any interpretive discipline that treats texts at all, it does not follow that formalism is necessarily reducible to close reading. It certainly was not for the New Critics, who employed close reading to further a highly particular notion of both literary texts and the function and significance of literature. Despite the fact that close reading is commonly regarded as the most enduring legacy – pedagogical legacy, at least – of the New Criticism, and despite contemporary claims such as Levinson's that it is "the single defining skill of our discipline," there was and is much more to formalist criticism than the thoughtful application of close reading techniques. And indeed, close reading itself is not a single, unitary mode of analysis, as Jonathan Culler makes clear:

> Partly because of our resistance to textbooks for literary study and explicit instructions, there exists a wide range of practices of close reading . . . The crucial thing is to slow down, though "slow reading" is doubtless a less useful slogan than either "slow food" or "close reading," since slow reading may be inattentive, distracted, lethargic. *Close* asks for a certain myopia – a *Verfremdungseffekt*. It enjoins looking at rather than through the language of the text and thinking about how it is functioning, finding it puzzling.[43]

To recognize that there are multiple practices of close reading – and that close reading itself is only a part of the critical methods in which it may be embedded – returns us to an earlier question, one that needs to be posed a second time and with a different sort of answer in mind. At first, "What do we want texts to be?" was a question that I tried to answer by claiming that formalists want texts to be linguistic objects, structures of language – a position that entailed, in turn, a mode of analysis appropriate to texts thus conceived: close reading. But now the question takes on a somewhat different and perhaps larger dimension, as it shades into matters of the value and function of reading, the uses of literature, and the relation of texts to their own era and context of production and to a reader's era and context of use. "What do we want texts to be?" but also, "What do we want texts to do for us?"

The New Formalism I am advocating wants texts to be, among other things, linguistic structures that in some sense speak to the condition of the readers who read them, in the present (whichever present that is), and that offer readers significant representations, or explorations, or rehearsals of a variety of existential situations, or roles, or attitudes, or issues. Discussing literary kinds in the eighteenth century, Samuel Johnson seconded Lord Monboddo's assertion that "The history of manners [human behavior, customs, modes of thought and feeling] is the most valuable. I never set a high value on any other history." Johnson responded, "Nor I; and therefore I esteem biography, as giving us *what comes near to ourselves, what we can turn to use.*"[44] This is not to say that texts ought to supply tidy morals, or overt lessons for life, or characters and situations available for simple identification, or exportable nuggets of wisdom. It is to say, however, that the texts we term "literary" can be expected to speak to the reader's own situation – real or merely imaginable – and in some way to deepen or refine or clarify or complicate that situation, or those situations.

The New Critics, too, expected a poem to illuminate the reader's experience, but theirs was a highly particular expectation, trailing clouds of literary and metaphysical assumptions. For them, the ironies and paradoxes of "the language of poetry" are emblems of a maturity of attitude that can negotiate competing or conflicting attitudes and emerge with a unified but complex point of view. Beyond this, poetry – or "the poet" – is to provide affirmations of the fundamental unity of experience. Unlike science (arguably the principal bête noire of the New Critics), which analyzes experience, breaks it up, classifies it, and in doing so thins it to a two-dimensional generalizability and abstractness, the poet's "task is finally to unify experience. He must return to us the unity of the experience itself as man knows it in his own experience."[45] Here is a fuller and even more metaphysically explicit formulation:

> If the poet, then, must perforce dramatize the oneness of the experience, even though paying tribute to its diversity, then his use of paradox and ambiguity is seen as necessary .... He is ... giving us an insight which preserves the unity of experience and which, at its higher and more serious levels, triumphs over the apparently contradictory and conflicting elements of experience by unifying them

into a new pattern.... [T]he poet can make his poem *one* by reducing to order the confusions and disorders and irrelevancies of ordinary experience in terms of one unifying insight.... The poet not only *may* do this; he must.[46]

In its shifts between "the experience" and "experience," its assumption that human experience was once unified but has become confused and contradictory (the poet works by "reducing" confusions – leading them back – to order), or that the disorder of experience is merely apparent, and that what "man" knows despite the evidence of fragmentariness and confusion is unity "in his own experience," the passage makes of poetry a guarantor – at least a revealer – of the coherence and meaningfulness of the cosmos. These are not claims that most contemporary formalisms would be likely to endorse. There are, for them, no constraints on what the poem may or must disclose about the coherence or incoherence of experience, or about anything else. There is only the expectation of using the poem as, among other things, a way of enlarging, or deepening, or clarifying, or rehearsing, or contemplating human attitudes and human experience – the attitudes and experience of the reader, and perhaps of others as well.

In the last quarter century or so, these older and newer sorts of formalist expectation have frequently been conflated, and the insistence that literature speak to the situation of its reader has been taken to be a sign that the poem is being naively conceived as a source of unearned metaphysical comfort or of merely aesthetic pleasure, or treated as a document that may be uprooted from its context of origin and applied to the reader's situation in a manner at once mystified, ahistorical, and slavishly appreciative of texts and their authors. The recommended alternative has not been a more rigorous formalism but some sort of historicizing imperative, from Fredric Jameson's "Always historicize!" in *The Political Unconscious* (1981) through New Historicism and Cultural Studies to various contextualizings and historical situatings performed by a variety of critical schools and trends, many identifying themselves explicitly or implicitly as "political," ideological, or otherwise demystificatory projects. The warrant for such analysis is almost always Marxist, and Jameson's quotation of and commentary on Benjamin's "Theses on the Philosophy of History" can serve as a terse representation of the view of culture, criticism, and especially non-historical criticism that frequently informs those projects. Here is Benjamin: "There has never been a document of culture which was not at one and the same time a document of barbarism." Here is Jameson: "Benjamin's slogan is a hard saying, and not only for liberal and apoliticizing critics of art and literature, for whom it spells the return of class realities and the painful recollection of the dark underside of even the most seemingly innocent and 'life-enhancing' masterpieces of the canon."[47]

As Jameson's self-applauding remark suggests, such historicizing approaches regularly characterize other – particularly formalist – projects of interpretation as labors of mystification that, unwittingly or not, foster belief in a variety of fantasmatic objects: in the autonomy of art and of culture generally; in the ahistoricality of human experience; in the myth of transhistorical cultural communication, as though one could actually imagine oneself part of the audience intelligibly addressed by texts of Plato or Pope; in the superiority of "high" or canonical art to popular or folk culture; in political quietism, since attentive, non-suspicious reading is taken to signify a thoughtless acquiescence in one's own exploitation (in contrast, relentless labor under the banner of exposé signifies liberation rather than uncritical entrapment by ideology); in myths of individualism and self-determination, because much literature and much traditional criticism treats characters as though their fates were somehow connected with their identity as relatively autonomous beings; and more. There is, of course, a case to be argued – better, a discussion to hold – about every one of these points, but it is rarely argued with much patience or tolerance.

This is itself a somewhat rash and ill-tempered summary, but I think it is important to try, however inadequately, to speak for those critics whom Marxist and some other forms of historical and ideological criticism would read out of court, and to assert that however "explainable" traditionalist annoyance may be as the expression of class interests (as in, "It's no accident that a mandarin professoriate promotes a bourgeois aesthetic"), an indissoluble component of that annoyance is outrage at the frequent crudities of historicist procedures: the tendentious allegorizing of texts so as to make them yield the required messages about class struggle and imperialism, for example, and the conscienceless characterization of traditional and formalist critics as simple apologists for exploitation. In a less polemical and more general and theoretical way, then, I want to ask what is lost or surrendered by certain kinds of historical approach, and whether there are not alternatives to historicist accounts of the rationale for non-historical criticism. My aim is not to argue that Marxist or ideological analysis is illegitimate in principle, or that it should be suspended forthwith, but to recall some of the tasks that such analysis cannot by its very nature perform, and to suggest some of the legitimate reasons why other sorts of critic – formalists included – engage in those tasks.

Certainly, anything can be historicized, and the question asked "Where did this come from?" That is, who or what produced it? by what means? to serve what ends? and so forth. But to ask this is not the same as to ask, "Is this true?" Of course, the question "Is this true?" – and the desire (or the belief that it is appropriate) to ask this question – can itself be historicized, but it is also true that the question "Where did this come from?" can be queried as to the truth, and the kind of truth, of the answer it supplies. The mistake is to think that one question simply dominates the other; each is the other's base, or each asks the question the other can't ask. What we often find in self-proclaimedly historicist theory and interpretation, however, is precisely a confusion of these two questions, and a critique – and a structure of value – built on that confusion. The demonstration of the historicity of formations is no indictment of their truth, and this is so even if the formations were indeed established by one or another kind of political, social, or cultural violence. For even though the establishment of norms by force – even by force of arms, let alone force of cultural signification – is a bad thing, this force has nothing to do with the truth or falsity of the norms thus violently established.

From another point of view, the claims of universality or naturalness that are part of the mechanism of ideology can indicate that the possibility of truth or belief and the inescapability of historicity are not necessarily at odds, though they belong to different conceptual spheres. One says "No knowledge or meaning or system is not produced historically," and the other says "No knowledge or meaning or system is exempt from – or should be deprived of – having its claims viewed as matters of truth and falsity, and of possible performability." The seemingly universalist claims are a reminder that there is another question besides "Where did it come from?" namely, "Is it true?" And a reminder, too, that discovery is experienced in the mode of truth and falsity, not in that of historicity. Even historicizing discoveries are experienced in this mode. After all, "Always historicize!" isn't a methodological imperative without an aim. Just as a stop sign says "Stop" but means "Stop, then go," so Jameson's cry means "Always historicize, because doing so will supply you with the truth." But it depends on what sort of truth is being sought – for example, a truth pertinent to the context, author, audience, and era of a text's writing and publication, or a truth pertinent to whoever happens to be reading the text, wherever and whenever. As John M. Ellis has remarked of some historicizing modes of interpretation,

Antiformalists were in theory right to insist that literary texts be related to life, but in practice did less to relate literature to life than their opponents, because they chose to relate them not to the life of the community but only to the limited context of life in which the texts originated.[48]

Ellis' is just one of many accounts of the limitations of a strictly historical approach to literary texts, and especially of the notion that such an approach is the sole rightful claimant to critical legitimacy. Lord Bolingbroke has been much derided by modern historians for saying that history is "philosophy teaching by examples," but it is no less one-sided to claim that our interest in a text and its meanings should never raise the question of their bearing on our own life and times, and on our own conceptions of truth and experience. Marjorie Levinson worries about a "contextualism that reduces artworks to bundles of historical content."[49] For Northrop Frye, historical criticism is by definition incomplete:

> From a purely historical point of view,... cultural phenomena are to be read in their own context without contemporary application. We study them as we do the stars, seeing their interrelationships but not approaching them. Hence historical criticism needs to be complemented by a corresponding activity growing out of tropical criticism.[50]

The "purely historical" point of view entails not simply a reduction of text to context and content, and not simply a loss of pertinence to contemporary readers, but – as I believe Levinson implies – a loss or deformation of the ontological status of the work itself, a dissolving of its present hereness or thisness into an instrumental transparence or translucence through which we seek to contemplate the past. It is partly as a reaction to these reductions and deformations that New Formalisms have posited and performed a variety of "historical formalisms" such as Stephen Cohen describes in his introduction to *Shakespeare and Historical Formalism*:

> [E]nmeshed in a web of institutional and cultural as well as social and political histories, literary forms are overdetermined by their historical circumstances and thus multiple and variable in their results, neither consistently ideological nor intrinsically demystificatory but instead reacting unpredictably with each other and with

other cultural discourses. The goal of a historical formalism is to explore the variety of these interactions, mutually implicating literature's formal individuation and its historical situation in order to illuminate at once text, form, and history.[51]

vi   "Universal" meanings, actual meanings

Even apart from questions of ideology, to insist on the pertinence to present readers of earlier texts is to re-invoke the specter of universalism. In this view, again, to read Plato or Sappho, Chaucer or Austen, we need only let them speak to us as though we were their original audience; their texts contain universal meanings available to all who read with reasonable care. For Samuel Johnson, there is a "uniformity in the state of man," present or past and presumably future as well. "We are all prompted by the same motives, all deceived by the same fallacies, all animated by hope, obstructed by anger, entangled by desire, and seduced by pleasure."[52] Few, of course, openly champion the idea of an essential and unchanging human nature (or human cultural identity), especially in the past half century or so. Nor, as I will try to suggest shortly, does the idea that literary texts or other cultural productions speak to us require the assumption of universalism. Certainly the perceived power and significance – in the present – of verbal and non-verbal art from the past still leads sensitive readers and critics to speak of "the uncanny problem of perceived historical continuity," or to argue that

> New Critical hypostatization of the text originates less with some fear of the difference that history threatens to unleash than with a need to address the unaccountable fact that texts from the distant past *do* continue to 'speak' – to come to terms with a temporal miracle that parallels the spatial miracle of the community of letters.[53]

But though the language here – "uncanny," "historical continuity," "unaccountable" – may seem to imply a vestigial universalism, the continuity of past with present is said to be "perceived," and the ability of past texts to speak to us is termed "unaccountable" rather than glibly explained by the assumption of a common human nature. In fact, passages like these register the fact that there is a dimension of textuality beyond the findings of historicism, that sophisticated readers and theorists consider this dimension to be of singular value, and that accounting for it requires a significant effort of theory and criticism and not an easy recourse to the fable of universalism, or any other fable.

Rather than being "universal," what formalist critics find in the texts they interpret is itself historical since what a given critic takes a text to mean is inescapably conditioned by his or her own historical situation. Even if a formalist foregoes historical accounts of authorial intention in favor of what used to be called an internal intention – that is, the inferred, linguistically enacted intention of the text's speaker rather than of its author – that internal intention is no more transhistorical or universal than anything else in the poem. The very language of the text to which we appeal in arguing for a particular internal intention will be read differently, will mean differently, will be different, in different historical periods. Appealing to "the text" can't circumvent the historical character of that appeal any more than it can circumvent the need for interpretation. Why, then, does it not seem to many interpreters that they are doing anything other than analytically and dispassionately discovering the meanings of the texts they interpret? Joel Weinsheimer paraphrases Gadamer's thinking about this question:

> The effect of history is manifest in every interpretation – or rather in every interpretation but our own. This exception may mean that the force of history has now been finally controlled by methodological safeguards conducive to objectivity. Gadamer concludes, however, that, quite the opposite, the transparency of our times to us is not the exception but the universal rule, for all responsible interpreters consider themselves to be telling the eternal truth.[54]

Just as Cassirer had argued that "the special symbolic forms are not imitations but *organs* of reality, since it is solely by their agency that anything real becomes an object for intellectual apprehension, and as such is made visible to us,"[55] so Gadamer contends that the historical shaping of our point of view is not the obstacle to an allegedly attainable "objectivity" (where "objective" commonly – and incoherently – means "understood, but from *no* point of view") but the condition of knowledge and interpretation at all. Thus, if New Formalism refuses to claim that the readerly perspective contemporary with the work's era of production is the most valuable, it also refuses both the false universalism that claims to find a timeless meaning in the text and the methodological naïveté that takes what is "there" in the text to be a meaning unshaped by the reader's historical determination. History, as Weinsheimer puts it, is "productive of knowledge and truth rather than the source of the relativism that precludes them."[56]

Another of Gadamer's formulations attempts to do justice both to readers' changing perceptions of a text and to their sense of its persistence through time. "The classic" he writes, "epitomizes a general characteristic of historical being" – a remark that Weinsheimer elaborates as follows: "historical being is the kind of being which, precisely by altering, comes into its own and is thus irreducibly both other and itself. Conceived in this way, the question of the classic and of history itself is how to think unity and plurality, sameness and difference, without denying either."[57] A statement like this can return us to Frye's effort to distinguish between "historical" and "tropical" criticism, but now in a different and more complex formulation. Frye first notes that what may have begun in the past as an object of utility (such as textiles, masks, clothing, armor, and so on) may be reclassified as an object of pleasure and thus a work of art, its identity being established not by anything intrinsic to the object but by the use that a given culture makes of it. Such reclassification is not confined to the "use/pleasure" or "not art/art" dualities, for it regularly takes place within the sphere of art itself as a new interpretation makes of a given text or painting or film a different sort of object, with different meanings. "Even the most fanatical historical critic," he writes, "is bound to see Shakespeare and Homer as writers whom we admire for reasons that would have been largely unintelligible to them, to say nothing of their societies."[58]

Having affirmed the modern understanding of earlier texts, Frye, like Gadamer, attempts to honor the historical as well as the "tropical" dimensions of critical analysis, pointing up the limitations of a rigorously ahistorical criticism:

> But we can hardly be satisfied with an approach to works of art which simply strips from them their original function. One of the tasks of criticism is that of the recovery of function, not of course the restoration of an original function, which is out of the question, but the recreation of function in a new context.

Drawing on Kierkegaard's concept of repetition, Frye describes this recreation of function as "not the simple repeating of an experience, but the recreating of it which redeems or awakens it to life…" He elaborates:

> [T]he goal of historical criticism, as our metaphors about it often indicate, is a kind of self-resurrection, the vision of a valley of dry bones that takes on the flesh and blood of our own vision. The culture of the past is not only the memory of mankind, but our own buried

life, and study of it leads to a recognition scene, a discovery in which we see, not our past lives, but the total cultural form of our present life....Without this sense of "repetition," historical criticism tends to remove the products of culture from our own sphere of interest. It must be counterpoised, as it is in all genuine historical critics, by a sense of the contemporary relevance of past art.[59]

The passage is remarkable for its flickering movement between historical and contemporary investments in the work of art, and for its refusal of more traditional accounts of the relationship between present readers and older texts. In Frye's formulation, we do not attempt to recreate or join the historical audience of Homer or Shakespeare, allegedly leaving behind our own contemporaneity. But neither do we simply "breathe new life" into older works, turning the dead letter into living meaning by an act of sympathetic understanding that is also an ascription of contemporary relevance. Older texts are indeed given a "recovery of function" – more precisely, a "recreation of function in a new context" – but what gets resurrected is not, as in traditional humanistic accounts, a previously moribund text but our contemporary selves. Our current life and cultural identity are themselves reborn, made new, by being seen in a context that now includes the dimensions of the past represented by the texts we read. As a result, we are changed, much as a word is changed when it is placed in a new and larger context, or viewed in relation to its earlier meanings and etymology.

Frye's discussion simply takes for granted that the past and its texts cannot be made present to us as they were present to readers contemporary with them, and the case he makes is not exactly what I meant earlier by the pertinence to present readers of earlier texts. But to my contention that "our interest in a text and its meanings should...raise the question of their bearing on our own life and times, and on our own conceptions of truth and experience," he offers a different and complementary model. In Frye's scheme, we can only know a work as we – not its contemporaries – know it, regardless of our efforts at historical scholarship; the alternative is a fantasy, simply "out of the question." But rather than drawing the work as we understand it into our own set of existential resources – "literature as equipment for living," as Kenneth Burke has put it[60] – Frye sees the interpreted work drawing us into *its* orbit, where we find ourselves newly expanded and redefined as dwellers in a larger and more complex cosmos than we had heretofore inhabited. In Hartman's succinct and related formulation, "Interpretation is bringing the poem forward into the present, which is acknowledging its historicity, which is grounding our terms in history."[61] It is almost as though Frye were rewriting Eliot's argument, in "Tradition and the Individual Talent," as an account of critical reading rather than of literary production, an account told from the point of view of the individual reader rather than of the order of existing works. Here is Eliot's famous formulation:

> [W]hat happens when a new work of art is created is something that happens simultaneously to all the works of art which preceded it. The existing monuments form an ideal order among themselves, which is modified by the introduction of the new (the really new) work of art among them. The existing order is complete before the new work arrives; for order to persist after the supervention of novelty, the *whole* existing order must be, if ever so slightly, altered; and so the relations, proportions, values of each work of art toward the whole are readjusted; and this is conformity between the old and the new. Whoever has approved this idea of order, of the form of European, of English literature, will not find it preposterous that the past should be altered by the present as much as the present is directed by the past.[62]

In Frye's discussion, what is not preposterous is that the present should be altered by the past. For him, present readers are altered by reading a work that discloses their place in a cultural and existential situation enlarged and modified by their critical understanding of that work.

In both Frye's account and in New Formalist versions of the ancient and traditional claim that literature is somehow pertinent to the reader's experience, no dreams of interpretive time travel are entertained: the past is visible to inhabitants of the present only as it is made intelligible by the historical forces that shape us and our investigations. And if one pole of critical fantasy is the historicist dream that we can know the past "in itself," or unconditioned by the present, or as its inhabitants knew it, the other pole is the universalist dream that historical distance is itself an illusion, that human nature is substantially the same in all eras and climes, and thus that the meanings we seek to derive from texts of the past, or of the present, are simply "human," conditioned insignificantly if at all by place, time, or circumstance. Neither of these fallacious assumptions is required for a formalist criticism that seeks to discover the pertinence to contemporary readers of works from the near or distant past, or that seeks to situate readers in a context enlarged and enriched by the ancient or modern texts they may read and interpret.

vii   Readerly distance, readerly nearness

When Frye notes that "from a purely historical point of view, ... cultural phenomena are to be read in their own context without contemporary application," but then adds that "historical criticism needs to be complemented by a corresponding activity growing out of tropical criticism," he raises – within the sphere of history and historical change – the question of the reader's distance from and nearness to the text. Quite apart from the historicist/formalist dialogue, this question bears generally on the kinds of criticism we want to produce and the kinds of experience we take reading and interpretation to provide. Moreover, there are several kinds of distance and proximity, and it is a mistake to lump them together. If the historicist, for example, seeks to distance the text by attempting to relocate it in its historical context, the formalist also holds the text at an analytical arm's length, investigating the details of its language and structure rather than concentrating on what it "says" or "represents."[63] Instead of looking *through* language, to borrow Richard A. Lanham's useful distinction, as though the text were merely a prose window on external reality (as with dosage instructions on a medicine bottle, for example, or a sign that says "Bridge Out"), formalists seek to look *at* language, noticing an instance of alliteration, or Latinate diction, or repetition, or sexual terminology, or any other feature of the textual surface itself.[64] At times, the second, formalist sort of distancing has been criticized as draining the text of human and/or historical interest, or reducing it to an object of chilly academic analysis, or uncritically elevating – fetishizing – it as an object of aesthetic worship: the "well-wrought urn" or "verbal icon" of the New Criticism. And historically speaking, the allegedly disinterested contemplation characteristic of some traditional aesthetics is indeed very much a secularized version of the characteristic posture of humans – contemplative and worshipful – before the perfection and self-containedness of the deity, as M. H. Abrams has deftly shown.[65]

While the arguments against disinterestedness and detachment have been plentiful if not remarkably varied, the opposite practice of taking the text directly to heart by drawing pat life-lessons from it or responding to its personages and events as though they were in some sense real has also come in for considerable criticism. There is a tradition of viewing this sort of relation to the text as amateurish, "book-clubby," unintellectual: a way of reading for (mere) pleasure rather than literary critical – or indeed, historical – understanding. Of particular interest, then, are those refusals of distance, or of distance alone, that arise not from the reading public in general but from the literary critical establishment, sometimes from the formalist wing of that establishment. For these critics, the detachment required for analysis is only part of the story, alternating or coexisting with the pleasurable and important ability to immerse oneself in a text, as we say, or lose oneself in a story, or inhabit the consciousness and experiences of a fictional character, or enter a fictional "world." This need not be conceived as a mindless confusion of fiction with reality. Even when spectators at a play are deeply moved by a performance, says Samuel Johnson, they "are always in their senses and know from the first act to the last that the stage is only a stage, and that the players are only players." "It will be asked," he adds, "how the drama moves [spectators] if it is not credited. It is credited with all the credit due to a drama."[66] While we may say, then, that there are no people, places, events, foods, crimes in a text, only verbal representations of such entities, we must also say that the experience of acting as though those elements of a text were real, even as we know them not to be, carries a particular value and power for even sophisticated readers and textual theorists.

Moreover, to deny or refuse such investments, yet insist that literary texts bear on readers' own experience, is almost inevitably to valorize the cognitive and intellectual import of reading rather than the experiential and emotive. But most contemporary formalisms do not urge an exclusively intellectual or cognitive model of reading. Quite the contrary. Most New Formalist interpretation is, precisely, a mode of criticism that recognizes the world as we experience it as well as the world as we know or analyze it, a criticism that envisions readers in a variety of subject positions and thus establishes a relationship of provisional identification as well as of critical distance. New Formalism thus "produces" a text that gives us not knowledge alone but a series of virtual positionings before (or in) virtual situations, and which thus permits us to rehearse or enrich or complicate or explore our relations to experience instead of simply analyzing them. In doing so, it of course assumes that our actual relation to experience is not purely analytical but, well, experiential: a matter of values, choices, sympathies, identifications, desires, aversions, and so on. It is a criticism responsive to the claims of experience, and not just those of knowledge.

A distinction like that between knowledge-based and experience-based criticism always runs the danger of looking anti-intellectual, as though one were trying to deny that knowledge is a good thing or – worse still – that it is itself a part of our experience. Perhaps this danger can be minimized by drawing a parallel between New Formalist analysis and different forms of psychotherapy. However valuable each of two therapeutic modes might be, there is a vast difference between a therapy that simply analyzes past experiences and coolly plans future ones, and a therapy that seeks to re-enact past experiences and thereby rehearse future ones. In the first case, the therapeutic session stands to future experiences as analysis to script, or as assessment to intention; in the second, it stands to future experiences as rehearsal to performance. Only the second kind would put one into the subject-position, insofar as that position is conceived to be more than an analytical posture, and only the second kind encourages a measure of identification as well as of distance in relation to the protagonists of that future experience – not least, oneself.

A criticism based on knowledge and a criticism based on experience are thus very different things. The former cannot conceive of litera-ture as supplying rehearsals of experience, an enlargement of freedom by a multiplication of imaginative possibilities, because the posture it encourages is not that of a potential experiencer but that of a knower or analyst of experience. This doesn't mean that such criticism is useless, or even secondary, only that it does one thing and can't do another. Whether the two systems or stances can be made to communicate, whether salutary leakage or benign contamination can be encouraged, is of course an important question, not just for literary study but for psy-chotherapies, philosophy, and indeed for education (does what we learn affect only our lives-as-knowers, or other aspects of our lives as well?). A Gestalt model suggests that the two stances "coexist" by alternation – faces *or* vase, duck *or* rabbit. The Johnsonian theatrical model ("It is credited with all the credit due to a drama") suggests the simultane-ity of a kind of double consciousness.[67] But the two critical stances are nevertheless distinct, and the activities I've designated by terms like "rehearsal," "modeling," "provisional," and "partial identification" all emphasize the experiential dimension of literary study and not simply the analytic.

Such a position, of course, presupposes the oblique or as-if character of literary works rather than taking them as direct guides for living, or as manifestos with claims on the reader – hortatory imperatives rather than models to be tried on and imaginatively lived into. It views the reading of literature as a project of enlarging imaginative possibility, of letting readers see and feel – without final commitment – what it would be like to inhabit a certain stance or view, whether that of a literary character, a narrator, or an internal "reader" or audience that a work creates by means of its structure of address. In this view, literature should provide, in Johnson's words, "what comes near us, what we can turn to use," and one of the ways it does so is by constructing numerous "subject positions" or alternative selves-in-situations with which we provisionally identify ourselves in the act of reading. As a result, reading enables us to enlarge our repertory of ways of being in the world. This is to many a crucial dimension of reading, even in the case of works whose narrators or characters are wildly repellent to us – not just works that entertain but ultimately criticize or reject repellent notions, but works that simply and unequivocally endorse them. Such works still allow us to rehearse, and not simply to appropriate or criticize, what it means to see things in a way that is not our own, to see things as a self that we are not sees them. Whether we end up simply approving or disapproving, or entertaining a more complex and nuanced response, it is the provisionality of our entering into the text that will lend the reader's response its freedom and earnedness.[68] Literature, as Derek Attridge notes, "can act powerfully to hold the political and the ethical up for scrutiny by means of its power of suspension, momentarily dissociating them from their usual pressing context, performing the ethical decision and the political gesture."[69] And earlier, Frye, in *The Educated Imagination*, had argued as well as anyone a somewhat different version of this case:

> In belief you're continually concerned with questions of truth or reality: you can't believe anything unless you can say "this is so." But literature ... never makes any statements of that kind; what the poet and novelist say is more like "let's assume this situation." ... So, you may ask, what is the use of studying the world of imagination where anything is possible and anything can be assumed, where there are no rights or wrongs and all arguments are equally good? One of the most obvious uses, I think, is its encouragement of tolerance. In the imagination our own beliefs are also only possibilities, but we can also see the possibilities in the beliefs of others.... What produces the tolerance is the power of detachment in the imagination, where things are removed just out of reach of belief and action.[70]

The ability to be changed by one's reading experience, to believe that literature can change us, is closely tied to the idea of an experience-based criticism. Bernard Sharratt writes interestingly about the way in which film and literature give us the double or complex pleasure of nearly losing ourselves in identification with one or another figure yet recovering ourselves through the re-establishment of a critical distance.[71] In watching a filmed conversation, for example, our perspective is frequently *almost* that of each character as he or she sees the other, but not quite. We see Y largely from X's point of view, but we also see a bit of X's shoulder or the back of X's head, and this leads us to oscillate between an intratextual identity that fuses with X and a coherent, extratextual identity or position that also looks at both X and Y. There is thus a play between the dissolving and the reconstitution of self, between identification and distance. Sharratt bases his argument on Marx, Freud, Plato (for whom the rhapsode's ecstasy is a matter of identifying with others, losing himself in roles he plays), and Lacan, but his central contention is much like the notion of provisional and partial identification that I have been describing. Since such reading both takes you out of yourself and provides pleasure, Sharratt calls it "extatic" [sic] reading.

A later formulation of Sharratt's turns to the possibility of being changed by what we read and thus resists the notion that to read as a subject fetishizes the text and confirms the reader in his or her ideological cloud of unknowing by producing simple identification and thus simple mystification:

> Insofar as extasie involves a vertigo of identifications, identities, projections, it calls into question the very notion of the "unity" of the person reading. To read Donne's "The Flea" "responsively," "fully," "appropriately" is to enter into a relationship with one's "self" that challenges the very coherence of that "self"; it is to create in the process of reading a palimpsest of "I's" and "Others" in which the known, stable, "I" we normally identify with, identify ourselves as, is constantly effaced and lost; yet in the same movement, in a fluctuating and flickering way, that coherent I is re-established, re-asserts itelf as the locus of control over the evanescence and vacillation. In subjecting myself to the reading I partially lose myself as subject, experience the "I" of the reading as constituted by and in the act of reading. Much of the time, that stable, everyday I is dominant; in reading extatically it is possible to glimpse the dissolution of that everyday I, to become aware of that I as always constituted. (p. 33)[72]

If Frye argues that literature and other imaginative experience allows us to see our actual beliefs as also possibilities, Sharratt extends this formulation, insisting that reading allows us to see *ourselves* as possibilities and, in consequence, lets us account for and value literature as something that can change us.

viii Rehearsing attitudes, realizing the text

The idea of reading as a provisional adoption of roles and attitudes that the text performs has been around for some time. In the twentieth century, it appears indirectly in T. S. Eliot's criticism when he discusses Coleridge on the "willing suspension of disbelief," or when – in an essay on Dante – he distinguishes between "philosophical belief and poetic assent."[73] It appears somewhat less obliquely in I. A. Richards' faith – itself part of an ambitious educational vision – that poetry might serve to "organize" impulses and emotions in such a way as to better fit readers to respond to experience. And in another guise, still oblique yet more insistent, it informs the New Critical emphasis on the essential presence of irony, paradox, tension, and complexity of attitude in the language of poetry. When Brooks says of Robert Herrick that, "Far from being unconscious of the contradictory elements in the poem ['Corinna's Going A-Maying'], he quite obviously has them in mind," or when he speaks of "the delicate balance and reconciliation of a host of partial interpretations and attitudes," or when he quotes Robert Penn Warren's claim that "The poet, somewhat less spectacularly [than the saint], proves his vision by submitting it to the fires of irony . . . to indicate that his vision has been earned, that it can survive reference to the complexities and contradictions of experience" – when Brooks does this, he is certainly arguing for the particular complexity of the New Critical idea of poetic language.[74]

But he is also suggesting, admittedly in a somewhat spectral way, a readerly attitude of non-appropriation based on what Hartman terms "the essential latency of what [the reader] finds, the quality of art's resistance to intimacy."[75] Brooks's language in these formulations, like Hartman's, largely operates within the discourse of the New Criticism: it assumes the existence of linguistic features specific and intrinsic to literature; it assigns the agency of meaning-production to the work itself, whether the "poem" or "art"; and if it speaks of a "vision" at all, it is that of the poet, not the reader. Yet in a later critical age such as our own, when the role of individual readers and particularly of what Fish terms interpretive communities has significantly shaped conceptions of both reader and text, it is not difficult to hear in such New Critical statements the desire for a salutary frustration of the reader's presumed eagerness for simple statements and meanings. In their regular, even ritual efforts to distinguish literature from political slogans and propaganda, in fact, the New Critics made it clear that direct action on – or simple belief in – the "statements" of a poem betrays an antiliterary and regressive mode of reading. While they rarely use the language of rehearsing or trying on roles and attitudes, then, their insistence on textual reticence, on ironic complexity, and on linguistic and existential contradiction opens a space in which we may find that possibility, or at least a significant precursor of it.

One of the interesting features of the current revival and revision of formalist criticism is the frequency with which the idea of reading as a rehearsal of attitudes appears. In some cases, the emphasis is on moving the perception of reality from a state of givenness to a state of possibility, thereby opening the world to change and the self to alternative attitudes and modes of agency. Such an undertaking may take a political form, though it need not do so. Robert Kaufman, for example, speaks of a readerly "construction of subjectivity," and a "capacity for *knowing* that is propaedeutic to knowledge, conceptual thought, and critical agency" rather than to political agency or social change alone.[76] The question of agency in this broader sense also lies at the heart of Knapp's notion of "literary interest," which posits the ability of the reader of literature to achieve self-discovery and "read herself as an instance of descriptive representation," an act that in turn provides "an unusually precise and concentrated analogue of what it is like to be an agent in general."[77] This is, as Culler says, an effort "to locate the distinctive features of literature not in particular qualities of language or framings of language but in the staging of agency and in the relation to otherness into which readers of literature are brought."[78]

The word "staging" in Culler's formulation returns us to the notion of rehearsing positions and attitudes, a dramatic and theatrical vocabulary that appears in Charles Altieri's discussion of "the delights of staging ourselves as different identities," a practice that makes possible the use of texts as "grounds for our taking certain dispositions as valuable without our having to derive the value by a chain of argument."[79] Levinson rightly notes the heavy emphasis on pleasure and affect elsewhere in Altieri's formulations, and the tendency of his vocabulary to imply, at times, a conception of simple identification with the subject positions made possible by reading a given text, rather than offering a more nuanced and more cognitive goal such as she finds in Shelley's *Defence of Poetry*: "We want [i.e., lack] the creative faculty to imagine that which we know; we want the generous impulse to act that which we imagine."[80] In all of these formulations, though, the value of literary texts is connected somehow to readers' provisional or exploratory relation to various subject positions as well as to the otherness those readers confront and negotiate, as in Knapp's account.

We have been considering different New Formalist descriptions of the relation between reader and text: as a rehearsal of virtual roles, or of one's agency and relation to otherness; as provisional identification; as an imagining of one's actuality as also a possibility (Shelley's "imagine that which we know"); as a multiplication of imaginative possibilities; or as a dynamic that puts readerly energies of identification and textual desire in tension with what Hartman terms "the quality of art's resistance to intimacy."[81] Formulations like these return us to the relation of doubleness between reader and text – a combination of nearness and distance, or identification and contemplation, or grasping at and "entertaining," or closing in on and closely reading. Such doubleness is, in fact, a central if frequently tacit assumption of much New Formalist criticism. It is something like the relation Emile Benveniste describes between a speaker's and a linguist's ideas of language:

> For the speaker there is a complete equivalence between language and reality. The sign overlies and commands reality; even better it *is* that reality.... [T]he point of view of the speaker and of the linguist are so different in this regard that the assertion of the linguist as to the arbitrariness of designations does not refute the contrary feeling of the speaker.[82]

This is an exaggeratedly stark account, but it accurately describes the opposition between a speaker whose language is scarcely distinct from the reality it designates – and is thus invisible – and a linguist for whom language enjoys a largely arbitrary and conventional relation to reality and is thus both visible and an object of analysis. Like Benveniste's speaker, the reader who identifies with a work, who seeks or simply finds intimacy with that work, approaches asymptotically a condition of fusion with the text that obliterates the latter's textual status entirely. Such a reader needs what Peter Brooks terms "the self-imposition of the formalist *askesis* because this alone can assure the critic that the act of interpretation has been submitted to an otherness, that it is not simply an assimilation of the object of study."[83] And like Benveniste's linguist, the purely analytic reader, who seeks to keep the text different from him or herself – to keep it at the distance of pure analyzability (like the stars, as Frye says) – approaches a condition that annihilates the text's bearing on experience, evacuates it of existential import.

Both terms of the relationship are necessary, in part because both intimacy and distance – when not pushed to their hypothetical end-states, as Benveniste and I have pushed them – are not grotesque abstractions from a more complex conception of reading but positive and essential modes of relation in their own right, however different from each other. Nearness is what makes the text real to readers, what gives it significance beyond the status of a work valued solely as a linguistic construct, or a fragment of history, or a cultural symptom, or an object of beauty that we contemplate with disinterested awe. It is what allows us to possess the text, in some sense, though not in the sense that we own it or crush it to our bosom so closely as to suffocate it or lose sight entirely of its difference from our actual, non-textual experience. Within a properly managed relation of nearness, that is, there is a dimension of restraint, of provisionality, of distance. Distance, on the other hand, is what allows us to see the text rather than naively strive to be one with it; it is what makes the text an object of interpretation, analysis, thought, and imagination. But this distanced, analytical, critical interpretation is more than an effort of scrutiny or taxonomy or dissection, though it may well include these and more, for such modes of analysis are means and not ends. In some sense, the end is certainly "To see what's there," as a naive empiricist might put it, but to see what's there in order to bring the text into fullest being, to help it to fulfillment of form and meaning, to realize it as a theater director realizes a play's text by interpreting it into stage life and existence.[84] So while distance is in some inescapable sense the condition of analysis, the ultimate goal of that analysis is not the flaying but the fulfillment of the artwork. The establishment of a critical distance thus has within it, as do teaching and parenthood, an ambition of nurturance, an investment in the realization of the other, a fostering energy of nearness.

ix The critique of the intrinsic, the objectivity of the text

This implicit rewriting of the intrinsic – "the language of paradox," "the language of poetry" – as a relation between text and reader is, as we have seen, a characteristic move of New Formalist criticism.[85] It is, for one thing, a way of revising and preserving a number of the most useful insights of the New Critical era without endorsing some of its highly problematic assumptions: about the unity of a text, about its total meaningfulness, about the intrinsic nature of textual or poetic meaning, about the distinguishability of literary from non-literary language by specifiable features, and more. This combination of valuable insight and problematic theoretical grounding marks Roman Jakobson's well known discussion of poetic language in his "Closing Statement: Linguistics and Poetics," which appeared in the 1960 collection *Style in*

Language.[86] Jakobson attempts there to distinguish poetic language – or "the poetic function" – from other forms of discourse, to isolate "the indispensable feature inherent in any piece of poetry" (358).

Jakobson first posits six distinct but overlapping "factors...involved in verbal communication" – Addresser, Addressee, Context (elsewhere, "referent"), Contact (mode of connection between addresser and addressee), Code (the "language" addresser and addressee must share), and Message (not the meaning, but the oral or written "text" itself). Jakobson elaborates the first five, and then turns to the sixth in order to define the essential character of the *poetic* text. While the poetic function operates in other modes of language in a subsidiary way, and while the others operate in a subsidiary way in poetic language, that function is the "dominant, determining function" of poetic language. "This function," he says, "by promoting the palpability of signs, deepens the fundamental dichotomy of signs and objects" (356). That is, it foregrounds the message as message, the words as words, the sounds as sounds, and thus enforces that attention to the verbal as such that many associate with poetry and other forms of "literary language" – what Nelson Goodman terms "the nontransparency of a work of art, ... the primacy of the work over what it refers to."[87] Elsewhere, Jakobson says that the "set (*Einstellung*) toward the MESSAGE as such, focus on the message for its own sake, is the POETIC function of language."[88]

In another formulation, using the vocabulary of linguistics, Jakobson first describes the "axis of selection" and "the axis of combination" and then proceeds to characterize their special relation in the language of poetry. The axis of selection is the virtual reservoir of words from which any actual word in a text has been selected. Thus in the sentence, "The cat is on the mat," "cat" has been selected from (that is, is grammatically interchangeable with) all the other words that might have filled that slot: "hat," or "spider," or "flame retardant," or "emphasis," and so on. The "axis of combination," on the other hand, is the speech chain (phrase, sentence, syntactic structure) in which that word is embedded and in which it functions. In the special case of poetic language, though, says Jakobson, "*The poetic function projects the principle of equivalence from the axis of selection into the axis of combination. Equivalence is promoted to the constitutive device of the sequence*" (358). In poetry, that is, the relationships among the various words in a given sentence are not a matter of grammatical and syntactic linkages ("combination") alone. Rather, just as the elements in the axis of selection display certain similarities and differences when compared, so – *in poetry* – the words in a phrase or line or sentence disclose their similarities and differences from each other.[89] In the example above, we might note that "cat" and "mat" are both monosyllables, both singular nouns, that they rhyme, that one names an animal and the other a floor covering or pad, that their first letters are different but their second and third the same, and so on. Non-poetic utterances do not display this quasi-metaphoric relation between and among their elements, in Jakobson's view, but poetic utterances do. That is why poetry is susceptible to the sorts of minute verbal and rhetorical analysis that Jakobson himself practiced when writing literary criticism and that marked the close reading of the New Criticism.

Jakobson's compressed and powerful formulations are not without their difficulties for a contemporary formalism. In the earlier claim about the "set (*Einstellung*) toward the MESSAGE as such, focus on the message for its own sake," it is impossible to say who or what does the setting or focusing. If it is "the poetic function" that does so, it is not clear how an aspect or function of the message can direct us to the message itself. In the second formulation, Jakobson says that "the poetic function" projects equivalence from one axis into the other, though he does not tell us how it does so, and he then obscures agency altogether by having recourse to the passive voice: "Equivalence *is promoted* to the constitutive device of the sequence" (my emphasis). Such linguistic choices enable him to bypass the roles of viewer or reader, or of conventions of viewing or reading, as sources of the poetic status of the object, relying instead on a mysteriously operating "poetic function" or an elided agent in order to insist that certain intrinsic features make some texts into poems.[90] Procedurally, Jakobson is certainly correct. A principal technique of critical analysis is indeed to look at the ways elements of a text are similar to and different from each other, and at how those similarities and differences work to generate meaning: differences of sound, grammatical status, semantics, linguistic register, origin (Latin, Anglo-Saxon, etc.), allusiveness to other texts, and so on. But Jakobson's implicit faith in the intrinsic, his insistence that such comparisons are performed by the poetic text itself, is something that New Formalisms must reject, along with the cognate notion of definitive and intrinsic differences between literary and non-literary texts.

This rhetoric of the intrinsic, which assigns to the work of art itself responsibility for its own artistic status and functioning, is both commonplace and often quite benign. In casual conversation, it is scarcely more harmful to say "This poem foregrounds its own uncertainty," or "That painting insists on its two-dimensional surface," than to reply, when a child concludes a lengthy string of questions with "But *why* are horses mammals?" that "They just *are*." When we are reflecting theoretically on the status of artworks and their interpretation, however, such shorthand misrepresents the character of critical interpretation by obscuring its disciplinary and epistemological underpinnings, just as the horse-mammal remark, appearing in a biology text, would obscure the humanly produced classificatory scheme that creates the horse's mammalian status.

Some readers, of course, feel that to insist on the constitutive role of reader and viewer threatens to obscure the force and significance and subtlety of the artwork and redefine these as mere products of critical stance or approach. The result, in their view, is a devaluing of art and artists – an outcome that actually pleases most New Formalists no more than it does anyone else. We should recall here, though, that the Kantian account of our knowledge of the world – that such knowledge is never and cannot be a knowledge of things in themselves but only of things as our consciousness shapes them in the act of apprehension – does not entail that the structure of the world should be *replaced* by structures of mind or of concepts or of symbol systems. The structure of the world is there; we need do nothing additional or different in order to perceive it. It may inescapably be generated by forms of consciousness, but the world was and is as solid as it ever was. If the noumena are unavailable, chimerical even, the phenomena are palpable, dense with actuality. The same is true, analogously, of literary and other artworks; they are as they are because of the conditions of our apprehension of them, but they are not reducible to those conditions, and they are not apprehensible without *some* conditions of apprehension. A critical rhetoric that eschews the language of the intrinsic in favor of a language of interpretive communities and disciplinary conventions may obscure that fact and therefore may seem to threaten to de-realize the objects it theorizes, but the threat is unreal and the works are solidly there. They do not require the indefensible rhetoric of the intrinsic to save them.

x   Hypotheses, interpretation, formalism

Interpretive conventions are something like metaphors in Frost's account: "I know the metaphor [of evolution] will break down at some point, but it has not failed everywhere. It is a very brilliant metaphor." And of the metaphor identifying reality as a process or event, he comments, "Everything is an event now. Another metaphor. Do you believe it is? Not quite. I believe it is almost an event. But I like the comparison of a thing with an event."[91] Two features of these statements seem particularly pertinent to our discussion. First, since one thing is never another thing, a metaphor's truth is unavoidably finite, limited. The metaphor must "break down at some point," or its assertion of identity must fall short of completeness: everything is "almost" an event. A metaphor, that is, cannot be true without also being in some way false. Second, while it is operative, the metaphor is a potential source of insight, illumination: it is "very brilliant." Frost may not be able to make metaphor "the whole of thinking," as he says he had wanted to do, but he does claim that powerful metaphors can at times do "all our thinking for us," and that they are capable of bringing us truth and supplying objects of belief.[92] Taken together, these two features of Frost's remarks imply something essential about not just metaphor but any explanatory system, conceptual lens, disciplinary discourse, or critical approach. Every interpretive method must be incomplete or limited or false in some sense, yet each can offer truth and insight if it is employed competently by a particular interpreter.

To say this is to recall, but also to go beyond, a remark of Burke's cited earlier: "Our instruments are but structures of terms," and thus reveal "only such reality as is capable of being revealed by this particular kind of terminology."[93] For Burke, our "instruments" are lenses that reveal some things and obscure what different lenses may disclose. But Frost suggests, as had Hans Vaihinger in his *The Philosophy of "As If"* (1935), that our instruments or explanatory schemes are not simply selective but to some degree fictional. Vaihinger speaks of "methods in which we operate intentionally with consciously false ideas," and of "thought-processes and thought-constructs" that "appear to be consciously false assumptions...but which are intentionally thus formed in order to overcome difficulties of thought...and reach the goal of thought by roundabout ways and bypaths." Such constructs "perform a *heuristic* service by...facilitating the discovery of a natural system"[94] – or, presumably, of a cultural artifact or system such as a poem. J. Hillis Miller describes a related literary critical process that rejects naive empiricism in favor of a model in which a construct or hypothesis or fiction precedes and enables analysis and discovery:

> Interpretation, "literary criticism," is not the detached statement of a knowledge objectively gained. It is the desperation of a bet, an ungrounded doing things with words. "I bet this is a lyric poem," or "I bet this is an elegy," or "I bet this is a parable," followed by the exegesis that is the consequence of the bet.[95]

This is not an overt language of fictions, but Miller's "bet," his "ungrounded doing things with words," is a close counterpart of Vaihinger's "As If" in that both entail treating the object of study as if it were a certain thing in order to approach more closely to the thing we ultimately discover it to be. More generally, we could say that the New Formalist critic bets that the text is an object most properly understood as a linguistic structure responsive to a close reading of its language, and holds that such an assumption or bet – and such a reading – will best disclose its meaning and significance.

2
Old and New Formalisms

i Sources of New Formalism: The New Criticism

The history of Anglo-American New Criticism has been recounted a number of times, and there is no need to recapitulate it in detail here, but a brief sketch may be useful since most contemporary formalisms do not simply abandon New Criticism but attempt to revise and reconstitute certain aspects of it. As John McIntyre and Miranda Hickman note, "today's reinvigorated forms of close and surface reading can valuably be informed by – in fact, need the support of – historically based reevaluations of the New Criticism."[1] We can start with a lightning prehistory. If the idea of the poem as an objective structure displaying a complex rather than simple unity is one concept at the heart of New Critical theory and practice, then it would be possible to begin a genealogy of the movement with Aristotle. As W. K. Wimsatt has remarked,

> The kind of oneness implied not only in Aristotle's general theory of organic form but in his theory of verbal mimesis is the oneness of a thing which has heterogeneous, interacting parts....He sees the whole as more than the sum of its parts if only in that it includes the relations among the parts.[2]

Later, in Plotinus' conception of oneness, we find the further claim that "It is in virtue of unity that beings are beings," for "What could exist at all except as one thing? Deprived of unity, a thing ceases to be what it is called."[3] One sort of unity, for Plotinus, is that of a simple and internally undifferentiated object, not complex or organic in the usual sense of those terms. But another sort is the unity of a compound, complex object, "the triumph of an ordering principle over multiplicity and diversity of parts," as Wimsatt puts it. It is this second, Plotinian sort of unity that looks back to Aristotle and – inflected by Spinoza's "[Omnis] determinatio est negatio" – forward to the dialectical unities of Hegel and the fully organic and Romantic unity of Coleridge, in which the imagination "reveals itself in the balance or reconciliation of opposite or discordant qualities."[4]

Before moving to the principal modern forebear of New Criticism, T. S. Eliot, it is worth recalling what literary study in American universities looked like prior to New Critical influence. With some exceptions, the study of literature at that time was divided between a mode of literary appreciation and evaluation – occasionally, of moralizing – largely untouched by textual analysis or historical scholarship, and a mode of philology and specialized historical scholarship largely untouched by interpretive criticism.[5] John Crowe Ransom in 1938 – the year Brooks and Warren published *Understanding Poetry* – quotes the head of an English graduate program addressing a student who wished to move beyond old-style scholarship: "This is a place for exact scholarship, and you want to do criticism. Well, we don't allow criticism here, because that is something which anybody can do."[6] A remark like that speaks volumes about scholarship, criticism, and the non-relation between them in the years before the New Criticism caught on – as does Alvin Kernan's memoir and meditation on modern literary study, *In Plato's Cave*. There, Kernan recalls that Williams College professor Nelson Bushnell was "known for walking through the English Lake District and writing *A Walk after John Keats* [pub. 1936]." "This was," Kernan adds, "the kind of thing literary criticism often was before the New Criticism."[7]

In another passage, Ransom more particularly and positively characterizes both the turn of literary studies in his time and the prominence of T. S. Eliot in that undertaking. Writing in 1938, he says:

> I suppose our modern critics have learned to talk more closely about poems than their predecessors ever did. The closeness of Mr. Eliot in discussing a text may well be greater than anybody's before him, and he in turn may now be even exceeded in closeness by Mr. [R. P.] Blackmur, and perhaps others. These are close critics, and define our age as one of critical genius.[8]

Eliot is certainly a close reader in several senses, though he performs little of the minute explication that we associate with New Critical analysis and critical modes influenced by it. Nor does he insist on the unity of the literary text, or on a specific language peculiar to poetry (cf. Brooks' "language of paradox," or Ransom's "structure" and "texture").[9] What he does do, consistently and energetically, is work to separate the poet from the person ("man"), thus implicitly bracketing questions of biography and intention and cutting the poem free from its origins.[10] His insistence, moreover, on the poet as a maker of poems, not of meanings or messages, foreshadows Cleanth Brooks' "heresy of paraphrase," reinforces the rejection of poems as acts of propaganda or calls to action, and emphasizes the poem as a verbal artifact that means, not a mere conveyor of meanings. The question of belief in poetry, for example, as opposed to what Eliot terms "poetic assent," rests upon a mistaking of the kind of discourse poetry is, since the significance of a poem lies not in some or all of its abstractable content or themes but in what happens to content and theme as they form part of the whole work.

The relation between theme and treatment, in turn, suggests another belief that the New Critics will inherit from Eliot: that all aspects of the poem from diction to meter to "music" must be interpreted or assessed in relation to each other rather than in isolation. The word "assessed," of course, suggests evaluation, but while Eliot certainly retains the critic's evaluative role, he attempts to tie the act of evaluating more closely to analysis of the work of art and exploration of its qualities, as will critics like Brooks, Ransom, and Wimsatt.[11] Some of those qualities most favored by Eliot, moreover, look forward to the tensional unions, the paradoxes and ironies, the "resolved stresses" of *The Well Wrought Urn* and other New Critical productions. Eliot particularly values such structures, verbal and attitudinal, locating them, for example, prior to the alleged "dissociation of sensibility," when playwrights like Chapman and poets like Donne and Herbert felt "their thought as immediately as the odour of a rose. A thought to Donne was an experience; it modified his sensibility."[12] After the dissociation, the story goes, exacerbated by the poetic habits of Milton and Dryden, English poetry no longer enjoys a "direct sensuous apprehension of thought" but undergoes a sundering of thought from feeling, thought from experience, mind from body, head from heart, and the head from even the "cerebral cortex, the nervous system, and the digestive tracts."[13]

History and the digestive tracts aside, it is to poetic language and attitudes intimating some such difficult fusion of heterogeneities that Eliot is particularly attracted. In the same essay, he generalizes Johnson's acerbic comment on the Metaphysical poets – "The most heterogeneous ideas are yoked by violence together" – to argue that "a degree of heterogeneity of material compelled into unity by the operation of the poet's

mind is omnipresent in poetry."[14] Eliot approaches New Critical formulations even more directly in an essay of the same year (1921) on
Andrew Marvell. There, he praises Marvell for his "wit," which takes the
tensional forms of an "alliance of levity and seriousness," and "a tough
reasonableness beneath the slight lyric grace." But he then explicitly
goes beyond the traditional (Lockean) understanding of wit to the
concept of imagination, and indeed to Coleridge's "balance or reconcile-
ment of opposite or discordant qualities," cited above, finally redefining
wit in an expansive and suggestive way that directly anticipates Brooks'
"irony" or Warren's image of the poet submitting his vision "to the fires
of irony...to indicate that...it can survive reference to the complexities and contradictions of experience."[15] Eliot claims that this expanded
conception of wit "involves...a recognition, implicit in the expression
of every experience, of other kinds of experience which are possible."[16]
It is arguable that the tensional and "ironic" poetics of the New Critics,
in particular of Brooks and Warren, find their most powerful source in
this strain of Eliot's criticism.

The importance for New Criticism of Eliot's near-contemporary,
I. A. Richards, is suggested by Brooks's remark that he "must have read
[Richards'] *Principles of Literary Criticism* through fifteen times in the
early thirties."[17] Indeed, Richards' biographer claims that "In the United
States, Richards was the unacknowledged 'father' of New Criticism."[18]
"Unacknowledged," perhaps, because many of Richards's literary critical remarks sound as though they are part of a larger psychological
or educational or social project, which they are. On the one hand, he
believed that the reading of poetry could encourage a harmonious yet
minimally inhibiting psychic equilibrium in the reader. In *Foundations
of Aesthetics*, written with C. K. Ogden and James Wood and first published in 1922, Richards and his coauthors describe what they term "the
theory of Beauty *par excellence*," the principle of synaesthesis: a psychic
"adjustment" that will "preserve free play of every impulse, with entire
avoidance of frustration. In any equilibrium of this kind, ... we are experiencing beauty...As we realise beauty we become more fully ourselves
the more our impulses are engaged."[19] This model has obvious analogies
to Eliot's "heterogeneity of material compelled into unity" and Brooks's
"pattern of resolved stresses," but in Richards it remains pretty resolutely
a psychological rather than textual phenomenon.

On the other hand, Richards saw literary criticism as part of a larger
promotion of literacy in the sense of reading with understanding and
subtlety. Reading, for Richards, is work, and it is a learned rather than
natural capacity.[20] Literary criticism in this context is a subset of and

a training for reading with rigor, accuracy, and nuance. It allows us to move beyond habitual "stock responses" – which shroud both text and reality in the comfortable and conventional – and thus to see what is actually there and to make informed judgments about it, in any field. This dimension of Richards' project responds to what he sees as a significant cultural neglect of accurate reading; he complains that the "technique of the approach to poetry has not received half so much serious systematic study as the technique of pole-jumping [pole-vaulting]," and that "there is no respectable treatise on the theory of linguistic interpretation" in existence, even though such interpretation is central to our education and to our free functioning in the world.[21]

While these investments in psychic equilibrium and in the social advocacy of accurate and strenuous reading are only obliquely related to the analytic practices of the New Criticism, many of Richards' particular ideas about literature and criticism harmonize with the proto-New Critical ideas of Eliot and help form the doctrine of the New Critics themselves. Even a bare list can suggest the range of Richards' influence. He insisted on the primacy of language, and on the necessity of close reading, often teasing out the numerous ambiguities in linguistic expression;[22] refused to equate paraphrase with the poem itself; argued for the subordination of parts to whole in poetic texts ("The blunder in all cases is the attempt to assign marks *independently* to details that can only be judged fairly with reference to the whole final result to which they contribute");[23] emphasized the "truth" of a work's *coherence* rather than the "truth" of its *correspondence* to extratextual reality; and conceptualized the literary text as the expression of a dramatized speaker (not the real-life utterance of an empirical person) moving through an array of tones and attitudes.[24] One educational effort can indicate Richards' embrace of these notions and his influence on the New Critical project of close reading. At Cambridge, he championed the examination paper (made compulsory in 1926) titled "Passages of English Prose and Verse for Critical Comment," which sought to bring into fruitful collision texts isolated for analysis and the critical powers of the students who were to interpret them (as did the lengthy Part Two of Richards' *Practical Criticism*).[25] That model is of course the fundamental unit of the kind of close reading that the New Criticism elaborated, theorized, and disseminated.

A Cambridge student of Richards', William Empson (1906–84), began as a gifted mathematician but emerged as one of the most original and idiosyncratic of the pre-New Critical analysts of poetry. His first and most influential critical study, *Seven Types of Ambiguity* (1930), arose in part from his reading of an analysis of a Shakespeare sonnet undertaken by Laura Riding and Robert Graves. Here is Richards' account of the launching moment:

> At about his third visit he brought up the games of interpretation which Laura Riding and Robert Graves had been playing with the unpunctuated form of "The expense of spirit in a waste of shame." Taking the sonnet as a conjuror takes his hat, he produced an endless swarm of lively rabbits from it and ended by "You could do that with any poetry, couldn't you?" This was a Godsend to a Director of Studies, so I said, "You'd better go off and do it, hadn't you?"[26]

Though engaged in no programmatic effort to improve the interpretive skills of citizens, Empson shared with Richards the idea of close reading as patient work, and he saw a cultural need to provide "the general assurance which comes of a belief that all sorts of poetry may be conceived as explicable."[27] His readings were often intricate, inventive, and minute, and they concentrated on teasing out multiple meanings of words and phrases: puns, paradoxes, syntactic ambiguities, and so on. The classification of ambiguities into seven types, though it forms the framework of his book, has seemed to many readers less important than the analyses of individual texts, which, as Wimsatt and Brooks note, "brought home to a whole generation of readers the fact of the manysidedness of language."[28]

Empson describes the phenomenon of ambiguity at a number of points: as a word or phrase of which "alternative views might be taken without sheer misreading"; as "a word or grammatical structure that is effective in several ways at once"; as a feature of "all good poetry" – even a feature whose "machinations ... are among the very roots of poetry" (recall Eliot's claim that "a degree of heterogeneity of material compelled into unity by the operation of the poet's mind is omnipresent in poetry"); as "any verbal nuance, however slight, which gives room for alternative reactions to the same piece of language"; and so on.[29] His formulations of the idea of unity – sometimes verbal unity, sometimes psychological – owe something to Richards' notion of a psychic equipoise of impulses, and something to Eliot's idea of a poem's unifying of heterogeneous materials.

But this relatively bland formulation does not suggest the depth and even mystery that Empson ascribed to the idea of textual and psychic "compounds." Just as Brooks (and Warren) moved from the language of paradox to the claim that poetry should "dramatize the oneness of ... experience, even though paying tribute to its diversity," so Empson makes a leap from verbal ambiguity to conceptual and existential contradictoriness. Where Brooks offers a quasi-theodicean image of the unifying power of poetry, Empson foregrounds the differing-from-itself that language and the conceptual order it brings into being sometimes display.

His seventh type of ambiguity – "the most ambiguous that can be conceived" – "occurs when the two meanings of the word, the two values of the ambiguity, are the two opposite meanings defined by the context."[30] But Empson then considers words that express opposites "without any overt ambiguity" ("Latin *altus*, high or deep, the English *let*, allow or hinder"), speculating that "words uniting two opposites are seldom or never formed in a language to express the conflict between them; such words come to exist for more sensible reasons, and may *then* be used to express conflict."[31] Having moved historically backward from ambiguity and contradiction to a more primitive semantic doubleness, Empson then turns to the *psychologically* primitive by invoking Freud and the sorts of non-contradictory doubleness through which the unconscious expresses itself in dreams.[32] On the authority of Freud's discussions of primitive languages, he cites the claim that the early Egyptians "wrote the same sign for 'young' and 'old,'" speculatively inferring from this that "When a primitive Egyptian saw a baby he at once thought of an old man, and he had to learn not to do this as his language became more civilized."[33] Empson is clearly moving from purely verbal ambiguity toward a conception of experience as fundamentally riven by irreducible doubleness.

Both the existential weight and the particular character of the meaning Empson ascribes to ambiguity appear forcefully in his ambiguity of the seventh type, which displays a kind of intensity "such as one finds in a gridiron pattern in architecture because it gives prominence neither to the horizontals nor to the verticals, and in a check pattern because neither colour is the ground on which the other is placed." He then adds, "it is at once an indecision and a structure, like the symbol of the Cross" – a remark that vaults from verbal ambiguity to theological mysteries like the Incarnation and the Fortunate Fall with remarkable aplomb.[34] While a critic like Brooks almost never imbues his notion of poetic unity with so intense a perception of fundamental contradiction, both he and Empson are concerned to formulate a definition of the poetic work that will intimate a particular kind of world, or view of the world.[35] Such a definition underlies many of Empson's close readings of ambiguity, and at times it enables fresh formulations about individual works and literary modes, such as the mock-heroic: the "idea behind MacFlecknoe and The Dunciad," he writes, is "that there is an ominous mystery in the way the lowest and most absurd things make an exact parallel with the highest... [T]he process of alternately identifying and separating a key pair of opposites is a fundamental one for the style."[36]

Despite the often brilliantly quirky character of Empson's analyses, there are important continuities between his work and that of the New Critics themselves: the centrality of linguistic analysis; the style of minute close reading – indeed, the intensification of the minuteness of his predecessors; the persistent attention to ambiguity and polysemy, to "the manysidedness of language";[37] the attraction to unities displaying a significant degree of internal stress, difference, and complexity; and, of course, the enabling assumption that patient attention to "any verbal nuance, however slight," can disclose important dimensions of meaning otherwise undiscoverable. In their extremely influential *Theory of Literature*, which was published in several editions during the 1940s and served as an unofficial guide to graduate study during and after the transition from scholarly to critical emphases, René Wellek and Austin Warren open the fourth section of their book, tellingly titled "The Intrinsic Study of Literature," by observing that "In recent years a healthy reaction has taken place which recognizes that the study of literature should, first and foremost, concentrate on the actual works of art themselves." They term the reaction "healthy" not just because it corrects "The Extrinsic Approach to the Study of Literature" (Part Three of *Theory of Literature*) but also, as their language suggests, because the intrinsic approach is already coming to seem "natural" – shedding its constructed and methodological character and acquiring the force of business as usual. "The natural and sensible starting-point for work in literary scholarship," they write, "is the interpretation and analysis of the works of literature themselves."[38] This historical moment, which coheres in the phrase that was to become the title of Ransom's 1941 book, *The New Criticism*, is scarcely thinkable without the rich, varied, and overlapping preliminary work of Eliot, Richards, and Empson.[39]

ii   New Formalist revisions of the New Criticism (1)

"The New Criticism," as a label, inevitably intimates a unity of aims and methods that simplifies the actual diverseness of the work of Brooks, Robert Penn Warren, Ransom, Allen Tate, Wimsatt, and others associated with that "school."[40] In what follows – an exercise in revision as well as exposition – I will compound that simplification by focusing largely on Brooks, who, with Warren in their *Understanding Poetry* (1938), and in his own *Well Wrought Urn* (1947), did more than anyone else to elaborate, disseminate, and give pedagogical force to the critical assumptions and reading strategies termed "New Critical." But I do not want to simplify the entire critical landscape of that period, for it is a simplification, as M. H. Abrams notes,

> to suppose ... that literary study in the mid-century was dominated by the New Criticism. What the New Criticism dominated was the pedagogy of courses designed to introduce undergraduates to the reading of poems, plays, and novels. But the era of the New Criticism was also the era of a great variety of enduringly important critical works that made frequent and diverse uses of the biographical, psychological, social, economic, and historical matrix of imaginative literature .... [F]or inventiveness, variety, and vitality, the literary studies of that time had no parallel in any earlier period.[41]

It is within this rich context that the New Critics emerged and "developed their distinctive practice of 'close reading,'" as Abrams puts it: a practice that "consisted of a detailed analysis of the 'ambiguities,' or multiple meanings, that in all good poems (it was claimed) interacted to compose a poetic structure of irony and paradox," a structure that expressed "an inclusive unity of opponent attitudes that is the mark of a mature and realistic stance toward reality."[42]

In a 1993 interview, Brooks looked back on the movement in which he had been so instrumental, noting that the critics associated with it "took the text very seriously."[43] Part of that seriousness was the well known refusal of a form-content dualism: "In poetry, I think form and content become pretty thoroughly merged and I prefer not to split them apart; they define each other. A good poem is an object in which form and content can be distinguished but cannot really be separated."[44] Many versions of this idea have been expressed in the literature of poetics and general aesthetics, among them Cardinal Newman's 1858 lecture, "Literature," included in *The Idea of a University*. There, ultimately basing his argument on the notion of "the two-fold Logos, the thought and the word, distinct, but inseparable from each other," he offers this famous formulation:

> When we can separate light and illumination, life and motion, the convex and the concave of a curve, then will it be possible for thought to tread speech under foot, and to hope to do without

it – then will it be conceivable that the vigorous and fertile intellect should renounce its own double, its instrument of expression, and the channel of its speculations and emotions.[45]

Whatever clouds of theology Newman's stirring assertion may trail are largely absent from Brooks' resolute insistence on the unity of content and form. That insistence, of course, enabled the New Critics to view the formal features of a text as carriers and performers of signification rather than mere ornaments and enhancements, which is all they are allowed by "the unphilosophical notion, that the language" is "an extra which could be dispensed with," as Newman puts it.[46] Thus when Brooks recalls that "The New Criticism was mainly concerned with *the detail of the text* which was very different from the kind of literary work that was going on before it," we can understand him in two different but related ways.[47] Most simply, he is claiming what Ransom claims when he uses the term "closeness," or Richards the word "details," or Empson the phrase "verbal nuance, however slight": that a new attention to minute details of language marked the emerging New Critical formalism of the 1930s and after. Beyond this, however, the New Critics sought not just to interpret in more detailed ways but to *view new details as interpretable*: the formal elements of texts as well as the semantic. They sought to understand those formal elements not as ornaments but as essential constituents of signification – conveying, performing, and shaping meaning both on their own and in concert with the semantic elements. This was not just to read closely but to find formerly decorative or inert elements of texts newly significant, newly readable. There are intimations of such readability – such attribution of meaningfulness to form and figure – in the more inventive passages of a Renaissance rhetorician like George Puttenham, or even in the early eighteenth-century essays of John Dennis. But in the realm of literary criticism, it was the New Critics who fully liberated form into meaningfulness.

Then there is the issue of value. An essay, titled "My Credo: The Formalist Critics" and originally published four years after *The Well Wrought Urn*, finds Brooks attempting to list some of the key principles or "articles of faith," as he terms them, of his critical stance. The first of these is explicit about value: "literary criticism is a description and an evaluation of its object."[48] Somewhat later, Brooks notes that "the formalist critic assumes an ideal reader: that is, instead of focusing on the varying spectrum of possible readings, he attempts to find a central point of reference from which he can focus upon the structure of the poem or novel." Here, the "ideal reader" seems principally a heuristic device designed to replace individual readerly prejudice and preoccupations with a focus on the text. In admitting as much, however, Brooks introduces another assumption: "There is no ideal reader, of course, and I suppose that the practicing critic can never be too often reminded of the gap between his reading and the 'true' reading of the poem."[49] The closing sentences of the essay obliquely echo this concern but in a different vocabulary: "Literature has many 'uses' – and critics propose new uses, some of them exciting and spectacular. But all the multiform uses to which literature can be put rest finally upon our knowing what a given work 'means.' That knowledge is basic."[50] The importance of critical evaluation, the fiction of an ideal reader, the notion of a true reading, and the distinction between meanings and uses are intimately linked in ways that can point toward a revision of certain New Critical assumptions so as to make them compatible with New Formalist criticism and theory.

Despite the difficulty of moving from description and analysis to evaluation – a difficulty memorably phrased by Northrop Frye: "The demonstrable value-judgment is the donkey's carrot of literary criticism" – most of the New Critics viewed the making of informed value judgments as part of the critic's cultural responsibility.[51] At the same time, evaluation has regularly been a problem for criticism of literature and the other arts, particularly in our own age where distinctions like that between "high" and "popular" culture, for example, have been frequently and often compellingly shown to express one or another sort of bias or unexamined assumption. As Frye says, "Every deliberately constructed hierarchy of values in literature known to me is based on a concealed social, moral, or intellectual analogy."[52] In response to such a challenge, one can claim that evaluation is inescapable since the very choice of this text rather than that text for analysis is an implicit judgment of value. Or one can believe it possible (at least desirable) to deploy a critical discourse that integrates the analytic and the evaluative – "a 'monism' of evaluation *through* explication," in Wimsatt's words.[53] Or one can contend, as I do, that the aim of the (formalist) critic is to interpret and thus to "realize" the text, and that doing so may allow other readers to understand it better and, perhaps, find value in the text thus realized.[54] In this last formulation, the critic does not so much evaluate as present the object in something like its fullness so that evaluation – should it take place – will be a response to an illuminated and maximized rather than an obscured and diminished object.

The notion of an "ideal reader" is connected to the New Critics' desire to accord the poem objective status, and to exorcise what Wellek and Warren routinely invoke as the specter of "scepticism and anarchy."[55]

But when Brooks concedes that there "is no ideal reader" yet adds that "the practicing critic can never be too often reminded of the gap between his reading and the 'true' reading of the poem," the ideal reader ceases to be merely a metaphoric reminder of the need to shed one's prejudices and singularity. Even restrained by quotation marks, the "true" in "the 'true' reading of the poem" can't help gesturing toward some poetic *Ding an sich* which we must always fall short of attaining to. Analogously, the distinction between the "uses to which literature can be put" and our knowledge of "what a given work 'means' " implies an understanding of the work that is prior to any critical framework and thus expresses a fantasy of knowledge that is "basic" because it is without a point of view. But a given work means one thing when the work is being "used" by a Marxist critic, say, and another thing when it is being "used" by a psychoanalytic or a deconstructive critic. There is no knowledge without some point of view, and any point of view is already, and inescapably, a particular way of "using" the work. What Brooks and some other New Critics take to be a sphere of pure, objective meaningfulness in which the work exists prior to interpretation must be rejected by New Formalism in favor of the inescapable positionality, the disciplinary and individual inflectedness, of any act of critical knowing at all.

The distinction between a critic's reading of a poem and the "true" reading is analogous to the distinction between different critics' assessment of a poem and its true value. If the former preserves the fantasy of a pre-interpretive intrinsic meaning, the latter preserves the fantasy of an intrinsic or objective degree of goodness. But a particular evaluation of a text can no more be compared with its "true" value than a particular interpretation of it can be compared with its "true" meaning. So there are at least two problems with evaluation. The first is that there is no degree of merit or value that is not the result of a human ascription. The second is that such an evaluation cannot logically grow out of the activity of interpretation. Again, this last is a particular instance of the fact–value split, which holds that the language of evaluation is incompatible with the language of description, analysis, and interpretation. The threat of evaluation is thus that it places critical discourse in an illogical and therefore untenable position. I do not see a satisfactory resolution to this difficulty, if "resolution" means finding a way to render the two languages compatible, but it may be useful to frame the problem somewhat differently. At one point, Frye says that "On the ethical level we can see that every increase of appreciation has been right and every decrease wrong: that criticism has no business to react against things, but should show a steady advance toward undiscriminating catholicity."[56] This seems at first a remarkable hymn to the abolition of standards, but Frye is using "ethical" in a special sense. Ethical criticism, for him, is criticism that "deals with art as a communication from the past to the present" and works to make that past available to present society.[57] Individual readers or consumers of past art are free to make any value judgments they please, but it is the "ethical" critic's job to transmit as much of the cultural heritage to the present as possible – whence the goal of an "undiscriminating catholicity."

This argument has an analogue within the sphere of individual interpretive activity. Negative and positive evaluations are interestingly asymmetrical. A positive evaluation not only argues that particular dimensions of the artwork are meaningful in a certain way; it also leaves open – even encourages – the opportunity to discover additional dimensions of that work. A negative evaluation, on the other hand, is a kind of dismissal; it encourages a suspension of precisely the sort of investigative and analytic exploration that might alter one's evaluation of the text – positively or negatively. Though one can never demonstrate that a particular textual element is *not* meaningful, since this would be an instance of the fallacy of negative proof ("You can't prove that white golf shoes are *not* causing teen pregnancy, so maybe they are"), an evaluative demotion of a work fosters a suspension of the kind of interpretive activity that could reverse such a judgment by producing fresh critical discoveries. Thus the principal reason for refraining from overt assertions of value may, perhaps surprisingly, have less to do with evaluation and more to do with the enterprise of interpretation. For this reason if for no other, evaluation has no serious place in the project of New Formalism.

iii New Formalist revisions of the New Criticism (2)

What are some other problematic features or assumptions of the New Criticism, and how can New Formalist criticism either avoid them or render them compatible with its aims? Of course, there is more than one brand of what Heather Dubrow seems to have first termed "new formalism."[58] To a number of critics, for example, the phrase implies "a critical genre dedicated to examining the social, cultural, and historical aspects of literary form, and the function of form for those who produce and consume literary texts."[59] Such a formalist project is sometimes conceived as an extension of New Historicism into more rigorously formalist territory, or as an incorporation of formalist analytic methods into historical, cultural, or political criticism. Other New Formalists, however, are wary of relegating "the formal to a secondary, supplementary role that neglects the depth and range of its contributions to style and meaning" and permits formalist exegesis only to provide "raw material that can be manufactured into the goods of political analysis."[60] Such distinctions can be explored later on. At this point, it is necessary to distinguish New Formalisms more fully from the New Critical practices and assumptions that they grew out of.

If meaning is not an intrinsic feature of texts but something that is produced by interpretation, the unity of the text is also not simply given, or simply discovered by readers. It is, first, an assumption or a working hypothesis governing and enabling the act of interpretation, and then it is something that interpretive activity discloses or produces – though not in order to simply revive New Critical faith in "organic unity." Although Mary Poovey argued in 2001 that "the trope of the organic whole continues to organize most of the strains of criticism that now dominate U. S. practice," in fact the dominance of organic unity has been repeatedly challenged within New Formalisms in several ways.[61] In some instances, there is an effort to retain the emphasis on forms but surrender the totalizations of New Critical conceptions of unity. "The rallying cry for *this* 'new formalism,'" writes Mark David Rasmussen, "might be 'literary reading without organic form.'"[62] Ellen Rooney similarly warns that "if a longing for the lost unities of bygone forms...is the impetus of a new formalism, the chances are not good for what is already an...urgent project: the revision and reanimation of form in the age of interdisciplinarity."[63] Like "intention" – surmised internal intention, not empirical authorial intention – unity exists initially as an enabling hypothesis, largely without content, and subsequently as a specific and individualized product of interpretation.[64] Recall Miller sketching the trajectory of a typical interpretive moment, one focusing on a text's generic identity:

> Interpretation, 'literary criticism,' is not the detached statement of a knowledge objectively gained. It is the desperation of a bet, an ungrounded doing things with words. 'I bet this is a lyric poem,' or 'I bet this is an elegy,' or 'I bet this is a parable,' followed by the exegesis that is the consequence of the bet.[65]

Even if we question the overwroughtness of "desperate" and "ungrounded," we can see that generic form, in this model, is an expectation or hypothesis enabling the subsequent analysis that will confirm, disconfirm, or transform it.

Such an investigative structure operates at several levels. Most generally, it bears on the very question of "literature" and "literariness," since we make such a bet when we interpret (that is, do literary criticism) at all. We assume or hypothesize that the text "is" literature: that it will, if interpreted by literary critical methods, prove amenable to those methods. We then conduct the exegesis that may confirm the hypothesis and establish the identity of the text. Since the distinction between literary and non-literary texts is not a matter of intrinsic differences but of certain uses of texts, when you "bet" that a work "is" literature and successfully show it to be so through interpretive labor, you are really showing that it may be put to one particular kind of use. There is, of course, nothing to say that it can't be put to others as well, under different assumptions and interpretive conventions; to demonstrate that a text is literature is not to preclude its also being other sorts of textual object.[66] A main reason for having the category "literature," even though texts of the most diverse kinds may fill it, and for having the procedures of literary critical interpretation, is that these make of texts the source of certain kinds of knowledge and experience and imaginative activity that many regard as culturally valuable, and that cannot be produced by other means.

Closer to individual acts of interpretation, we make a comparable bet when we hypothesize that a given poem treats its subject ironically, or that it rewrites and responds to an earlier text, or that it displays a curious swerve from this poet's characteristic stance or concerns, or that its medical or nautical metaphors signify in such and such a way. What is important in each case – genre, literariness, interpretation of an individual poem – is the replacement of a naive empirical model with a model acknowledging the role of an expectation, a forestructure, that does not simply constrain analysis but gives it an arena in which to perform. Paul de Man indicates such a forestructure when he says, "I have a tendency to put upon texts an inherent authority . . . I assume as a working hypothesis (as a working hypothesis, because I know better than that), that the text *knows* in an absolute way what it is doing."[67]

More recently, Caroline Levine has proposed a "strategic formalism" that seeks to blend the post-New Critical troubling of organic unity with a sense of the *methodological* work that the idea of unity performs:

> [R]ather than discarding the notion of wholes altogether, we might do best to approach it strategically. After all, even those critics

who are most dedicated to investigating diversity and marginality must posit temporal and spatial boundaries around their objects of analysis.... The strategic formalist would invite a self-consciousness about the act of positing the provisional "whole" object of analysis, rather than imagining that it is possible to do away with totalities altogether.[68]

This is a sensible formulation, nicely sidestepping the cruder aspects of the unity/heterogeneity polemics. Indeed, the methodological dimension of this notion of unity can be expanded beyond the contemporary quarrel with "organic unity" and even beyond literary criticism. For to undertake work in just any discipline at all requires one or another assumption of unity. This may be the disciplinary unity that circumscribes "anthropology" and distinguishes it from "psychology" or "anatomy," or the unity/homogeneity of the posited object of study (matter and energy for physics; one or another natural language for historical linguistics, etc.). Or – to return to literary and art criticism – it may be the common-sense assumption of wholeness that would render incoherent a study of *Paradise Lost* that assumed the meaningfulness of only every other word, or a study of Constable's painting *The Hay Wain* that ignored the bottom half of the canvas.

Whatever particular hypotheses or positings or expectations of unity a given analysis may invoke, to have a field or discipline at all – whether literary criticism or any other science – requires what Frye terms "the assumption of total coherence."[69] As Wimsatt and Beardsley note in a Jamesian moment, "For all the objects of our manifold experience, for every unity, there is an action of the mind which cuts off roots, melts away context – or indeed we should never have objects or ideas or anything to talk about."[70] From this perspective, the persistence of the question of organic unity may be less about interpretive assumptions and more about the maturing of literary criticism as a discipline. Formalism, as Poovey puts it,

turns out to have been the prerequisite for literary study's professionalization in universities in the 1930s and 1940s.... In order to understand how formalism triumphed... it is necessary to explore how a rudimentary project of grouping and classifying literary effects gave way to the objectification of the literary text, which resulted in both an ideology of aesthetic autonomy and a discourse about literature as specialized as the discourse about science.[71]

In another contrast to New Critical concerns, at times more thematic than methodological, New Formalism follows in the wake of criticism and theory from the late 1960s to the present that is interested in kinds of dissonance, contradiction, and disharmony in the text that go beyond New Critical "irony" and "tension," which almost always enriched rather than impeded or troubled final unification. New Formalism admits more and different sorts of tension – largely derived from the textual practices of deconstruction and to some extent of Marxism, psychoanalysis, and (more recently) Queer Theory – and is far less concerned that these be gathered into a comprehensive totality or last roundup. Related to this expectation – even assumption – of thematic or rhetorical or semantic tension and disharmony is an increased awareness of the operations of power in texts: strategies of exclusion, marginalization, hierarchy, legitimation, and illegitimation, and so on. This awareness comes from a variety of sources: from deconstructive analyses of hierarchy; from feminist and other modes of attention to strategies of exclusion; from Marxist alertness to the political and hierarchical significance of masked or seemingly innocent deployments of power; from Foucault's analyses of the production of knowledge and knowledge-spaces within which certain kinds of fact or assumption are possible or impossible. And, of course, from the renewed interest in rhetoric, itself generated by various sources including belated appreciation of Kenneth Burke, new work by theorists of composition, and others.

These are often, as I have noted, matters of shifting thematic attention (recall the search for "Christ figures" in the 1960s and 1970s), only sometimes opening onto methodological or theoretical issues, but they nonetheless mark a difference between post-structuralist New Formalisms and the typical concerns of the New Critics. And at times, they are indeed methodologically as well as thematically engaged. Eric Savoy, for example, describes his work as "an effort to recuperate the uses of rhetorical criticism for queer theory," based on what he regards as the "more general queerness that is implicit in formalism's work" – particularly, the formalist concern with tropes and their linkage in turn to the figure of catachresis, understood in its contemporary senses.[72] His concern goes well beyond the thematics of queerness, resting on the formalist assumption that "the most valuable and hard-won political lessons accrue from a patient attentiveness," from "the specific complexities of textual engagement, of really reading."[73] From another perspective, Savoy's turn to New Formalist analysis, like Best and Marcus' advocacy of "surface reading," is part of his effort to counter the misleading belief "that the things worth knowing are not on the surface, not enmeshed in the *différance* of language," a belief whose principal interpretive consequence is that "one remains blind to the text and concentrates on the murky and illusory depths of the work."[74]

A similar effort to ally formalist methodological investments to contemporary thematic concerns occurs within the field of ecocriticism. In an essay on "Ecocriticism, Literary Theory, and the Truth of Ecology," Dana Phillips cites Lawrence Buell's commentary on Hopkins' "Pied Beauty" and then remarks on its relative inattention to formal features: "It seems to me that if this commentary is intended as ecocriticism, then ecocriticism may benefit from a strong dose of formalism. Otherwise, it may lapse into the merely appreciative mode formalism – and after it, theory – was originally intended to correct and improve upon."[75] More recently, Sarah Ensor's strikingly original essay "Spinster Ecology: Rachel Carson, Sarah Orne Jewett, and Nonreproductive Futurity" attempts to demonstrate "how the problem of a queer ecocriticism might in fact have formalist answers." Here is her summary of the reading of *Silent Spring* with which the essay opens:

> I have opened my discussion of spinster ecology with *Silent Spring* in part to emphasize the surprising fact that a text which could be blamed for inaugurating (or at least fortifying) the heterosexist bias of contemporary ecology also provides one basis for developing a queer ecocriticism. Implicit in that discussion, however, is an assertion that this more radical basis is found not simply in the thematic dimensions or explicit argumentation of Carson's book but also in its style, its grammar, and its form.

She generalizes in a footnote, "An implication of my argument is that ecocriticism, a field whose focus has largely been on the thematic or mimetic representation of the environment in literature, also stands to benefit from an increased attention to literary form and style."[76]

New Formalism has also learned, from structuralism and, more recently, from ideological criticism and cultural studies, to pay closer attention to the cultural significance or valence of literary forms and conventions. Onto the pre-formalist and formalist interest in genres and conventions has been grafted an attention to their cultural, social, and political weight. Here is Debra Fried addressing the sonnet form as a literary-historical nexus of genre, gender, and poetic power in the works of Edna St. Vincent Millay:

Millay addresses the Romantic myths of the sonnet as liberating prison and pleasing fetters, the figurations governing Wordsworth's "Nuns Fret Not" and Keats's "If by Dull Rhymes." Her sonnets reshape those myths with the revisionary force of a woman poet who, however rearguard in the phalanx of modernism, recognizes that she has inherited a genre laden with figurations exclusive to a male poetic authority, and who knows that her adaptations of that genre must engage those very myths and figurations that would bar her from the ranks of legitimate practitioners of the sonnet.[77]

And here is a later, more general meditation on the stanza as such:

Not a genre, but a marker for many poetic genres, the stanza is a workhorse not much written about aside from its labor within individual genres and poems.... Divider and connector, trellis and climbing vine at once, the stanza is as subject to the individual poet's crafting as the line, as freighted with the history of its uses and as ripe for reinvention.[78]

To see the sonnet and the stanza – or form and genre generally – in this way is to remark their embeddedness in a history of use and semiotic import that is part of a writer's repertoire of signification whenever a traditional genre is chosen. As Stephen Cohen puts it,

Unlike the historicity of texts, the historicity of form emphasizes the particularity of literary discourse, insisting not only that literary texts have historical roots and functions, but that they do so by virtue of their discourse-specific forms and conventions as well as their extratextual or interdiscursive ideological content. For the literary scholar, this understanding invites the historicization not only of generic and prosodic forms but of many of the other concepts and practices associated with traditional formalism.[79]

Contemporary formalisms also look well beyond specifically *literary* history, and beyond traditional assumptions that literary and cultural forms will mirror or reproduce social formations. Such forms may actually, as Caroline Levine puts it,

participate in a destabilizing relation to social formations, often colliding with social hierarchies rather than reflecting or foreshadowing them. Literary forms, that is, trouble and remake political relationships in surprising, aleatory, and often confusingly disorderly ways. A range of critics in recent years—including Heather Dubrow, Dorothy Hale, Ellen Rooney, Herbert Tucker, and Susan Wolfson— have urged a new attention to form as part of a politically aware historicism.[80]

Indeed, in her studies of English Romanticism, Susan Wolfson argues that formalism has been assigned a grotesquely diminished place in contemporary representations of critical modes, and that the tedious antitheses used to describe the relationship between formal analysis on the one hand, and cultural-historical-political analyses on the other, are both misguided and stumbling blocks to productive criticism. In "the most critical turns of Romantic and post-Romantic poetics," she contends, "formal elements do not exist 'apart' from but play a part in the semantic order." That is because "choices of form and the way it is managed often signify as much as, and as part of, words themselves."[81] In addition to deeming formal elements as significant as semantic, she demonstrates that "Romanticism's poetic forms take shape within complicated literary *and cultural* contexts" – indeed, that "Romanticism's involvement with poetic form... participates in central discussions of its historical moment."[82] This moves the study of forms beyond significative parity with "the semantic order" to claim that poetic form signifies "in different textual sites and within different contextual pressures"; as a result, "Cultural knowledge is not excluded but informed."[83] Such a statement harmonizes with Culler's remark that "formalism does not involve a denial of history, as is sometimes claimed. What it rejects is historical interpretation that makes the work a symptom, whose causes are to be found in historical reality."[84] Like Dubrow, Wolfson wants finally to insist, refreshingly, that formalism does not exist merely to provide "raw material that can be manufactured into the goods of political analysis."[85] Avoiding that needless subordination of formal to political or ideological concerns, her criticism repeatedly demonstrates again and again that the formal and the contextual (cultural, historical, political) are kept apart only to the detriment of critical analysis.

Indeed, fresh configurations of such modes of analysis are an important feature of the New Formalisms of the past decade or so, as is suggested by Robert Kaufman's 2001 review of Wolfson's *Formal Charges*: "[R]eports of the demise of historically and theoretically inclined literary scholarship may be premature," he writes, adding wryly that "it would prove no small measure of poetic justice and post-Romantic irony if concerns for history and theory should in turn find themselves inextricably bound to the survival of form and formalism within literary studies."[86] And, in a 1999 essay that predates both Kaufman's review of Wolfson and Levine's "Strategic Formalism" essay, Jonathan Loesberg argues for a "recognition of the continuity between" what he terms aesthetic formalism and "the Foucauldian, historicist, and cultural readings to which they are [sic] ostensibly opposed" – a recognition that chimes with the bold suggestions of Kaufman's review and the stronger claims in Kaufman's "Everybody Hates Kant: Blakean Formalism and the Symmetries of Laura Moriarty."[87] For Loesberg, "one can offer a justification of literariness or formalism as a perspective having certain advantages for regarding a given period, genre, structure, or discursive formation."[88] Moreover, this justification suggests a certain reshuffling of the relations among rival critical perspectives:

> since cultural studies would now have to recognize its own formalist procedure, its imperialistic tendency to see itself as its own pan-disciplinary discipline would cede to the more modest claim of being a perhaps somewhat peculiar permutation of formalist analysis whose results other disciplines may usefully add to, dispute, or appropriate for their own ends.[89]

It is clear that relations among New Formalisms and various historicist modes of analysis – cultural studies included – are the object of sophisticated rethinking that is satisfyingly unsettled, promisingly dynamic.

iv New Formalism and contemporary aesthetics

At the opposite pole from history and politics, at least ostensibly, some modes of New Formalism have presented themselves as engaged in a recovery of the aesthetic from the commandeerings of literary texts performed by various modes of political, theoretical, historical, and ideological criticism. In this view, formalist analysis allows a liberation on "aesthetic" grounds of textual beauty, readerly pleasure, identification, disinterested contemplation, even the elevation of one work over another – all of which, it is claimed, have been held hostage to the various content-oriented and paraphrase-based utilitarianisms of ideology critique, demystification, etc. As Mary Janell Metzger puts it in her contribution to a recent volume advocating historical formalism, "Critiques of literature as ideology are both necessary and insufficient. Aesthetic form as a vehicle of dialectical consciousness, when understood in the light of material history, seems well worth recovering."[90] Indeed, Marjorie Levinson has written that "the most general feature of critical work in the humanities right now seems to be its *wish to re-enchant the object* (often seen to have been reductively demystified over the past 20 years)."[91] Elsewhere, she contends that

> one could construe new formalism as itself a kind of aesthetic or formal commitment. It seeks to fend off the divisiveness encouraged by the kinds of cognitive, ethical, and juridical commitments – as it were, content commitments – rife among and effectively defining all the critical practices summed up by the term new historicism.[92]

This aesthetic "movement" is interestingly regressive and progressive at the same time. On the one hand, it seeks to revive some of the New Critical respect for the poem's singular status: its use of a unique, literary language; its transcendence of paraphrasable statements, exportable *sententiae*, and propagandistic aims; its distinctness from the rational discourse and programmatic abstraction of science; its reliance on the significative energies of formal and not just semantic features; and more. On the other hand, this revival jettisons much of the caution or obliquity of the New Critical language of implicit evaluation and enjoyment, substituting emphatic vocabularies of emotion, readerly identification, response, volition, and desire (even bodily response and desire), and of the discourse of traditional aesthetics, especially Kantian and post-Kantian. If re-enchanting the object, though, means encouraging readers to submit to the spell of beauty or pleasure or sensation or evaluation instead of the spell of a demystified politics or history or ideology, New Formalisms will need to proceed in a clear-eyed and somewhat wary fashion, and with a firm commitment to preserving the literary specificity – the textual and significative character – of that object.

Contemporary formalist critics making use of aesthetic theory tend to take either of two general positions. One group works to explore and elaborate the Kantian idea that "an aesthetic judgment ... is a judgment which is based on feeling, and in particular on the feeling of pleasure or displeasure."[93] For Kant, this pleasure

> is of a distinctive kind: it is disinterested, which means that it does not depend on the subject's having a desire for the object, nor does it generate such a desire. The fact that judgments of beauty are based

on feeling rather than "objective sensation" (e.g., the sensation of a thing's colour) distinguishes them from cognitive judgments based on perception (e.g., the judgment that a thing is green). But the disinterested character of the feeling distinguishes them from other judgments based on feeling.[94]

The other group seeks to extend the Kantian position in the direction of the cognitive, and/or in the direction of the constitution of human agency, having recourse to Kant's derivation of morality from aesthetic experience. As Hannah Ginsborg frames Kant's argument, "Aesthetic experience serves as a propadeutic for morality, in that 'the beautiful prepares us to love something, even nature, without interest.' "[95]

The first group can be represented by Charles Altieri, especially his *The Particulars of Rapture*, the subtitle of which clearly indicates the position he will elaborate with ingenuity and complexity: *An Aesthetic of the Affects*. Altieri's book "originated as a reaction against dominant tendencies" in criticism: both an emphasis on context over text, and a contrary textual focus justified only by "attributing to the text some kind of moral wisdom or ethically enlightened attitude." If the first group reduces texts to their historical or other contexts, the latter gives prominence to the works themselves but only by being "too eager to equate texts with the interpretive frameworks we could put around them."[96] Too much history, in short, and too many reductions of texts to "meanings" and morals generated by readerly need. What is Altieri's alternative? At one point, he says it is to explore "specific modes of affective engagement presented by works of art," affects being "immediate modes of sensuous responsiveness to the world characterized by an accompanying imaginative dimension."[97] Elsewhere, he argues that the arts

inspire accounts that make affective experience not just something we understand, but something that we pursue as a fundamental value.... I want to use aesthetic models to foreground conative experiences of affective states as ends in themselves.... An aesthetic perspective invites us to ask what states, roles, identifications, and social bonds become possible by virtue of our efforts to dwell fully within these dispositions of energies and the modes of self-reflection they sustain. Rather than asking what we can know about the affects, or how they contribute to the work of knowing, we begin to ask who we can be by virtue of how we dispose our self-consciousness in relation to affective experience.[98]

This position clearly has some connections with the idea of reading as provisional identification: the viewing of texts as linguistic structures that allow readers to explore or rehearse a variety of existential situations, or characters, or attitudes, or issues. But Altieri differs sharply from most New Formalisms in his insistent focus on the senses, and on desire and emotion (and value), and in his resistance to traditional emphases – literary critical as well as philosophical – on the cognitive.

The other group of "aesthetic formalists" seeks to develop the cognitive or moral or agential implications of Kantian aesthetics, relying on the argument paraphrased by Ginsborg above: "Aesthetic experience serves as a propadeutic for morality, in that 'the beautiful prepares us to love something, even nature, without interest.' " The moral focus is perhaps most striking in an account like Elaine Scarry's *On Beauty and Being Just*, in part because the claims for the moral implications of aesthetics are so grand yet the derivation of moral awareness from the sense of beauty is so fragile, rhapsodic, and untroubled by example. Equally curious is the fact that Kant appears in the book exactly once, and not as a philosopher leading us from beauty to morality but as one of those deplorable eighteenth-century theorists of the sublime who allegedly diminished and trivialized the idea of the beautiful by conceding its charm but pilfering its thunder and conferring it on sublimity instead. In Scarry's vision, the beautiful and the sublime, meadow flower and magnificent tree, were formerly not distinct but continuous.[99] Indeed, before the fatal sundering of beauty from sublimity, "the magnificent tree had itself assisted, or at least not interrupted, the passage from blossom to... " To what? To fullblown flower? To magnificent tree? No, to "something beyond both meadow flower and mighty tree,... [to] *the mental realm where, with or without a god's help, the principles of justice and goodness hold sway.*"[100] One can be forgiven for desiring a somewhat stronger bridge linking the beautiful blossom with "principles of justice and goodness."

Elsewhere, she contends that "beautiful things hold steadily visible the manifest good of equality and balance." (Scarry terms this particular argument "almost self-evident," which perhaps accounts for the paucity of citation and logic in her exposition.)[101] The claimed, though dubious and tenuously argued, identification between the "symmetry" of the beautiful object and the very different "symmetry" of just and fair human relations is only part of Scarry's attempt to find in beauty the source of a sense of justice and equality ("[B]eauty... assists us in the work of addressing injustice"). She asserts, further, that the "willingness to continually revise one's own location in order to place oneself in the path of beauty is the basic impulse underlying education."[102] If sublimity, for Scarry, has appropriated the dignity of beauty, the beautiful, in her account, expands to encompass much that humans hold valuable: fairness, equality (political, social, economic), justice, pleasurable selflessness, education, aliveness, and more. In consequence, *On Beauty and Being Just* can stand as one extreme case of the contemporary effort to redeem the aesthetic by asking it to perform beyond its traditional sphere of beauty, pleasure, the affects, and bodily sensation.

One critic who takes a more measured approach to the recovery of the aesthetic, and to its connections with New Formalist criticism, is Dubrow. In an economically argued section of "The Politics of Aesthetics: Recuperating Formalism and the Country House Poem," Dubrow rehearses some of the standard charges against the aesthetic (it mystifies the role of politics and power; it implicitly celebrates individualism; it reinforces class hierarchies and their attendant artistic rankings; it subordinates history and contingency to fantasies of universality; etc.) and offers suggestions toward a revised view of Kant that would permit his aesthetic theory a richer pertinence to contemporary formalisms. Her detailed readings of some English country house poems make good on the title of her essay, bringing an inventive textual attention to the form and politics of those poems and both arguing for and demonstrating a New Formalism that can be linked creatively to historical and political concerns without surrendering its own distinctive explorations of "style and meaning."[103]

v New Formalism, aesthetics, and contemporary ideas of form

Contemporary aesthetic revisions of the concept of form are at times surprisingly far-reaching. Arguing a more sweepingly "cognitivist" account of aesthetics, Robert Kaufman recapitulates Dubrow's recital of contemporary distrust of Kant's aesthetics and the formalism they are supposed to entail, but with a different twist. For Kaufman, the assumption of a "coterminous" relation of Kantian aesthetics with "that baleful phenomenon, formalism," betrays an inattention to several key issues.[104] The notion that Kant's third *Critique* puts in place "an essentialist or transcendental theory of cultural value, a theory based in literary or aesthetic form," and that such a theory "ideologically deforms" "the material, the social, and the historical," both simplifies Kant and ignores the light shed on his aesthetics by some Frankfurt School theorists – notably Adorno, who makes the third *Critique* "virtually a cornerstone of his negatively dialectical final statement, *Aesthetic Theory*."[105] At the heart of Adorno's interpretation of Kant, for Kaufman, is the idea that "aesthetic thought-experience in some way *precedes* objective, content-and-use-oriented thought; in that sense, aesthetic experience is 'formal' because it provides *the form for* conceptual, 'objective' thought or cognition."[106] In this account, "aesthetic form" contributes to "the possibilities of critical thought and agency."[107] As Angela Leighton paraphrases, "Form, then, ... starts to alter the very thing we mean by knowing. To be a 'capacity for,' rather than an object of knowledge, shifts attention towards a kind of knowing which is an imaginative attitude rather than an accumulation of known things."[108] Kaufman does not shrink from the fullest implications of his argument:

> Via Frankfurt Critical Theory or other methodologically available restatements, ... Kantian formal aesthetics reveals its kinship rather than hostility to Blakean poetics.... [F]ar from having its unruly heteronomy whipped into shape by the abstract force of formal discipline, *the material (or materiality) gets to count as material in the first place by virtue of its relationship to an act – however provisional – of framing, an act of form.*[109]

Such a revision echoes, first, Focillon's characteristic remark that "Between nature and man, form intervenes," and "what we call 'natural life' is in effect a relationship between forms, so inexorable that without it this natural life could not exist."[110] It also recalls a more recent and very different sort of text: Marshall Sahlins' powerful critique of materialist explanations of social and cultural forms in his *Culture and Practical Reason*, a book whose title obviously evokes Kant's third *Critique*.[111] Working to "suggest the symbolic structure in material utility," much as Saussure had suggested "to an unsuspecting Western world that its ostensible quest for the material is mediated by the symbolic," Sahlins cites approvingly these remarks of Habermas:

> While epistemologically we must presuppose nature as existing in itself, we ourselves have access to nature only within the historical dimension disclosed by labor processes.... "Nature in itself" is therefore an abstraction, which is a requisite of our thought: but we always encounter nature within the horizon of the world-historical self-formative process of mankind.[112]

"Formalism," then, in Kaufman's neo-Kantian account, neither mystifies nor simply reveals the social, historical, and material worlds. Instead, it interprets and gives an account of the forms through which those worlds are known and apart from which they cannot be known at all.[113]

Obviously, the opposition between the formal and the material, on which much antiformalism (and some formalism) is based is profoundly troubled by a perspective from which the material – or materiality – is a category that is formally[114] produced before it is the name for a collection of actual material objects.[115] From such a perspective, as Kaufman shows, the dualism that grounds the critique of Kantian aesthetics and the formalism which that aesthetics is alleged to sponsor become incoherent.

With this expanded, cognitivist notion of aesthetic form, traditionally restrictive ideas of form's *givenness* (whether as container, or adornment, or genre, or verse-form, or speech act) make way for innumerable particular forms, and kinds of form, that result from individual critical interpretations of particular works. In addition, then, to critical propaedeutics such as Miller's " 'I bet this is a lyric poem,' or 'I bet this is an elegy,' or 'I bet this is a parable,' " any number of individualized forms may emerge from the analysis that follows an aesthetic apprehension of the text or artwork. Thus, "I bet these hints and clues ('My top is dull black, and my sides glimmer gaily; / I never grow tired though I'm worked almost daily...') only superficially mimic a traditional riddle but actually constitute a lament about the unknowable inwardness of other persons." Or, "I bet these accounts of woods and fields are not instances of natural description as such but description commandeered by the speech of pathology: inventions of a dissociative fugue state masking trauma." And, of course, one work may disclose many forms and kinds of form depending on the interpretations it supports and the forms cognate with – produced by – those interpretations. Take this brief poem of Alexander Pope's:

EPIGRAM

Engraved on the Collar of a Dog which
I gave to his Royal Highness.

I am his Highness' Dog at *Kew*;
Pray tell me Sir, whose Dog are you?[116]

Conventionally, and accurately, the poem is likely to be termed an epigram, or a closed octosyllabic couplet, a brief satire, perhaps an inscription, or a prosopopoiea, depending on which traditional elements we choose to emphasize. But what form does the poem take if we note that its title has a disproportionately large number of syllables (twenty-one) in relation to the text it designates (sixteen)? Or that it is a poem of double or contaminated authorship since the title implicitly marks the text as a human production while the couplet presents itself as a canine utterance? Or if we focus on the contrasts among the gift-relationship between author and recipient ("a Dog which I gave to his Royal Highness"), the author–reader relationship implicit in the poem's explanatory title, and the asymmetrical, open-ended relationship between the canine speaker and the unspecified, indeterminate male audience the dog addresses ("Sir")? Or if we emphasize the presumed material contrast between the leather collar on which the poem allegedly first appeared and the paper on which the poem-plus-title appears after the fact? Or between both leather and paper and the voiced utterance we infer from the material text?

In cases like this, there need not – or need not only – be a traditional name like "elegy" or "epigram" or "sonnet" for the text's form. Indeed, such labels belong to an extremely valuable but limited system of literary designations whose deployment is often nearly pre-interpretive – at times, just short of *a priori*. Kaufman's understanding of "the aesthetic" allows us to see that interpretation produces not only meaning but the forms(s) of that meaning, and thus the authentic identities of the text. As Denis Donoghue puts it in his study of Walter Pater, "The part of Aestheticism which should now be recovered…is its concern for the particularity of form in every work of art." "Form," Donoghue elsewhere elaborates, "is the distinguishing characteristic of art; there is no reason to assume that it is unproblematically given, like the counting of syllables in an iambic pentameter."[117] If, for Kaufman, "the material (or materiality) gets to count as material in the first place by virtue of its relationship to an act – however provisional – of framing, an act of form," the text gets to count as an instance of a certain kind of form – gets to have a certain formal identity – by virtue of its relationship to an act of interpretation that produces both the meaning of that text and its identity as a certain kind of text.[118] This is a definition of "form" that, in Douglas Bruster's words, "emphasizes qualities that disclose themselves during the reading process."[119] Nor do those forms need to be specified within a purely literary register. It is entirely possible to produce a mode of New Formalist analysis that understands not just literary but "any authority as structured and informed as well as individually exerted[,] and the articulation of form, not merely as a product of social evaluations, but as a social evaluation itself, one of the texts in which culture is written."[120] An aesthetics that can take us to such a point of interpretive fertility and specificity – not re-enchanting the object or fixating on sensation, pleasure, and beauty, or tendentiously allegorizing the beautiful as the moral, but theorizing the work's significative and thus formal constitution – makes an important contribution to New Formalist criticism and theory.

The recognition that interpretation produces what Donoghue terms "the particularity of form in every work of art" requires a revision of older claims that form and meaning are two inseparable aspects of a single thing (recall Newman on "the convex and the concave of a curve"). Such claims, of course, have both echoed and varied from the New Critical assertion that "A good poem is an object in which form and content can be distinguished but cannot really be separated."[121] To take just one example, there is the writerly claim that form and meaning do not exist separately in the writer's consciousness. In Valéry's view, for example, "The philosopher cannot easily comprehend that the artist passes, almost with indifference, from form to content and from content to form; that *form comes to the artist with the meaning that he wishes to give it.*"[122] For New Formalism, however, the fusion of form and content is neither intrinsic to the artwork nor a particular feature of the artist's mode of conceptualization. Recall that Levinson, paraphrasing Rooney's argument in the latter's valuable "Form and Contentment," understands "form" as "the effect of reading," and that Fish argues that "formal units are always a function of the interpretive model one brings to bear (they are not 'in the text')."[123]

And not just "formal units." In Fish's account, "the [entire] text as an entity independent of interpretation and (ideally) responsible for its career drops out and is replaced by the texts that emerge as the consequence of our interpretive activities."[124] Fish is willing to go to the end of the line in this argument, contending that even the individual letters on a page of text are not elemental givens but objects *construed as letters by acts of interpretation*. It is readers, for example, who – however habitually, instantaneously, and therefore invisibly – construe a capital T as that letter rather than as one of two supports holding up a clothesline, a capital O as that letter rather than as a cross-section of a garden hose, a capital L as that letter rather than a right angle or an uncompleted triangle.[125] As with the unity of form and content, the formal identity of the text at all levels – from individual letters to particular forms to traditional genres – is the result of interpretive expectations and interpretive procedures. As Leighton paraphrases Focillon, "The life of forms... is simply the innumerable ways in which the artwork comes to life through interpretation."[126]

vi New Formalism, intention, reference, back-formation

For New Formalisms attempting to reground some of the textualist imperatives of New Criticism in contemporary theory, it is not just a text's formal identity and its unifications of form and content that come to life through interpretation. New Formalists also have something to say about the long-lived and contested topics of intention and reference. The New Critical position on intention was formulated by Wimsatt and Beardsley in 1946, with both evaluative and explicative consequences. First, "the design or intention of the author is neither available nor desirable as a standard for judging the success of a work of literary art"; second, "We ought to impute the thoughts and attitudes of the poem immediately to the dramatic speaker, and if to the author at all, only by an act of biographical inference."[127] Although intention might have seemed a non-problem after Wimsatt and Beardsley's essay, in the ensuing years their analysis has been both misunderstood and misrepresented. The anti-intentionalist position has been challenged on the grounds that it is complicit with an apoliticizing flight from history and biography, or (a related charge) that it represents an aestheticizing effort to insulate and fetishize the artwork, or that it contradicts the notion formulated by Burke, among others, that "the main ideal of criticism... is to use all that there is to use."[128] For this reason, and because a criticism calling itself "New Formalist" can hardly avoid taking up one of the founding notions of the old formalism, it is necessary to say a few words about the modern fate of the concept.

The issue loomed large in the 1980s in Walter Benn Michaels and Stephen Knapp's once-controversial article "Against Theory."[129] In their discussion, they conduct a thought-experiment in which the words of "A Slumber Did My Spirit Seal" appear inscribed in the sand of a beach immediately after a wave recedes. Michaels and Knapp will consider these markings in the sand to be the text of "A Slumber Did My Spirit Seal," a genuine (poetic) piece of language, only if the inscription in the sand is intended – whether by the sea, Wordsworth's ghost, or anything else imagined capable of intending. But if its appearance is a wild statistical fluke, the product of sheer unintended accident, they regard the markings as distinctly not a text – indeed, not as a piece of language at all – but only its simulacrum. In that case, there is no speech act, no poem – indeed, no words: just marks that "will merely seem to resemble words" because "marks without intention are not language either."[130] For the New Formalist, however, the text is indeed language, its intention not being an external and prior cause but one dimension of a speaker internal to and constituted by the language itself. Indeed, the second case (marks in sand produced by chance) is the crucial one and actually subsumes the first because it is according to this same internal intention – not that of the sea, or Wordsworth's ghost – that we should also read the *first* example in which we discover the words to have been inscribed by the sea, or Wordsworth's ghost, or even Wordsworth himself. That is one part of what it means to read it "as literature." This feature of writing, its ability to produce linguistic counterparts or analogues to the contextual features of historical or non-literary discourse – speaker, audience, context, and so on – is what permits literature to be read outside of its original, historical context of utterance. Indeed, it is what permits a text to be read in this way not just at some later point in time but also at the very moment when it was produced within that original context. In this sense, the text was distinct from that immediate context at the moment it was written.[131]

Thus confronted with "A Slumber Did My Spirit Seal" inscribed on the shore by chance, Michaels and Knapp can do nothing, because for them it lacks an intention and is therefore not a poem and not even language. Less radically, P. D. Juhl would regard this text as an instance of language but not a speech act: it is language, but language without an intention and thus uninterpretable. Juhl can do nothing with it either because "marks without intention are not speech acts."[132] A New Formalist, of course, can do something with this text: interpret it.[133] Not that there is a link between the New Formalist claim for an internal intention and the evidence for any *particular* intention or interpretation. It is always possible to read badly, to ascribe intention incompetently, to misinterpret. The argument that intention is internal is a way of locating it, not of determining or describing it. Thus while the positing of an intention is one of the first, enabling acts performed in an interpretation, the description of that intention, or the conviction that one has adequate understanding of it, is in some sense a significant goal of the interpretation, or one of its main results. And while we make assumptions, guesses, and conjectures all along the way, the interpretation is "done" (insofar as it ever is) only when we feel that we know, with satisfying detail and completeness, what kind of intention governs the text. In this sense, a specific intention is no more prior to interpretation than it is to the text itself.

The philosopher Alexander Nehamas, in "What an Author Is," makes this point from another angle in the course of contesting Foucault's claim (in "What Is an Author?") that an author is a readerly construction that we use in order to outlaw interpretive possibilities and thereby exercise power over the text. The historical author may indeed be used in this way, says Nehamas, but the author constructed by the text is not a means to exclude interpretations but itself a product of interpretation. (That this internal "author," too, may be used to exclude or rule out interpretations is beside the point, since any act of interpretation necessarily entails the exclusion of some meanings.) To clarify his point, Nehamas distinguishes between a *text* (any piece of writing) and a *work* (an interpretable and interpreted text). "Writers produce texts; some texts are interpreted and are thus construed as works; works generate the figure of the author manifested in them." Thus, "to determine what work a text constitutes is the very object of interpretation."[134] We begin, therefore, by hypothesizing that a given text may constitute a work – that it is "literature" – and that it has an internal author or intention. If this hypothesis proves correct, we will end by being able to give an account of what kind of work that text is, and what kind of speaker/author it generates.[135]

For Juhl, then, marks without intention, like those left on the shore, are language but not speech acts; for Michaels and Knapp, they are not even language. For a New Formalist, they are language and they produce an internal intention (and speaker, audience, context). Even historical-intentionalists of the old and not-so-old kind should acknowledge this, since they inevitably make use of this internal or text-constructed intention, perhaps without realizing that they are doing so. Imagine, for example, that someone announces a particular intention.[136] The intention as verbalized may be: "I intend to suggest politely to my supervisor that I deserve a higher salary." But now imagine that the text or utterance subsequently produced contradicts this intention, that the actual utterance is, "Hey, am I getting a raise or what?" In such a case, it's not just that the text or utterance contravenes the announced intention, for the internal intention of the utterance does so as well. The intention that we are likely to infer from this text is one of belligerence, bullying, and impatience; the internal speaker does *not* intend to suggest politely. The constructed or rhetorical or linguistic or textual intending doesn't square with the historical. Thus the problem is not that some texts lack an intention, as Michaels and Knapp assert, but that no text – taken as an object for interpretation – does. Whatever the empirical author's intention, the one discovered by interpretation will be produced internally and construed from the text itself.

How does a text produce its own intention? Barbara Johnson offers this paraphrase of Paul de Man's views on the topic:

> [I]t looks as if a text is produced to express the desire of a subject; but, since the only desire we *know* has been expressed is that of the text's own self-constitution, what legitimates our belief that the text is the product of a subject's desire, rather than, let's say, the subject being an effect of the text's desire? Not that he's substituting the second for the first, but he's saying, "*What prevents us* from seeing this as equally possible?"[137]

For New Formalism, the crucial point is not that it is "possible" to consider the text in two different ways (though that is true) but that the text becomes either of two different objects, depending on how we view and approach it, and that each of those objects reveals a different relation between the text and the intending author or "subject." Viewed as a biographical production, an authorial creation, the text is by definition "the product of a subject's desire." But the "subject" of a literary text is always a textual effect – an effect perhaps best understood on the model of what linguists call back-formation, a particular mode of coining words by inventing new forms based on the presumed priority (logical, morphological, historical) of one form to another. For example, it is a common though unreliable assumption that the verb form precedes the noun form (whether as historically anterior, or as in some sense prior because more linguistically primitive).[138] Relying on an assumption like this, "back-formation creates *what are supposed to be* primitives," and in doing so entails "the reinterpretation of a given form as derivative."[139] "Thus," remarks Esko Pennanen, "if in a language the verb is accepted as primitive in comparison to the corresponding agent noun, a verb that can be proved to be later in appearance than its agent noun may legitimately be looked upon as a back-formation from the noun."[140]

The production of such *faux* primitives produces examples like the following. Given the noun "liaison," *presumed* to be a secondary or derivative form, we produce the verb, "liaise." Given "burglar," we produce "burgle." Ditto "enthusiasm" and "enthuse." In each case, the noun form is in fact historically prior, but the implicit justification for the production of the verb form is the presumption that the noun form "must have" derived from a prior verb form. The verb is formed by a leap "backward" to a stage preceding the noun form – whence "back-formation." (We can think of back-formation as the linguistic equivalent of the "prequel," in which narrative B, produced at a later date than narrative A, nonetheless tells the story of events *preceding* A.) Another example is the invention of "monokini" from "bikini." The joke here – for linguists and literary critics, at least – is that the "bi" in "bikini" has nothing to do with the Latin prefix for "two." Rather, "Bikini" is the name of an atoll in the Marshall Islands where atomic bomb tests were performed in the 1940s, tests whose devastating effect on men or on society in general was jokingly presumed to have a counterpart in the impact of the two-piece bathing suit (cf. "blonde bombshell"). Nonetheless, since "one" is taken to be more "primitive" than "two," "bikini" generated "monokini." Can the still more primitive – and revealing – "kini" be far behind?

Back-formation is a useful model to New Formalist thinking about the way in which texts generate not only their speakers or personas or subjects but also their effects of reference – the things the texts seem to be about. In the case of reference, the implicit justification is not a fantasy of linguistic or historical priority but the widespread everyday notion that language and speech are referential, mimetic; that they are called into action by the effort to refer to an *already existing* reality; and thus that language is a secondary form while experience (reality, life, history) is a primary form. In response to a friend's utterance, "I went shopping and found some really fresh ginger," it is natural – that is, conventional – to ask "When?" or "Where?" In response to the opening of Wordsworth's *Resolution and Independence*, "There was a roaring in the wind all night;/The rain came heavily and fell in floods," it can seem similarly natural to wonder "When and where was that roaring, that rain?" Indeed, Wordsworth seems to anticipate such wonderings in a later, highly "circumstantial" note:

> Written at Town-end, Grasmere. This old Man I met a few hundred yards from my cottage; and the account of him is taken from his own mouth. I was in the state of feeling described in the beginning of the poem, while crossing over Barton Fell from Mr. Clarkson's, at the foot of Ullswater, towards Askham. The image of the hare I then observed on the ridge of the Fell.[141]

Similarly, given this sentence from a more recent prose text – "So now at last the City was besieged, enclosed in a ring of foes" – it is natural to want to know who is speaking, to whom, about which city and which foes.

But while the questions about shopping for ginger are indeed answerable if the initiating remark is part of an everyday, real-life conversation, it will not be useful to rely on Wordsworth's note when we approach "Resolution and Independence" as a poem, nor will it help us as formalist critics to investigate the life and times of J. R. R. Tolkien, from whose *Lord of the Rings* that sentence about the besieged city comes.[142] All of the elements seemingly referred to are in fact produced by back-formation from a text that *acts as though* it were reporting on a prior and/or anterior reality. But in the case of a literary text, there is no such reality.[143] And even though there is indeed a village named Grasmere and a lake named Ullswater, the fictionality of the city Gondor in *The Return of the King*, and its production by back-formation, are no different from the comparable fictionality and production of the characters, settings, and events in Wordsworth's poem, or in literary texts that speak of Carthage or Cathay, Bridgeport or Binghamton. If interpretation produces form, interpretation also produces the peculiar ability of literary texts to generate the reality they seem merely to describe after the fact.[144] Wallace Stevens intimates something of this process, and of its power for readers, in "The Idea of Order at Key West":

> It may be that in all her phrases stirred
> The grinding water and the gasping wind;
> But it was she and not the sea we heard.
> For she was the maker of the song she sang.
> She was the single artificer of the world
> In which she sang. And when she sang, the sea,
> Whatever self it had, became the self
> That was her song, for she was the maker. Then we,
> As we beheld her striding there alone,
> Knew that there never was a world for her
> Except the one she sang and, singing, made.[145]

If the literary text is for New Formalists fundamentally a linguistic object, it is also a linguistic object that generates the reality it purports – and is often taken – to represent or describe. As Wittgenstein wrote, "Do not forget that a poem [or 'work of literature'], even though it is composed in the language of information, is not used in the language-game of giving information."[146]

I am aware that it may seem counterintuitive, or the gesture of a spoilsport, to compromise the status of the empirical reality to which the text seems so clearly to refer. One can, after all, actually visit Grasmere and Ullswater, if not Gondor. Yet Grasmere and Ullswater in the poem are different from Grasmere and Ullswater in the English Lake District, which are, after all, never named in the text of the poem. And in any case, the absence of these place names from the poem is far from the heart of the matter, for simply to name "Grasmere" or "Ullswater" is to evoke each in only a minimal, even preliminary, way – not so much to refer as to offer a kind of promissory note of reference. What these places are, what they mean, what they shall count as, can only emerge from a perception or a representation or an imagining of them by some particular consciousness, just as the actual rather than potential meanings of any word – "drink," say – can only be determined by examining that word in the context of whatever text or utterance it occurs in. "Give me to drink Mandragora." "Drink to me only with thine eyes." "They slipped on the muddy bank and landed in the drink." "Drink in this gorgeous sunset." " 'Drink' in German is 'Trinken.' " "He's a long, tall drink of water." Simply saying "Grasmere" is like simply saying "drink": each scarcely nudges the signifier from the potentiality of *la langue* into the actuality of *la parole*; each scarcely begins to signify. Yet when each word is embedded in a significant stretch of discourse, its meaning is chiefly constructed by the numerous and minute particulars of context and characterization, and by the word itself only in some attenuated, indexical way – a way that is less a meaning than a vector of reference. Thus "the actual Grasmere" cannot be "in" *Resolution and Independence*, whether its name is present or not, because there are innumerable actual Grasmeres produced by individual acts of apprehension and representation, and the only ones pertinent to Wordsworth's poem are those inferred or construed or constructed by particular interpretations of that poem.[147] As William Galperin complains in *The Historical Austen*,

> in making Austen's oeuvre a social or political text permeable to elements or influences from which it can no longer beg severance, historical readings invariably make Austen's writings answerable to a given context instead of appreciating the degree to which the novels are just as much a context *in themselves* where matters of history, ranging from the literary to the social to the very reality on which the narratives dilate, work to complicated, if often antithetical, ends.[148]

To quote David Lodge once again, "every imaginable utterance is an 'appropriate' symbolization of the experience it conveys since there is no possible alternative symbolization of 'the same' experience."[149] For New Formalism, reference, like intention, is a textual effect that follows from acts of interpretation.

vii   Reference and rhetoric in New Formalist interpretation

If we can call the traditional idea of textual reference "referential" or "mimetic," and the contemporary formalist idea "textual" or "rhetorical," we can begin to follow out some larger implications for interpretation of the distinction between them. Let's start with a question about an apparently marginal sort of text. How would the mimetic/rhetorical distinction operate in a text that, whatever its real source, set out to imitate or be the utterance of a non-linguistic thing or creature – say, one of Ted Hughes's animal poems, such as "Hawk Roosting," which opens this way?

> I sit in the top of the wood, my eyes closed.
> Inaction, no falsifying dream
> Between my hooked head and hooked feet:
> Or in sleep rehearse perfect kills and eat.[150]

Most likely, we would want to treat it as both the utterance of a human trying to give voice to a non-linguistic creature and as the actual utterance of a speaking animal. And we would want to explore the relations between these two perspectives, as we would in reading Pope's poem on his Highness' dog at Kew. "Mimetically," we recognize that the prior reality can't be an introspective talking hawk so must be something else – in this case, a human pretending to be a speaking hawk – while rhetorically or textually we explore the hawk's utterance and attitude. To do only the latter is to ignore the evident impossibility of the situation; to do only the former is to ignore the gain for vision of the "as if" perspective, the view of the human world from a hawk's (or a dog's) point of view. Examples like these suggest that the mimetic and rhetorical perspectives are, in pure form, each other's limiting cases, or – more usefully – that both perspectives are necessary if we are to bring new experiences in line with our present sense of reality and possibility and enlarge that sense of reality and possibility as well: to comprehend but also to expand experience. And this is true not simply of special cases such as these but of recognizably central or mainstream texts as well. It is important to say, for example, not simply that Shelley's "Ode to the West Wind" treats the West Wind *as though* it were sentient but also that in this poem what is called the West Wind *is* a spirit, a sentient being.[151] Poems like Pope's or Hughes's show us the referential/rhetorical tension in a particularly vivid way – seem almost designed to tease out the possibilities of that tension. But it is a tension that marks any text that we view from these two perspectives, and one of the goals of New Formalist analysis is to take account of it and of other tensions like it.

It may be helpful to look at a poem in which the play between the two perspectives does not lie quite so near the surface: Keats' "Bright Star." I'll begin with a compressed summary from the mimetic or referential perspective and go on to develop, at slightly greater length, both the rhetorical-textual perspective and some of the interesting tensions between these two accounts of the poem.

> Bright Star! would I were stedfast as thou art–
> Not in lone splendor hung aloft the night,
> And watching, with eternal lids apart,
> Like nature's patient, sleepless Eremite,
> The moving waters at their priestlike task
> Of pure ablution round earth's human shores,
> Or gazing on the new soft-fallen mask
> Of snow upon the mountains and the moors;
> No – yet still steadfast, still unchangeable,
> Pillow'd upon my fair love's ripening breast,
> To feel forever its soft fall and swell,
> Awake forever in a sweet unrest,
> Still, still to hear her tender-taken breath,
> And so live ever – or else swoon to death.[152]

"Bright Star" is the expression of a wish – the wish that the human experience of sensuous intimacy might be extended forever, that the eternity of the star might be wedded to the "sweet unrest" of human, physical passion. But though the speaker wishes for the eternity of the star, he rejects most of the other attributes of that distant luminary: thus "would I were stedfast as thou art" means as steadfast as the star, not steadfast *in the way that* the star is steadfast. For in addition to its steadfastness, the star displays many traits that sharply contrast with the kind of experience that attracts the speaker. The opposition between star and speaker, or between the star's relation to the world and the speaker's relation to his "love," is in fact almost diagrammatic in its clarity. The star is distant; the speaker wishes for intimacy. The star relies solely on visual knowledge ("watching," "gazing"); the speaker wishes to hear and feel. The star seems beyond time and change ("stedfast," "eternal lids"); the speaker inhabits a world in which enjoyment is intimately bound up with time and change ("ripening," "fall and swell," "sweet unrest," "breath"). The star's splendor is lone and ascetic ("Eremite");

the speaker longs for nearness and sensual enjoyment. Initially, at least, the speaker's intimate and time-engaged knowledge seems preferable to the passive ("hung") and impassive solitude of the star. Relying solely on the visual, gazing through interstellar distances, the star sees "the new soft-fallen mask/Of snow upon the mountains and the moors." It sees, that is, imperfectly ("mask"), and perhaps with a precision inferior to that available to the speaker's multi-sensory, intimate, and tactile awareness. From those heights, can the star tell the difference between those similar because alliterative "mountains" and "moors" when they are masked by snow – the alliterating "mask" further blending mountain and moor in a kind of consonantal white noise?

In contrast (also brought out by phonetic similarity) to the "soft-fallen mask," there is the "soft fall and swell" of the lover's breast, a bodily landscape whose undulations are neither masked nor known only visually.[153] What the speaker wishes for, then, is the star's apparent eternality, but that eternality translated to the sphere of human passion, temporality, and sensual intimacy. Such a wish is, of course, incapable of fulfillment, since it is a wish for contradictory things, and the speaker seems to recognize its impossibility. He does not claim to experience eternal temporality and steadfast unrest but to wish for it (*"would* I were stedfast"), and he also envisions an alternative to this dream: he would "so live ever – or else swoon to death," a romantic ending (in both senses of both words) which replaces the wish for eternity with a death that is scarcely distinguishable from overpowering bliss. With this alternative, the poem shifts from one paradoxical and borderline experience (temporality/eternity) to another (life/death), and in so doing partly disengages itself from the imagined bliss it has explored and longed for. It is a poem of desire, and it seeks to enlarge our image of desire by imagining its way into a territory that lies beyond the boundaries of actual experience. From this point of view, "Bright Star" is a particular version of a larger Romantic project: the recovery for imagination of an idealized world, a world of romance, of the possibility of extraordinary "joy," and of an expanded sensory, emotive, and imaginative life. So, in embarrassingly rough outline, might run a fairly standard reading from the mimetic perspective.

To begin to read from the rhetorical perspective is in a sense to introduce a deconstructive element by virtue of the incompatibility of this perspective with the referential. If some contemporary formalist approaches entertain, if only in a regulative fashion, the concept of unity, deconstructive approaches generally gravitate to disunity and contradiction – not the random contradictions of ordinary absent-mindedness, but contradictions that bring us up against the limits of the ways we make sense of things: contradictions, especially, between two or more necessary yet incompatible systems of signification.[154] Such clashes between two systems of meaning can show us with great clarity the form of these systems even though, much of the time, we need not pay close attention to them. When we turn to "Bright Star," we find that many of the contrasts on which a reading from the mimetic perspective is based are capable of being construed quite differently in a rhetorical reading. First there is the question of distance and nearness. From one perspective, the star's remoteness from the earth ("lone splendor," "aloft") contrasts with, for example, the speaker's intimate pillowedness on his love's "ripening breast." But from another point of view, these relations are precisely reversed, for it is the star that is addressed, apostrophized ("Bright star!"), treated as a present "thou," while the love, desirable as intimacy with her may be, is distinctly offstage, excluded from the one-sided colloquy that constitutes the poem – a third person grammatically as well as numerically.[155] The apostrophe is especially striking since the star is not only physically distant but also, though manifesting only the sense of sight, addressed by the poet as though it could hear. It could even be argued that, in addition to being absent, the "fair love" is also invoked only partially by the poem's rhetoric since the speaker isolates her (arguably synecdochic) breast and focuses on its "fall and swell," and on a "sweet unrest" that seems syntactically (what is the antecedent?) as much her breast's and the speaker's as it is hers. The speaker's nearness or intimate attention to the star is emphasized in other ways as well: by his detailed elaboration of those features of starhood he does not wish to possess (2–8); by the power and beauty he finds in the star's visual seizing of earthly pattern, "The moving waters at their priestlike task/Of pure ablution round earth's human shores"; and by the phrase "lone splendor," which insists not simply on solitude and brightness but on magnificence and eminence as well. A letter from Keats to his brother Tom, written during the poet's tour of the north country, reflects biographically what the poem has begun to suggest about the poet's identification with the star:

> ... the two views we have had of it ["this lake"] are of the most noble tenderness – they can never fade away – they make one forget the divisions of life; age, youth, poverty and riches; and refine one's sensual vision into a sort of north star which can never cease to be open lidded and stedfast over the wonders of the great Power.[156]

We have, then, an interesting critical crux. Clearly, the speaker privileges intimacy, temporality, and earthly warmth over the star's distance, and he wants to graft only the star's "stedfastness" onto that earthly experience, to enjoy an unending state of ecstatic pillowedness. As clearly, though, he admires the star's splendid aloftness, and the vision it makes possible, even as he also claims ("Not...") to reject them. And from a grammatical and rhetorical point of view, he is considerably "nearer" to the star, whom he addresses, than to the "fair love," who remains an absent object of desire for the entire poem. That is, we can treat the poem as though it were the utterance of a person presumed to exist outside and prior to the text, in the empirical world, even if that person is only imaginary. Thus we say that a speaker "speaks" the poem and uses the first person of himself ("would I were stedfast"). This is the referential perspective. But we can also treat the poem as a linguistic and rhetorical construct whose speaker is precisely *created by* the poem. From this point of view, we don't have a speaker who uses the first person but an instance of the power of the first-person pronoun and other deictics to create a speaker. The conflict is a matter of two antithetical – not simply different – ways of conceiving discourse.

The referential perspective shows us a speaker with an assumed life and context apart from and prior to the utterance of the poem itself. This speaker is mortal, sensual, pleasure-seeking; he longs for the eternal enjoyment of an intrinsically finite condition; and he refers to a woman who is presumably absent from him at the moment of his utterance. He wishes for an experience that he does not in that moment have, an experience from which he is distanced. From a textual or rhetorical point of view, however, this distance is not simply the product of human mortality (eternal love is not available to mortals) or of chance (his love happens not to be with him at the moment) but of a particular necessity: this speaker's distance from experience is the result of his existing as a rhetorical rather than an empirical entity, an "I" rather than a person in the world, marks on the page rather than a mind–body complex in life. Put crudely, "he" is distant from the empirical world because deictics like the first-person pronoun can't be pillowed on anything – because even if he began as an empirical person, he has undergone an ontological transformation as a result of the move from the referential to the rhetorical perspective. Such a transformation is glossed over by phrases like "putting oneself on paper" or "getting more of yourself into your writing." What such formulas obscure is the yawning chasm between the referential and the rhetorical, the utterance of the self and the self as created by utterance. This chasm is unbridgeable in a way that even the gulf between mortal speaker and immortal longings, or between present speaker and absent lover, is not. It is an image of utter experiential deprivation, absolute distance from the empirical world.

But it is also an image of the distance from experience that makes discourse – as an act of conception and articulation, an act of signification – possible: discourse like that, for example, which constitutes "Bright Star." Such distance, or "lone splendor," as we might now term it, is the inescapable condition of a text – including a textualized self or subject – and it is not surprising that Keats should have recognized its antithetical relation to experience or that he should have found this distance attractive and compelling, as well as problematically anti-experiential.[157] The star in "Bright Star," then, like the speaker, is an image of double aspect. From a referential or empirical perspective, it is an image of the poet in his detachment from the experience he would make into poetry. It is thus a kind of antithesis to the poem's speaker understood as a poet wishing to be immersed in, or pillowed upon, that worldly experience – living it, as we say, rather than watching it. From a rhetorical perspective, the star is an image of a different kind of detachment from experience: not that of the empirical person in a reflective moment, or even in a life extraordinarily devoted to reflection, but the detachment of the rhetorical sphere itself from the empirical sphere. Here the star is an image not, say, of Keats' speaker thinking about his love rather than experiencing her, but of the "I" and "she" that are created by, exist only in, and can never leave behind the verbal construct that is "Bright Star" (compare the lovers on the Grecian Urn). As empirical person, the speaker wishes to be steadfast "as thou art" in the sense of being as steadfast as the star, though not in the same way. As rhetorical person, however, the speaker is steadfast "as" – that is, *in the way that* – the star is, since both belong to the same sphere, that of rhetoric or textuality. From this perspective, it makes perfect sense for a (grammatical) person to address a star ("I," "thou") since there is absolutely no discontinuity between them; physical distance doesn't apply in this sphere, nor is there an ontological gulf.

The star is significant, then, apart from its steadfastness, because its almost inconceivable distance from the earthly world is an emblem of an experiential deprivation that, from another point of view, is an affirmation of one of the realms in which utterances such as poems exist – the textual or rhetorical. Only here, if anywhere, can anything like eternity be attained (the poet is dead but his poems still address stars, urns, seasons, us). Only here can stars that one has "hung" there oneself by the very act of apostrophizing them be meaningfully addressed.[158] And only here can sensual passion – which, since it marks us as human and thus mortal creatures, is a dedication to the passing world and thus to our own mortality ("swoon to death") – be countered by the ascetic perpetuity of textuality itself. Indeed, if one wanted to write a poem expressing simply the wish to graft eternity onto the sensual experiencing of the beloved, one could hardly pick a less apt image than Keats's star, most of whose attributes he must in fact reject for half the poem. One might choose, rather, something like the sea that the star watches, something "eternal," in a loose sense, and yet – in its earthliness, movement, and physical contact with the shore – closer to the sensuous temporality of here-and-nowness. But such an image would not have served the very different purpose that I am trying to outline here.

Does the exploration of these two perspectives unify the poem or set it against itself? Is Keats' sonnet a harmonious exploration of the tension between the referential and the rhetorical, or is it simply the localizable site of an irremediable, contestatory doubleness? To be sure, we haven't tried to reduce the poem to indeterminateness or undecidability, but neither have we found unity of the kind usually sought in older formalist readings: "an inclusive unity of opponent attitudes that is the mark of a mature and realistic stance toward reality," in Abrams' words, or Brooks' "pattern of resolved stresses."[159] But questions of unity and difference are rarely if ever simply descriptive or empirical questions; the decision to promote either to a commanding position is usually a way of signaling one's critical sympathies or affiliations rather than of telling us anything about a given text, or texts in general. Thus the decision to describe a text like "Bright Star" as a unified exploration of contrasts or a site of unrecuperable differential energy is largely a terminological decision, and it may well depend, at bottom, on a temperamental or fantasized preference for the beautiful or the sublime. What a New Formalist criticism seeks to establish is not the definition of this or that text as finally unified or finally self-contestatory, but the perpetual availability of the mimetic and textual – or referential and rhetorical – perspectives to critical analysis, and the specificity and detail of their varied implications for particular texts. It is to some of those texts that we must now turn.

3
New Formalist Interpretation

i Reference and rhetoric in Williams, Milton, and Browning

The preceding chapters have tried to present, theorize, and argue for some of the contemporary critical practices known as New Formalist or New Formalism. They have also attempted to situate these practices in relation to formalist criticism of the twentieth century as it evolved from the essays of T. S. Eliot to the New Critics themselves, and in relation to some other theoretical and philosophical projects such as contemporary critical theory, Cassirer's philosophy of symbolic forms, and Gadamer's "philosophical hermeneutics." Except for the discussion of Keats's "Bright Star" that closes Chapter 2, the textual analyses have been extremely brief and subordinated to one or another theoretical or methodological argument. The present chapter will try to present a more concrete and circumstantial case for New Formalist criticism by offering a variety of textual analyses, and by exploring – with examples – the place of close reading in New Formalism, in critical practices that do not claim to be formalist, and indeed in a variety of non-literary disciplines. In I. A. Richards' quaint but still useful terminology, this chapter marks a transition from an emphasis on principles of literary criticism to an emphasis on practical criticism – criticism or interpretation in practice.

Readers of the "proof of the pudding is in the eating" persuasion may expect that the present study will stand or fall by the spectacular freshness and convincingness – or absence thereof – of the textual interpretations offered below. This expectation is misplaced, I think, and for two reasons. First, it is no argument against a method that it may be incompetently or uninterestingly employed. If I assert that the sum of nine and seven is eighteen, my error is no indictment of arithmetic procedures generally, or of the system of natural numbers. The method is a matter of principles and procedures; the application is a matter of particular abilities and performances. Second, in the case of New Formalism, what is being proposed is not an entirely new interpretive method built on a dramatic deciphering of textual elements but a renewed and revised commitment to the principles and practices of the close reading that has regularly been a staple of formalist, deconstructive, and other modes of textual analysis. Sometimes in dialogue with other critics and sometimes not, these analyses attempt to illustrate some particular meanings and some kinds of meaning that contemporary formalist interpretation can hope to elicit from various texts.

We can begin by extending the discussion of reference and rhetoric in Keats' "Bright Star" to a Modernist poem that more overtly stages their confrontation, William Carlos Williams' "This Is Just to Say."

> This Is Just to Say
> I have eaten
> the plums
> that were in
> the icebox
> and which
> you were probably
> saving
> for breakfast
> Forgive me
> they were delicious
> so sweet
> and so cold

Williams' short poem has spurred a number of interpretations, some of them resolutely biographical (the poem is a note to his wife, whose understanding and forgiveness he could count on), and some literary-historical, focusing on the poem's connections with Modernism, with Imagism, or with Williams' published ideas about poetry and perception. Others are ethical and linguistic, concerned with the acts – and speech acts – of apology and forgiveness that the poem performs or requests. A few are simply bizarre: the poem is about nothing; it's about the uselessness of sexual desire; it's about a boy's Oedipal quest to learn of his own origin from his mother. A sophisticated and deeply meditated essay by Charles Altieri uses Williams' poem to explore larger questions of "Presence and Reference in a Literary Text," investigating the status and character of the poem's oblique apology, teasing out possible meanings of "Just" and of "just saying," and offering a notion of literary reference as a mechanism for picturing experiences but not for denoting "specific states of affairs."[1] I want to take Altieri's line of analysis in a slightly different direction while still hewing closely to the reference/rhetoric opposition.

Handwritten on a narrow piece of paper and discovered on a kitchen table or an icebox door, Williams' text approaches the status of an every-day note – a terse admission, a recognition of likely implications of trespass, an appeal for forgiveness, and then what sounds half like a promotion of physical pleasure to the status of an excuse and half like a curious taunt. Printed in a book of poems, however, the text looks like a poem: title, three four-line stanzas, unjustified right margins, and so on. As a note, the text implicitly claims referential status, designating plums, icebox, some empirical "you" and "I." As a poem, it "refers" only by back-formation and requires no anterior persons, plums, or other props. Williams constructs clues that point in both directions, offering his short text as an object lesson in the relations between reference and rhetoric, non-literary and literary texts.

The title, for example, can be paraphrased in several ways, among them: (1) "This relatively unimportant utterance simply wants to express..." – a familiar formula often introducing letters, notes, or tele-phone messages of no great import. As such, it belongs to the realm of the referential, and what is subsequently said is presumably about the real world: there were some plums, I ate them, and at this later point in time I am telling you about that act. (2) "This is just to *say* I have eaten the plums – it is not to refer to any actual plums or actual eating. My aim is not to represent an anterior real-world situation but to *say these words*." Here the line becomes a rhetorical rather than referential act. By a kind of syntactic or idiomatic pun, moreover, the title permits both of these antithetical readings – as though each were a latent feature of the text waiting to be liberated by one or another act of interpretation.

An additional and analogous ambiguity governs the status of the clause in question, "This Is Just to Say." These mostly capitalized words are at once a title designating a separate rhetorical structure, the poem – as the phrase *Paradise Lost* designates the 12-book poem that follows it – *and* the first line of a note beginning with these five words. As title, the line is spatially distinct from the three stanzas and helps to establish the visual format we recognize as "a poem." But syntactically, and aurally, it is continuous with the rest of the text and pulls it toward the status of a (referential) "note." There are two different sorts of utterance or text here, then, but no secure boundary definitively distinguishes them. And if the title's textual distinctness is eroded by its syntactic continuity with the rest of the utterance, other boundaries are similarly compromised. Stanza three begins with a capital letter, but no period precedes it; in consequence, the single sentence stretching from the title through the end of stanza two does not definitively conclude, even though stanza three definitively re-begins – or almost definitively, since a capitalized word of this kind conventionally follows a period or inaugurates a new text entirely. The sentences are separate and not separate.[2] Similarly, the entire text concludes without any punctuation, even though the two parallel descriptive phrases, "so sweet/and so cold," intimate a conclusive-sounding cadence. The text undeniably ends, yet it is also not conventionally demarcated from other texts, or from the discourse and the world that are its contexts.

In numerous ways, the text invokes and compromises the very idea of boundaries and distinctions, most pointedly in its systematic enactment of the textual capacity to function both referentially and rhetorically. Indeed, if moving from a referential to a rhetorical reading of Keats' "Bright Star" drastically changes the speaker's relation to the star he addresses, such a move in the case of Williams' poem dramatizes the co-presence of two kinds of verbal status and – historically speaking – the Modernist preoccupation with the definition of art, verbal and pictorial. Of Eliot's famous phrase in "The Love Song of J. Alfred Prufrock," "Like a patient etherised upon a table," John Berryman once remarked, "With this line, modern poetry begins"[3] – a bold exaggeration making an important point. One might similarly claim that with "This Is Just to Say," Modernist poetry requires its audience to meditate on the question, "What is poetry?" and on the problematic relations between literary and non-literary texts.

Tensions like these between referential and rhetorical modes of understanding a text can manifest themselves in a variety of ways. In the case of Keats, the focus is on relations between speaker and addressee, and between empirical and rhetorical existence; in the case of Williams, relations between non-literary and literary modes of textuality. It is possible to explore different but related kinds of tension: for example, between a rhetorical reading in which speaker and world are generated by the text, and a traditional referential reading relying directly on biographical and historical information. Consider, for example, Milton's Sonnet 19:

> When I consider how my light is spent,
> E're half my days, in this dark world and wide,
> And that one Talent which is death to hide,
> Lodg'd with me useless, though my Soul more bent
> To serve therewith my Maker, and present

My true account, least he returning chide,
Doth God exact day labour, light deny'd,
I fondly ask; But patience to prevent
That murmur, soon replies, God doth not need
Either man's work or his own gifts, who best
Bear his milde yoak, they serve him best, his State
Is Kingly. Thousands at his bidding speed
And post o're Land and Ocean without rest:
They also serve who only stand and waite.[4]

Often titled "On his Blindness" by editors and anthologists (though not by the author), Milton's sonnet indeed makes sense when read as referring to the author's own physical blindness. True, taken biographically (the poem's likely date is in the 1650s; Milton was born in 1608; line 2 speaks of "half my days"), the poem raises questions either about textual dating or about the author's sanguine view of seventeenth-century life expectancy. In response to these questions, some scholars have speculated that Milton – like Pope – predated his poems to underscore his precociousness; or that in line two the poet meant "half my *working* days"; or (still less plausibly) that he derived confidence from his father's having lived some 84 years. Even so, tradition has made it difficult to read the poem biographically and not think that it probably refers to the poet's growing blindness. Even read from a New Formalist perspective, it is reasonable to understand the poem as generating a speaker who is troubled by his failing vision, and by the possibility that this condition will keep him from performing the work to which he is called.

But it is also reasonable to understand it in another way. If we can focus on the text and put aside our knowledge of its author, making of it – to misappropriate John Crowe Ransom's words about *Lycidas* – "a poem nearly anonymous," things look rather different. Bracketing chronology, Milton's beliefs and career, idiom, and more, we could conduct a kind of thought experiment in which we imagine the poem to be anonymous, or even to have been written by, say, Keats – the speaker or author fired by poetic ambition, haunted by the threat of early death (intensified by the fate of his brother, if we read biographically), and finding himself and his hope or guidance or talent or poetic illumination ("light") stranded in the metaphoric hopelessness of a "dark world and wide." The warrant for doing so would be, first, that nothing in the poem requires the imagery of vision, light, and darkness to be read literally, and, second, that literary history is more than abundantly marked by metaphoric uses of such imagery.[5] I suspect that if this poem had never been linked to Milton but treated as anonymous or ascribed to Keats or another poet, the question of physical blindness might never have arisen. That is, once Milton is out of the picture, it is not obvious that this is a poem about literal blindness at all. The goal, of course, is not to replace Milton with Keats, or the biographical reading with a New Formalist analysis, or a poem about literal with a poem about metaphorical blindness. It is rather to see what the text itself tells us and to put that structure of meaning into play with the structure of meaning generated by the poem seen as an autobiographical document. What we do in such a case, when the text has been allowed a voice, is up to individual readers. What is essential is that the text be permitted to have its voice, or its voices.

An interesting variant on this situation is offered by a poem like Browning's "My Last Duchess," in part because it is a dramatic monologue, a poetic form that is commonly defined in two different ways: as a poem spoken by a single speaker to a silent but physically present addressee, and as a poem definitively not in the author's voice.[6] In the case of this particular text, there are significant links between some of its formal and thematic features and its status as a dramatic monologue. First, there is what we might call the "iron fist in a velvet glove" dimension of the Duke's personality, the way in which his mania for control couches itself in polite, decorous, and ostensibly accommodating forms. Every reader will recall the Duke asking the visiting envoy, "Will't please you sit and look at her?" – an utterance that is technically a question but functionally a command, since one can hardly imagine the envoy replying, "I think not – I'd prefer to get directly to the negotiations."[7] The same is true of the later question, "Will't please you rise?" Then there is the Duke's remark that strangers viewing the portrait of the Duchess for the first time always turned to him,

> And seemed as they would ask me, if they durst,
> How such a glance came there; so, not the first
> Are you to turn and ask thus.[8]

Has the envoy in fact asked? Perhaps, but it seems at least as likely that the Duke has ventriloquized the utterance, acting as though the envoy has said precisely what the Duke requires him to say at that moment – in effect, commandeering the envoy's being and volition or constructing it by a kind of patrician interpellation. An analogous moment occurs near the end of the conversation when the Duke says, "Nay, we'll go/Together down, sir," presumably in response to the envoy's deferential gesture inviting the Duke to precede him.[9] The Duke here feigns a gesture of equality that is undercut by the sheer reality of rank, by the structure of power relations that has pervaded the entire scene, and of course by the fact that it is he who imposes the egalitarian charade.

This thematic dramatization of masked power has a formal counterpart in Browning's versification. Though the poem is written in heroic couplets, someone hearing it recited might easily fail to notice its meter because of Browning's resolutely anti-Augustan management of the couplet. The wildly varying lengths of the units of meaning (entailing their frequent non-coincidence with line or couplet); their at times tortuous syntax and intense hypotaxis; the chaotic placement of caesuras; the extravagant variations of stress veiling the iambic pentameter norm; and of course the frequent enjambment over one, two, or more lines – these, combined and often reinforcing each other, work to mute the heroic couplet, to render it nearly unhearable, even though it remains the metrical organizing principle of the entire poem. This feat of versification is clearly a formal analogue to the Duke's ever-present but camouflaged and covert controllingness – an instance of sound echoing sense, of form reinforcing meaning by performing it in another textual modality.

But to turn to the non-formal definition of dramatic monologue – as a poem not in the author's voice – is to understand the poem's versification, and indeed the totality of its discourse, in quite another way. This may seem to move from a formalist to a biographical perspective, but that is not quite accurate. In fact, "auctorial" is a more accurate term than "biographical," since it is not Browning's particular authorship of the poem that is at issue but the fact of our taking it as being authored at all by someone – anyone – other than the Duke. One could even take the "poem markers" of the text – the unjustified right margin, the title and scene-setting epigraph, the fictional Pandolf and Claus, the couplets, the reliance on the text itself to generate its setting, and so on – as indicators that this monologue and its speaker are discursive constructions produced by someone who may have been Browning but who is in any case not the Duke. In making this move, then, we are not so much relinquishing the New Formalist perspective as insisting on it in a different way: as an approach allowing us to suspend the referential perspective that the poem in other ways seems to invite, as we did with Hughes's "Hawk Roosting" and with Pope's dog-collar "Epigram."

When that perspective is suspended, the free, manipulative, and self-determining source of the poem's magnificent rhetoric, the Duke, is immediately reduced to an effect – an epiphenomenon – of that very rhetoric: its product rather than its producer. Thus the poem's closing and presumably cautionary hierarchy of control, ranging from the lowly tamed sea horse on up to the Duke – "me!" – could be thought of as having an additional, invisible and unspoken agent at its apex of power: the text's author, or the very fact of the text's having been authored. From this perspective, the disguised control that the Duke exerts in his interview with the envoy is massively trumped by the textual force that not only generates the Duke and his discourse but also ensures that the Duke does not – cannot – know of that force: cannot, in a sense, know that he does not exist. Just as the Duke likely ventriloquizes his guest's question about the portrait, commandeering the envoy's subjectivity, so the text's source performs the same action on the Duke it creates and to whom it gives voice. This reversal creates an irony with devastating implications for the independent and imperious figure we had taken the Duke to be.

Thus, the "auctorial" claim made earlier is from another perspective a textual or rhetorical claim since we have moved from a referential perspective to a rhetorical one – in Barbara Johnson's terms, from seeing the text as the product of a subject's desire to seeing the subject as an effect of the text's desire.[10] This move is not peculiar to the dramatic monologue form, of course, for it would be equally applicable to a lyric poem addressed to an audience both unparticularized and not imagined as physically present – "A slumber did my spirit seal," for example. But the seeming autonomy as character of a speaker addressing a present audience in a shared and highly specified setting adds a certain heft and thickness that make all the more dramatic their evaporation by a change in readerly perspective. Nor can we assume that what has been said here of "My Last Duchess" applies to the dramatic monologue form generally, for – with its particular strategy of characterization and its particular thematic structure – this poem puts its dual textual status into play in a highly individual way. The same opposition of perspectives would yield very different interpretive results if applied to "Fra Lippo Lippi" or "Porphyria's Lover" or Tennyson's "Ulysses." Analyses such as these are often less concerned with shared features of genre than with what Donoghue terms the "particularity of form."

It is possible to explore any number of different but related kinds of tension or disharmony – for example, between the visual and aural dimensions of a text. In his detailed and sophisticated essay " 'Words Are Things': Romantic Ideology and the Matter of Poetic Language," William Keach attempts to "critically rethink and affirm the materiality of formal articulation in art and literature," and – more particularly – to explore Romantic "efforts to validate as well as to escape from the materiality of form in artistic representation."[11] This effort leads him to tease out in an especially detailed and acute way the tensions between eye and ear in Byron's language describing the pirate Lambro:

Lambro is "a man who seldom used a word/Too much," we are told, preferring instead to move men "with the sword": the odd way in which *word* gets taken up into *sword* in this stanza and yet rhymes with it only to the eye, not to the ear, bears a diacritical relation to the *ink/think* rhyme in *Don Juan* 3, st. 88 (and to *Childe Harold* 3, st. 97, where *word* also gets taken up into *sword* but to quite different effect).[12]

It is worth noting that Keach not only registers and interprets the eye/ear tension in these lines, but also notes that such effects mean differently in different particular contexts. His example can encourage us to discover analogous tensions between still other dimensions of the text. Discussing the "words are things" passage in *Don Juan* 3 from which he takes his essay's title, Keach cites the following stanza, which meditates on human mortality and the material textual survival enabled by paper and ink (st. 89):

And when his bones are dust, his grave a blank,
His station, generation, even his nation,
Become a thing, or nothing, save to rank
In chronological commemoration,
Some dull MS oblivion long has sank,
Or Graven stone found in a barrack's station
In digging the foundation of a closet,
May turn his name up, as a rare deposit.[13]

In order to pronounce the fifth line of the stanza with metrical accuracy, "MS" must be voiced not as "manuscript" but as the constituent letters of the abbreviation: "M, S" (Byron uses this device elsewhere). This pronunciation produces a tension between letters voiced as parts of the words they constitute (as when we read poetry or prose) and letters voiced as alphabetical building blocks (as when we recite the alphabet). This is not an eye/ear distinction, but it is a comparable unrecuperable disharmony, and it, too, can be interpreted differently in different contexts. In moments such as these, one can see – among other things – the way deconstructive criticism has inflected New Formalist critical procedures and assumptions.

ii Interpretive "patience": Jonson and P. B. Shelley

The relation between referential and rhetorical readings as they affect the status of a text, its speaker and audience, or other dimensions of a verbal structure, is only one opportunity for the kind of close reading that marks New Formalist analysis. Another dimension of New Formalist practice revises and extends the New Critical concern with ambiguity, and New Critical belief in the privileged (some would say "sacrosanct") status of the text. It does so, however, while rejecting the notion of a literary or poetic language that is intrinsically meaningful or ambiguous or both ("the language of poetry is the language of paradox")[14] and by treating each textual element *as though* it might prove meaningful and/or multivalent. The aim here is not to enshrine or fetishize the poem, or textuality generally, but to avoid the foreclosing of interpretation entailed by the assumption that a given element is non-meaningful. Such an aim has at times been associated with deconstructive as opposed to "humanist" modes of interpretation – for example, by Barbara Johnson in 1985: "Deconstruction is a reading strategy that carefully follows both the meanings and the suspensions and displacements of meaning in a text, while humanism is a strategy to stop reading when the text stops saying what it ought to have said."[15] But at the present moment, when deconstructive and other modes of formalist criticism have significantly interpenetrated, Johnson's acerbic and polemical distinction can be generalized into a more comprehensive critical guideline. Whatever the particular approach, alertness to the openendedness of a text's significative possibility amounts to a kind of interpretive patience – a patience that must, of course, wear thin at some point, but which interpretive curiosity, formal exploration, and a respect for the immeasurable variety of textual meaning work to sustain as long as possible.

Two brief and problematic examples will suffice, the first focusing on a lyric moment that has commonly been taken to contain an authorial error, and the second on a hybrid sonnet that has been understood in very different ways: either as the announcement of a "revolutionary explosion," or as "a political poem whose chief interest seems to be that of self-arousal."[16] Here is Ben Jonson's "Song," "To Celia":

> Drinke to me, onely, with thine eyes,
> And I will pledge with mine;
> Or leave a kisse but in the cup,
> And Ile not look for wine.

> The thirst, that from the soule doth rise,
> Doth aske a drinke divine:
> But might I of *Jove's Nectar* sup,
> I would not change for thine.
> I sent thee, late, a rosie wreath,
> Not so much honoring thee,
> As giving it a hope, that there
> It could not withered bee.
> But thou thereon did'st only breath,
> And sent'st it backe to mee:
> Since when it growes, and smells, I sweare,
> Not of it selfe, but thee.[17]

Empson observes that lines seven and eight – "But might I of *Jove's Nectar* sup,/I would not change for thine" – "say the opposite of what is meant... [O]ne has already decided from the rest of the verse that a simple lyrism is intended; there are no other two-faced implications of any plausibility, and the word *but*, after all, admits of only one form for the antithesis."[18] So Jonson meant to say that he would *not* exchange his lover's cup even for one containing Jove's nectar, but he mistakenly says just the opposite: If I could have Jove's nectar, I wouldn't exchange it for yours. There seem to be two critical possibilities, neither particularly satisfying: (1) we presume an authorial slip and tacitly correct the line to make it harmonize with the rest of the poem; or (2) we insist on the integrity of the text as given and confront a contradiction that seems interpretively unpromising in the extreme, even "unreadable."

For Empson, the "simple lyrism" of the poem discourages an elaborate search for ambiguities, but if we are willing to entertain a lyrism slightly less simple, we may get somewhat further. We notice, first, that the poem, however cavalierly, sets up a series of antitheses. Jove, the god of sky and thunder, is set in opposition to the heavenly "Celia"; additionally, "The thirst, that from the soule doth rise" (5) and the "drinke divine" it desires are opposed to the salute of eyes and kisses that itself displaces literal wine in the poem's opening conceit (1–4).[19] At first, the contrasts seem patently a strategy of invoking the first term in each antithesis in order to make of it a courtly sacrifice to the secular divinity of Celia and desire. But consider the possibility that the poem entertains, however glancingly, two different kinds of "divinity" and the desire to pay homage to each. In this view, the lines in question – "But might I of *Jove's Nectar* sup,/I would not change for thine" – articulate a singular exception to the poet's adoration of Celia rather than an ineptly phrased elevation of it, an exception that could be paraphrased thus: "Only ['But'] if I could have Jove's nectar would I refuse to exchange it for yours."[20] The tacit assumption is that in every *other* case, Celia wins.

Reading the poem in this way does not exactly solve the problem Empson notices, but it does significantly transform it. It gives us a pair of lines in which the speaker claims that he would not exchange the woman's nectar for Jove's, *and* that it is only Jove's nectar that he would prefer to hers. We move from a case of amorous lyric plus error to an ambiguity that certainly enlists Jove's nectar in hyperbolic praise of Celia but also entertains the possibility of divided and conflicting loyalties. Since these differing accounts of the relative attractions of Jove and Celia are framed by verses that venerate the woman with courtly intensity – her eyes, her kiss, her life-renewing breath (13–16) – Empson is understandably tempted to replace Jonson's phrasing with contrary words that "ought to" have been there, and perhaps to curtail his usual interpretive patience.[21] But this is not to say that the question of Jonson's "Song" is now closed in a new way, only that it may prove productive to keep it open. Like a negative determination of literary value, interpretive closure is a form of dismissal suspending just the sort of analytic exploration that might alter one's understanding of the text. True, the critic – New Formalist or not – must stop somewhere, but there is more than one way to do so. We can stop finally, freezing the text in a determinate mode of unchanging meaningfulness, or we can stop provisionally, securing a particular structure of textual meaning but tacitly retaining the option of reopening or reconsidering that structure.[22] The choice is not really between a humanistic rush to finality and a tedious because endlessly deferred deconstructive dithering. What is needed is a fictive mode of concluding, a critical procedure that remains open but necessarily acts *as if* analysis has concluded so that assertions and formulations are not reduced to mere asymptotic unreachability. From this perspective, Henry James' remarks about the literary artist are also pertinent to the critic: "Really, universally, relations stop nowhere, and the exquisite problem of the artist is eternally but to draw, by a geometry of his own, the circle within which they shall happily *appear* to do so."[23]

The other poem, the sonnet of "revolutionary explosion" or "self-arousal," is Percy Shelley's, known by the title that Mary Shelley gave it in 1839, "England in 1819":

> An old, mad, blind, despised, and dying King;
> Princes, the dregs of their dull race, who flow
> Through public scorn, – mud from a muddy spring;

Rulers who neither see nor feel nor know,
But leechlike to their fainting country cling
Till they drop, blind in blood, without a blow.
A people starved and stabbed in th'untilled field;
An army, whom liberticide and prey
Makes as a two-edged sword to all who wield;
Golden and sanguine laws which tempt and slay;
Religion Christless, Godless – a book sealed;
A senate, Time's worst statute, unrepealed–
Are graves from which a glorious Phantom may
Burst, to illumine our tempestuous day.[24]

My concern here is not principally with the poem's uncertain status as versified revolutionary tract or ineffectually angelic meditation – an uncertainty about (among other things) public and private that is replayed by Shelley's equivocal remark to Leigh Hunt when sending him the sonnet: "I do not expect you to publish it, but you may show it to whom you please."[25] Nonetheless, it is a fixation on that binary choice that I think has foreclosed more patient and probing analysis. And while there are many fascinating features of this text, from its hybrid sonnet status, to its identity as both catalogue and periodic sentence, to its management of singular, plural, and collective nouns, my focus is mainly on the final couplet, with its delayed verb ("are") and envisioned "Phantom."

Discussion has usually focused on the when and whether: *when* the revolutionary transformation will occur, or *whether* it will do so.[26] How, for example, are we to take "may" (13)? Wolfson tersely summarizes the chief possibilities: "If it means 'perhaps,' it is tentative, whether optimistically or skeptically … But if it means 'is enabled,' or even 'is empowered to,' then it is energized in the way that Curran suggests."[27] In his book-length study, James Chandler works to get us beyond this dilemma. He first reviews the positions Wolfson describes, noting that for some readers, the body of the sonnet expresses "the woes of English society," and the final couplet "a hope of their being overcome."[28] On this reading, Chandler says, the sonnet seems "to confirm those commentators who would dismiss Shelley's politics as so much wishful thinking. After all, when this sort of resolution occurs in comedy we call it 'deus ex machina' and label the work sentimental."[29] For others, however, England's "present dark moment holds out the possibility of a millenarian illumination that will mark its general rebirth."[30]

After a dialectical account of the poem's imagery, Chandler goes beyond Curran's "revolutionary explosion" to read the poem in a somewhat different way. What occasions "a resurrection" is not a spirit of revolution or liberty, some potent and liberatory historical force waiting in the wings before striding onto the stage of history. It is nothing other than "the act of reading the first twelve lines" of the poem. And the " 'glorious phantom' of the closing couplet is, from this perspective, just the meaning of the terms that come before." To understand those terms in the correct way is to grasp the poem's "apparent commitment to the notion of changing history by interpreting it."[31] This Phantom will not transform "our tempestuous day" but "illumine" it, reveal its true nature, and it is only the truth about how things are that will enable Britons to move beyond those things to better ones.[32] Whatever social or political instrumentality may be required to accomplish this end, the poem's chief investment, in its closing couplet but not only there, is that "Ye shall know the truth, and the truth shall make you free."[33]

If the glorious phantom is "just the meaning of the terms that come before," those terms nonetheless have more than one meaning.[34] The poem proceeds, in fact, according to a structure of doubled or progressive metaphor whereby a series of metaphoric identifications is replaced by a second and final identification that sweeps them all, as it were, into a single mass grave. At first, princes are actually dregs, and mud; rulers are leeches; the army is a two-edged sword; laws are personified beings of gold and blood that tempt and slay; and so on. But this diversity of corruption and devastation is reduced, in a second metaphor, to deathly uniformity: all "Are graves." So it is only the first part of readerly recognition to replace conventional notions of king, army, laws, and the rest with the underlying realities of dregs, leeches, swords, and sealed books. This initial disclosure is like the revelatory moment in earlier political satire, as when Pope – boasting of the courage to "strip the gilding off a knave" – announces that he will "Dash the proud gamester in his gilded car," and "Bare the mean heart that lurks beneath a star."[35]

In Shelley's poem, however, the satiric re-description of the vilified objects then gives way to a second revelatory metaphor which subsumes those re-described objects into a universe of death that is also the precondition for rebirth. At that prophetic moment, we will not see rulers or an army or religion, but neither will we see leeches or a two-edged sword or "a book sealed." We will see graves, and only when we see them will we be able to feel the need for new life, let alone imagine the as yet unshaped forms of that life. The sonnet thus constructs a two-stage scene of instruction in which the conventional is first replaced by the scathingly satiric, then the scathingly satiric by a visionary perception of spiritual death. Yet "scene" is a static and thus inaccurate term. The poem's forward-pressing grammar actually creates a dynamic trajectory whose penultimate stage is the poet's awareness that these "are graves." Its true conclusion can only be supplied by the poem's readers, who "may" come to share this knowledge the poet has made available, but who also may not. If the accreted nouns of the first twelve lines require the postponed verb ("are") to supply their context and identity, the sonnet as a whole requires the answering understanding of readers to liberate its truth. But just as the next (compound) verb vibrates with the uncertainty of possibility ("may/Burst"), and the final verb resides in the perpetual deferral marking the infinitive form ("to illumine"), so readerly understanding is inescapably shadowed with uncertainty and futurity. As Keach says, a "liberatory but indeterminate future possibility" is "stretched across the line-ending of the couplet."[36]

This textual and rhetorical situation is neither the announcement of a "revolutionary explosion" nor a political assertion aimed at self-arousal. It is, instead, a hybrid of prophecy and plea, or heralding and hope, and it creates space for a readerly response that can be envisioned but neither reliably compelled nor certainly predicted. Most optimistically, the poem resonates with the closing lines of Shelley's *Defence of Poetry*:

> Poets are the hierophants of an unapprehended inspiration, the mirrors of the gigantic shadows which futurity casts upon the present, the words which express what they understand not, the trumpets which sing to battle and feel not what they inspire: *the influence which is moved not, but moves. Poets are the unacknowledged legislators of the World.*[37]

But it also recalls the plangent open-endedness of the "Ode to the West Wind," with its concluding combination of imperative and beseeching, and its unanswered question:

> Be through my lips to unawakened Earth
> The trumpet of a prophecy! O Wind,
> If Winter comes, can Spring be far behind?

That poem's central plea "hear, O hear!" reiterated three times as "O hear!" seems to conjure the West Wind, as "England in 1819" conjures its audience, not only to hear but also to be "here" rather than elsewhere. In doing so, Shelley's sonnet shows us the Romantic poet poised between the magical verbal efficacy of legendary seers and shamans and the mere speech of demystified modernity in which "poetry makes nothing happen: it survives/In the valley of its saying."[38] It is as though the Romantic bard's assertion, "I can call spirits from the vasty deep," were met by the skeptical reply, "Why, so can I, or so can any man,/But will they come when you do call for them?"[39] In its formal performance of this poetic and political liminality, Shelley's sonnet emerges as a somewhat more complex and somewhat more moving speech act than it has sometimes been taken to be.

iii Form and "politics": heroic couplets in Pope's *The Rape of the Lock*

Before considering the role of New Formalist analysis in non-literary disciplines, I want to look at two different instances of what could be called "political" criticism – the first, an exploration of some historical and political implications of the heroic couplet in Alexander Pope, and the second, a brief discussion of race and gender in a short poem by Phillis Wheatley. One of the problems that have dogged political and ideological interpretations of a poem's formal features is what might be called the Fallacy of Formal Generalization: the mistaken assumption that the meanings, or associations, or symbolic valences of a given formal feature are intrinsic to it and thus inseparable from it in any given appearance. If the *terza rima* rhyme scheme – aba bcb cdc, etc. – allegorizes a fascist lockstep, or a sober forward progress retaining elements of the past, or a repeated promotion from contained to container, or the movement of Ptolemaic epicycles, then it does so in every instance, regardless of the particularities of one or another text. If slant rhyme and enjambment subvert or ignore conventions and boundaries, then they do so in much the same way each time they are employed. Despite the fact that formal patterns can acquire thematic meaning or symbolic force only in a particular instance or in the history of particular instances, the desire to claim intrinsic and general status for the import of form often seems nearly irresistible. We may say of form what George Levine says of the aesthetic: it "has no particular political commitments. It leaves itself open to endless and indeterminate interpretations."[40] Or, in another formulation, "the aesthetic leads neither to the left nor to the right. It is politically unaffiliated, and can be put to use for any politics."[41]

Such easy formal generalization often accompanies a comparably easy historicism, usually Marxist at base, that finds entire eras – almost always, the repression or conservatism or hegemonic quietism of those eras – emblematized by one formal feature or another.[42] In the case of the seventeenth- and eighteenth-century English heroic couplet, the story told is usually one in which formal regularity and boundedness express sociopolitical and ideological investments in the rigid and contained. Here is Antony Easthope:

> The couplet form is ideologically significant, its rhyming uniformity having strong connotations of order, as has often been noted. In 1694 Dryden writes that rhyme "bounds" what would otherwise be "wild and lawless" ... and it is in this spirit that Christopher Caudwell (for example) says that after the blank verse of the Civil War period, poetry between 1650 and 1688 "indicates its readiness to compromise by moving within the bounds of the heroic couplet."[43]

And here, much more recently and announcing a "more subtle attention to form," is Terry Eagleton: "the elegance and economy" of the couplet, he writes, "with its trim balances, inversions and antitheses, its sense of words locking with preordained precision into their allotted places, reflects a certain notion of order, reason, harmony and cosmic necessity. It would not be difficult to relate this notion in turn to the traditional world-view of the English landowning and patrician class of which Pope is so eloquent a spokesman" – if not exactly a member. "What we get" in these couplets, concludes Eagleton, "is nothing less than a whole social ideology."[44] The words in heroic couplets know their place, these poems say, and so should you.

Such glib allegorizing of form as social ideology requires a corresponding simplification of the formal patterns themselves.[45] Without a crude understanding of the couplet as a simple and unproblematically binary structure – two rhyme words, balanced and antithetical elements (couplets, lines, half-lines, chiasmus, zeugma) – a more accurate and nuanced vision of the politics of form in any given poem would be much more difficult to evade. J. Paul Hunter works to resist and complicate simplifications like these, in part by arguing that binarism is more complex than it has been taken to be, and that even when it is relatively simple or diagrammatic, it functions as a formal means to explore greater complexity. Simple binarism, he says, is precisely what much eighteenth-century discourse...opposes, corrects, or modifies. Proving that the world is not "binary," despite appearances and prevalent linguistic habit, is what much couplet poetry (and much eighteenth-century philosophical and political discourse) is about, as recent discussions of the private-public dichotomy dramatically suggest.... [I]t is to correct this simplistic popular thinking that discourses such as the couplet and the dialogue came to define their ways of working.[46]

This intriguing argument acknowledges the evident binarism of the couplet but views it as something like the rectilinear scaffolding from which workers construct a variously shaped and textured edifice. Hunter's main focus is on Pope, who "blurs and reconfigures binaries and develops a rhetoric of complex redefinition... [that] challenges the transparency of the apparent rhetoric and blurs and bleeds images of plain opposites into one another."[47] He argues that the complex binarism of *The Rape of the Lock*

> sorts out...what it means to play male or female roles, to be witty or witless, to be powerful or powerless, to negotiate between punishment and reward, to know the difference between metaphor and action. Nearly everything is set up in terms of polar oppositions: past and present, permanence and triviality, private and public, value and appearance, material and spiritual, temporality and eternity, grounded reality and heavenly hopes. It is a world of contrasts and clear distinctions, one by one, but cumulatively, the sorting is complex and over-lapping.[48]

To this list of binaries one could add: the tension between the high and the low of the mock-heroic itself; the rhetorical parallelisms and antitheses of lines and half-lines, and of figures such as zeugma and chiasmus; the symmetry of Belinda's "two Locks, which graceful hung behind/In equal curls" before the Baron's attack; even the central opposition between the manifest world of courtly politeness and sublimation and the social unconscious represented by the anarchic Cave of Spleen – the latter a realm where gender boundaries readily dissolve and where the desire for hermetic inviolateness and the desire for penetration are expressed by a single cry: "Men prove with child, as pow'rful fancy works,/And maids turn'd bottles, call aloud for corks."[49]

From a New Formalist perspective, the mock-heroic is a more complex binary structure than it once was taken to be, deploying both categorical oppositions and the simultaneous violation of those oppositions in works like *The Rape of the Lock*, "Mac Flecknoe," *The Dunciad*, and *Peri Bathous*. There is "an ominous mystery," as Empson put it, "in the way the lowest and most absurd things make an exact parallel with the highest."[50] The mock-heroic is not just a mode in which the everyday is mocked by the elevated (or the reverse) but also a mode in which the everyday operates as a sort of stand-in for the elevated – much as "mock-turtle soup" signifies not mockery of real turtle soup but an act of substitution or surrogacy. Like the word "faux" in such formulae as "faux leather" or "faux pearls," "mock-" designates substitutability rather than mere inferiority, as the 1960s advertising motto of the synthetic fur fiber Dynel™ makes clear: "It's not fake anything. It's real Dynel." High and low, genuine and fake are thus problematized rather than simply separated and clarified by the binary structure of the mock-heroic.

Much the same can be said of the opposition between courtly society and the Cave of Spleen in Pope's poem. For it is the contents of the "wond'rous Bag" which the goddess Spleen prepares for Umbriel that drive Belinda to burn "with more than mortal ire" and initiate the chaotic fracas of the poem's final canto.[51] Here, too, a boundary has been transgressed rather than simply indicated or affirmed; the materials of the social unconscious have spilled into the world of social performance. It is significant that Umbriel is the agent of this transgression, for he is himself an amphibious or boundary-transgressing figure. For one thing, his name links him to the shadowy world of the Cave of Spleen, though he mainly inhabits the courtly sphere. For another, as a gnome – the transmogrified soul of a (female) prude who is nonetheless referred to consistently as a male – Umbriel embodies the gender crossing that we find in the Cave of Spleen and elsewhere. Beyond this, Umbriel's name also links him to the game of Ombre, which is in French "shade" or "shadow," but in Spanish (*hombre*) "man." This can remind us that Belinda's real crime in the poem, for which the Baron punishes her by snipping her hair, is to be a woman who beats him at the game of man, as the conventional rhetoric of male ambition and conquest emphasizes in these and other lines:

> Belinda now, whom *thirst of fame* invites,
> *Burns* to encounter two advent'rous Knights,
> At Ombre *singly to decide their doom*;
> And *swells her breast with conquests* yet to come.[52]

Nor does she soften her victory by means of the traditional feminine ploys of minimizing its significance, or ascribing it to chance rather than merit or achievement, or apologizing for it:

> An Ace of Hearts steps forth: The King unseen
> Lurk'd in her hand, and mourn'd his captive Queen:
> He springs to Vengeance with an eager pace,
> And falls like thunder on the prostrate Ace.
> *The nymph exulting fills with shouts the sky;*
> *The walls, the woods, and long canals reply.*[53]

It is to rectify this unseemly transgression of gender boundaries and to reassert a conventional and unproblematic binarism of male and female that the Baron performs the act that gives the poem its name.

Like the treatment of genre in much of the work of the Scriblerians, then, the representation of gender in *The Rape of the Lock* entails both the establishment and the erosion of the conventional dyad, at the level of the couplet as well as in the narrative and symbolic structures at which we have glanced. Consider these lines from the poem's introductory verses:

> Say what strange motive, Goddess! could compel
> A well-bred Lord t' assault a gentle Belle?
> O say what stranger cause, yet unexplor'd,
> Could make a gentle Belle reject a Lord?
> In tasks so bold, can little men engage,
> And in soft bosoms dwells such mighty Rage?[54]

Hunter says that in this passage, "the 'gentle' and 'bold' sexes are ... polarized, teasingly reversed, then complicated," and that is undeniably the case.[55] But the details of the final couplet, especially, present a more exact and nuanced image of the poem's gender politics than Hunter's "complicated" suggests.[56]

> In tasks so bold, can little men engage,
> And in soft bosoms dwells such mighty Rage?

This couplet seems initially structured by an antithesis equitably assigning one line to each gender, but that tidiness breaks down when we look at its grammar and figurative language. If the men are "little," they are at least entire males rather than synecdochic substitutions; the women are represented merely by their "soft bosoms." The effect is not one of crisp antithesis but of figurative asymmetry – whole male ver- sus female part. Then there is the similarly asymmetrical antithesis of the main verbs: the activity of "engage" as against the static inhabiting of "dwells." But the ostensibly antithetical structure of the couplet is most powerfully undone when we turn to the grammatical subject of each line. The subject of the first is of course "little men," and we might expect this phrase to be countered by the synecdochic "soft bosoms." But the asymmetry is even more striking than that gender-biased oppo- sition would suggest, since the grammatical subject of the second line is "mighty Rage." In contrast to "little men," it turns out, "Soft bosoms" don't do anything at all; they are simply the place where mighty Rage "dwells."

Somewhat like the asymmetry of linguistically unmarked and marked terms in the pair "poet/poetess," Pope's couplet gestures toward a tra- ditional structure of equivalence and antithesis but undoes it with a grammatical and figurative strategy that puts male and female in a relationship of grotesquely one-sided heterogeneity. The details of that heterogeneity, and of the poem's complex representation of gender pol- itics and power relations, are not arrived at by easy analogies between poetic forms and social ideology or by a priori notions of how the couplet must signify. As with the very different couplets in Browning's "My Last Duchess," or indeed with any element of form, only close, patient exploration of the particular features, functions, and meanings of a given formal pattern in a particular text can disclose its workings and its range of significative nuance. And this is as true of textual anal- ysis in the service of political or gender or other kinds of ideological criticism as it is of any other sort of critical practice.

iv Form and "politics": heroic couplets in *The Dunciad*

It is true even when we move from one poem in a given form to another in that form, both by the same author. Eagleton attempts to adapt his reading of the heroic couplet as the ally of "order, reason, har- mony and cosmic necessity" to the anarchic energies of *The Dunciad* by claiming that the verse-form of that poem operates as a "riposte" to its "carnival of unreason." The ideology he finds in the verse-form is unchanged by context; the "conservatism" of the couplet is preserved whether it is enlisted to support an ideology of patrician conservatism or to counter a cultural disruption of apocalyptic scope. But in fact the couplet rhetoric of *The Dunciad* is very different from that of *The Rape of the Lock*, and it is more complexly related to the poem's "carnival of unreason" than Eagleton begins to suggest. *The Dunciad*'s rhetoric at once establishes and erodes the distinctions on which Pope's verse usually depends because the poem suggests – remarkably – that the creation of meaning derives as much from the power to undo distinctions as from the power to establish them.[57]

Dulness is the force of the single, the uniform, the undifferentiated: pure energy of identification. As such, however, she is an unrestrained or unbound (therefore personified) form of precisely that combinatory energy which in bound form is the predominant element of Locke's "wit," the tacit component of Locke's "judgment," and an indispensable constituent of any figure of speech or unit of meaning that is even minimally combinatory, minimally structured. To claim so much may seem to venture dangerously near the abyss of Dulness itself, for it is to assert not just that "there is an ominous mystery," as Empson says, "in the way the lowest and most absurd things make an exact parallel with the highest," but also that there is a greater mystery still in the *dependence* of the highest things on the lowest. Yet the force that Dulness represents can undergo a crucial transformation from a free, unbound form into the bondedness of relationship. By means of that binding, Dulness is not simply restrained, as "rebellious Logic" is "gagg'd and bound" at the opening of Book 4. Rather, she becomes a positive and indispensable part of a structure of signification inconceivable without her, much as chlorine, in bonding to sodium, sheds its toxicity to become a necessary and benign component of common salt, not simply a captive, quiescent ingredient.[58]

The Dunciad, then, aims not at annihilating but at binding Dulness, and Pope's object of satire is not Dulness herself but that failure to resist, bind, transfigure, and draw strength from her which is caught in the monstrous mindlessness of Cibber. That there is almost no Cibber to focus on, that his passivity renders him a transparent nonentity through whom we view Dulness unbound because of just such passivity, is what the poem is largely about. Pope, in other words, wishes that Cibber existed, not that Dulness did not. One modern critic has said that Pope's "way with Chaos…is to keep his distance," but such a view is precisely half true.[59] Just as rhetoric is a system neither of combinatory force alone nor of divisive force alone (it could not be such and be a "system") but one in which sameness and difference together generate meaning, so the poet, for Pope, is not a hero of univocal stamp who slays the dragon of chaos once and finally – "For, born a Goddess, Dulness never dies" (1.18). The poet is rather a more complex and dialectical figure who binds and turns to significance powers that would, if they were simply released or simply annihilated, destroy the structure of meaning – and the very possibility of meaning – that he continually works to create. In consequence, the poem's securely mock-celebratory narrator and its securely distinguishing rhetorical structures are like secondary inscriptions on a palimpsest whose primary inscriptions are a sincere celebrant of Dulness and an unrestrained combinatory energy. Not only are those primary inscriptions still visible, they are necessary to a structure of meaning that the secondary layer completes by establishing the very possibility of structure. Dulness is in this sense the poet's, and the poem's, secret sharer: isolated and unbound, an outlaw; internalized, and bound, a constituent of meaningfulness itself.

Heroic couplets gesturing toward – at times enacting – such a conception of meaning operate very differently than the couplets in a poem like *The Rape of the Lock*, despite their metrical and other similarities. The semiotics, valence, and politics of a form are neither intrinsic nor invariable. Two examples will have to suffice. Dulness' first action in *The Dunciad* is, appropriately enough, the contemplation of her own chaos:

> Here she beholds the Chaos dark and deep,
> Where nameless Somethings in their causes sleep,
> 'Till genial Jacob, or a warm Third day,
> Call forth each mass, a Poem, or a Play:
> How hints, like spawn, scarce quick in embryo lie,
> How new-born nonsense first is taught to cry,
> Maggots half-form'd in rhyme exactly meet,
> And learn to crawl upon poetic feet.
> Here one poor word an hundred clenches makes,
> And ductile dulness new meanders takes;
> There motley Images her fancy strike,
> Figures ill pair'd, and Similies unlike.
> She sees a Mob of Metaphors advance,
> Pleas'd with the madness of the mazy dance:
> How Tragedy and Comedy embrace;
> How Farce and Epic get a jumbled race;
> How Time himself stands still at her command,
> Realms shift their place, and Ocean turns to land.
> Here gay Description Egypt glads with show'rs,

> Or gives to Zembla fruits, to Barca flow'rs;
> Glitt'ring with ice here hoary hills are seen,
> There painted vallies of eternal green,
> In cold December fragrant chaplets blow,
> And heavy harvests nod beneath the snow. (1.55–78)

We notice the pervasively physical language leveling thoughts, persons, and things; the emphasis on the unformed and half-formed; the chaotic vitality, the outline-obscuring profusions of alliteration and assonance. The passage also unites what are opposites from a traditional point of view, though not from Dulness': tragedy and comedy, farce and epic, Zembla and fruits, one moment and another, and so on ("Time... stands still" for Dulness since temporality requires difference). There is a different kind of joining in the syntactic ambiguity of certain lines. It is not clear whether Dulness herself or the mob of metaphors is "Pleas'd with the madness of the mazy dance," but since the chaos of which the metaphors are part *is* Dulness, it should not be clear. None of Dulness' creations ever really breaks free from her maternal adherence, as none ever really wishes to; thus Pope's ambiguity of reference is a major trope – both figure of speech and epistemological schema – of the duncely world.

Moreover, though it may not be clear at first glance, the couplet rhetoric in this passage accomplishes just such a joining or merging on a larger scale. Its structuring partly mimics the failure of antithesis, for – in sharp contrast to most of Pope's other poems – it depends on an oblique or slack coordination of verb and direct objects at two key points. Dulness first beholds (1) "the Chaos" and (2) "How hints... in embryo lie," and she later sees (1) "a Mob of Metaphors" and (2) "How Tragedy and Comedy embrace." In each pairing, the crispness of parallel direct objects is eroded by the alignment of a strong noun with an adverbial phrase introduced by "how." (The same construction appears at 11.273–86 and elsewhere.). This syntactic slackness further weakens the opposition between chaos and the "works" that proceed from it, dissolving antithesis into parallel and, beyond that, into simple iteration or apposition, as in the two series beginning with "how." The productions called forth from chaos – "each mass, a Poem or a Play" – seem to be just other names for chaos, as though there were, finally, only one "thing" and the possibility of repeating it. Even the meanings of "here" and "there" (55, 63, 65, 73, 76) are finally unspecifiable. "Here" might refer to the chaos and "there" to what lies outside chaos, but they do not; the intrauterine is the extrauterine. Or "here" and "there" might refer to different locations in chaos, except that location has no meaning in chaos, which Milton calls

> a dark
> Illimitable ocean without bound,
> Without dimension; where length, breadth, and highth,
> And time and place are lost.
>
> (Paradise Lost 2.891–94)

"Here" and "there" have lost all but a serial or itemizing function and no longer serve as specifiers of location. "Here" and "there" are also deictics or shifters, singularly relational parts of speech: my "here" is your "there." The undoing of their directional significance is therefore an undoing of their deictic force and of the relation of self to world – the world as place but also as "position" in the metaphoric sense: "Here I stand."

It is thus an annihilation of individual identity as well, since the "individual" implied by these specters of deixis is as much here as there. In losing all stability of self, he becomes at once utterly fragmented and demonically at one with himself, incapable of being in relation – critical or otherwise – to "himself" at all. The self as chaotic nonentity and the self as tautological vacuity are extremes that meet, and at their meeting point there is no one.

For a passage that treats mainly chaos and undifferentiation, then, this one exhibits a remarkable amount of structuring, because Pope's goal is an image not of the unstructured but of the undoing of structure by undifferentiation: not of meaninglessness but of the partial subversion of meaning. Virtually all of the structural, metrical, and rhyming binarisms that we find in *The Rape of the Lock* appear here as well, but shadowed by the anti-matter of rhetorical decreation. Only because Pope establishes a secure rhetoric of antithesis – an apparently combinatory rhetoric that structures distinct items – can he subvert the passage so dramatically and, in dramatizing the dissolve of structure into undifferentiation, show us that rhetoric is also the dividing (therefore, the structuring) of an undifferentiation it cannot do without. The structuring effected by a rhetorical figure, that is, results from an energy that both joins and distinguishes (there can be no purely combinatory or purely distinguishing figure); any particular employment of a figure will to some degree suppress, but not annihilate, one or the other of these impulses. What brings about this suppression is not the figure itself but the meaning of the elements it structures. Parallelism and antithesis, for example, differ only in the semantic import of their

elements; they do not differ structurally any more than the alliteration that enforces contrast differs structurally from the alliteration that
enforces likeness. Virtually every figure holds within itself such a mirror
image or inverted twin.

When it is not clear whether two elements – two words, say – are
similar or opposed in meaning, then contradictory capacities of the
figure they are part of are brought equally into play, and we have either
nonsense or an utterance that we must understand at another level
altogether – in the case of *The Dunciad*, at the level of a dramatized
poetics that discloses the mysterious relations between meaninglessness
and meaning. This startling rhetoric of Pope's couplets can remind us of
Donoghue's assertion, cited earlier, that the "part of Aestheticism which
should now be recovered . . . is its concern for the *particularity* of form in
every work of art." If form is "the distinguishing characteristic of art," as
he says, "there is no reason to assume that it is unproblematically given,
like the counting of syllables in an iambic pentameter."[60] And as that
last phrase suggests, it is only the brute numericality of the pentameter line (or couplet) that in some sense remains constant from text to
text or author to author. New Formalist explorations of the politics of
form with respect to versification or any other formal pattern need to
move away from general and generic claims, whether poetic or political, to the details of a particular form as they are enacted in a particular
poem.

v   Form and "politics": race, religion, and syntax in Wheatley

A different sort of "political" problem is posed by Phillis Wheatley's
short poem, "On being brought from AFRICA to AMERICA":

> 'TWAS mercy brought me from my *Pagan* land,
> Taught my benighted soul to understand
> That there's a God, that there's a *Saviour* too:
> Once I redemption neither sought nor knew.
> Some view our sable race with scornful eye,
> "Their colour is a diabolic die."
> Remember, *Christians*, *Negros*, black as *Cain*,
> May be refin'd, and join th'angelic train.[61]

The problem and its history are discussed at length in Henry Louis
Gates, Jr.'s *The Trials of Phillis Wheatley*, where he notes that the reason Wheatley is "not a household word within the black community is

owing largely to" the poem just cited.[62] Wheatley "fits the Uncle Tom syndrome," says one of Gates' sources; is "oblivious to the lot of her fellow blacks," writes another; and, worse still, the self-hatred evident in her writing expresses "the nigger component of the Black Experience."[63] More temperately but no less witheringly, Addison Gayle remarks that Wheatley was the first black writer "to accept the images and symbols of degradation passed down from the South's most intellectual lights and the first to speak from a sensibility finely tuned by close approximation to [her] oppressors."[64]

Noting in summary the historical irony that Wheatley was rejected by white critics in the eighteenth century and by black critics in the twentieth, Gates seeks to redirect the conversation: "What would happen if we ceased to stereotype Wheatley but, instead, read her, read her with all the resourcefulness that she herself brought to her craft?" Our task, he continues is "to learn to read Wheatley anew, unblinkered by the anxieties of her time and ours."[65] Fair enough, and sufficient to quicken the New Formalist pulse. Yet the only alternative Gates offers is an ingenious anagrammatization of Wheatley's poem submitted by one Walter Grigo – a rearrangement that entirely overwrites Wheatley's poem with Grigo's politicized fantasies, even changing the title from "On being brought from AFRICA to AMERICA," to "Bitter, Go I, Ebon Human Cargo, From Africa."[66] Gates's little book ends on the next page, so no rereading of Wheatley is offered apart from Grigo's, and the unfortunate effect is to trivialize rather than redeem the poem and its author.

The "problem" posed by Wheatley's poem is real enough, and turning elsewhere in her writings complicates it somewhat but does not dispel it. In "To the University of CAMBRIDGE, in NEW-ENGLAND," probably written a year before "On being brought from AFRICA to AMERICA," she seems to anticipate some of the sentiments of the later work:

> 'Twas not long since I left my native shore
> The land of errors, and *Egyptian* gloom:
> Father of mercy, 'Twas thy gracious hand
> Brought me in safety from those dark abodes.[67]

A slightly more complex sentiment appears in "To the Right Honourable WILLIAM, Earl of DARTMOUTH, His Majesty's Principal Secretary of State for North-America, &c." Here, Wheatley explains her "love of *Freedom*" this way: "I, young in life, by seeming cruel fate/Was snatch'd from *Afric's* fancy'd happy seat." True, she acknowledges that "tyrannic sway" "seiz'd" her from her father, who suffered "pangs excruciating" as a result. But at the same time, her fate was only *"seeming* cruel," and Africa is only *"fancy'd"* a "happy seat."[68] It was cruel to snatch her from Africa, but it is also good to be free from "the land of errors" which, though "fancy'd happy," consists of "dark abodes." (A similar ambivalence marks her celebration, in the poem to the Earl of Dartmouth, of the newly appointed overseer of the North American colonies and President of the Board of Trade and Foreign Plantations. Unlike the "wanton *Tyranny"* of crueler governors, the "reins" that the Earl holds in his hands are "silken" – though they are no less reins for that.)

"On being brought from AFRICA to AMERICA" shifts somewhat abruptly at its midpoint from a focus on religion (pagan versus Christian) to a focus on race, the poet ventriloquizing the voice of white racism in the latter half of the poem only to answer it with a reminder that "Negros, black as *Cain"* can find redemption as well as white persons. The apparent suggestion is that such Christian redemption is a kind of transcendence of race as well: "Remember, *Christians, Negros,* black as *Cain,*/May be refin'd, and join th'angelic train." Christianity's metaphoric promise of washing its adherents' robes, thus making them "white in the blood of the lamb," is in some sense literalized by Wheatley, who promises both spiritual and racial whiteness.[69] But this ambiguity about a whiteness literal or metaphoric, racial or spiritual, opens onto some further possibilities. For one thing, it allows us to think of blackness or darkness as in some sense not intrinsic but superadded to a prior humanity. "Sable," after all, is a color term borrowed from a furry mammal rather than a foundational human feature, much as "benighted" implies an imposed condition, an ignorance that is applied to or that has overtaken those originally not thus darkened. Something similar could be said of the "diabolic die" in line 6, since a dye is an added color or tint that is not the object's original, an added color whose secondariness or redundancy is caught in the sonic supererogation of "di[-abolic] . . . die." Such details at least begin to drive a wedge between the personhood that Wheatley depicts and the modes of blackness that in her view seem to beset it.

The syntax of her final couplet seems to hesitate in an analogous manner, depending on where we punctuate it (or how we voice it). If we place the main caesura after the second word, we get: "Remember, *Christians – Negros,* black as *Cain,*/May be refin'd, and join th'angelic train." But if we move that principal caesura one word earlier, the couplet becomes: "Remember – *Christians, Negros,* black as *Cain,*/May be refin'd, and join th'angelic train." In the second version, Christians as well as "Negros" may receive refinement, and are presumably equally in need of it. The blackness referred to here becomes the darkness of sin or ignorance rather than of skin color as racial difference is finally trumped by the gulf separating the saved from the condemned.[70] Reading the poem in this way will not instate Wheatley as "a household word within the black community," as Gates puts it, nor instantly redeem what he terms "the most reviled poem in African-American literature."[71] But it may allow us to remain open to a certain political, racial, and religious complexity – indeed, a certain *poetic* complexity – in a text that has been more frequently dismissed impatiently, or at best apologized for, than read carefully.

If the text emerges from this analysis as a kind of verbal double-exposure, that may be less a problem than a plausible formal mode for a gifted young female poet at once admired and distrusted, both prodigy and kidnapped slave, and a woman, in her editor's words, interested in "the reality of strength underlying apparent weakness, and in confidence beneath professed diffidence."[72] Even biographically considered, that is, the tensions and doublenesses of the poem seem entirely understandable. Beyond that, our discussion of Wheatley's poem can illustrate the role of formalist analysis in modes of criticism deemed "political" or "ideological." There is no reason to think that formalism is a practice limited to texts treated purely as aesthetic objects, any more than it is limited to texts understood on a New Critical model of tensional unity, or harmonious discord, or "resolved stresses." The close analysis of language enables a richer and more precise grasp of textual meaning, and that goal should not be limited to particular subdisciplines of literary criticism, or to any other discipline that relies on textual analysis.

vi   Formalist analysis of non-literary texts: periodical essays, political rhetoric, semiotics of medicine/the body

Paying closer attention to the historical, cultural, social, and political significance of various literary forms and conventions has been one principal effort of New Formalist criticism. To quote Stephen Cohen again:

> Unlike the historicity of texts, the historicity of form emphasizes the particularity of literary discourse, insisting not only that literary texts have historical roots and functions, but that they do so by virtue of their discourse-specific forms and conventions as well as their extratextual or interdiscursive ideological content. For the literary scholar, this understanding invites the historicization not only of

generic and prosodic forms but of many of the other concepts and practices associated with traditional formalism.[73]

This is a note sounded with some regularity in New Formalisms. Richard Strier, for example, echoing Cleanth Brooks, asserts that the "results of a formal analysis...may themselves be *data* for historical understanding."[74] The suggestion is that formalist attention of various kinds may not only deliver textual analyses to non-literary disciplines and practices but play a significant part in the work of those disciplines themselves.

As John McIntyre and Miranda Hickman put it, in their epilogue to *Rereading the New Criticism*, "In recent years, methods of close reading in particular have been increasingly invoked as they bear not only upon the category of 'literature' but also on a much wider range of verbal text in various media, as well as on the semiotics of cultural texts more broadly."[75] And while some scholars have lamented the migration of close reading and other literary critical practices to fields like history, philosophy, and anthropology as an undermining of the methods, insights, and truth claims of those fields (and perhaps of the hegemony of literary studies as well), such views are countered by others – perhaps surprisingly, by Fredric Jameson himself:

> Textuality may be rapidly described as a methodological hypothesis whereby the objects of study of the human sciences are considered to constitute so many texts that we *decipher* and *interpret*, as distinguished from older views of these objects as realities or existents or substances that we in one way or another attempt to *know*.[76]

Jameson describes a shift whereby documents and other objects of study, once considered knowable in their empirical givenness, come to be considered as texts requiring interpretation to disclose their meaning and significance. Such interpretation or deciphering need not be literary critical, or even verbal; "textual" in Jameson's account seems to mean simply "in need of interpretation" rather than "made of language or images or other media."

But for our present purposes, we can stop well short of the global hermeneutics implied by Jameson's conception of postmodern disciplinarity to look at some texts from non-literary fields and to ask whether reading them with a New Formalist investment can yield results pertinent not only to criticism, formalist or otherwise, but to the interests and aims of the fields themselves, and to students of texts in those fields. Of course, opportunities to mediate historical and theoretical issues through the linguistic must rigorously respect the latter. How, as Garrett Stewart laments, "can [interpretive] opportunities be responsibly cultivated when novels or poems... are increasingly taken as mere cultural symptoms, the way one takes a temperature, without being noticed first as verbal objects?"[77] And Ellen Rooney offers a sharp assessment of the damage inattention to form can inflict well beyond the discipline of literary criticism: "The extinction of an entire range of modes of formal analysis has eroded our ability to read *every genre of text* – literary texts, nonliterary texts, aural and visual texts, and the social text itself."[78] Nonetheless, it is within the power of New Formalist critical procedures to address texts beyond the literary without scanting the linguistic and formal specificity of those texts – to effect what Jane Gallop terms "a generalizing of literary reading so that, rather than a way to read a particular kind of text, it becomes a particular way to read all texts."[79]

Recently, for example, Anthony Pollock has turned a formalist perspective (and interpretive rationale) on English eighteenth-century periodicals – a set of texts as much social, cultural, and political as literary, though traditionally studied in literature classes. In "Formalist Cultural Criticism and the Post-Restoration Periodical," he attempts to show "how and why we should read the early periodical from a rhetorical-formalist perspective, one that is attentive both to the performative dimension of these texts that gives them their *effet de réel*, and to the ideological import of these papers' tendency to allegorize their own operations."[80] Arguing against the notion of transparency and simple historical reference in these publications, Pollock teases out their "rhetoric of authenticity," their "rhetoric of referentiality," and makes these part of a more sophisticated and textually alert New Formalist cultural studies. "This is not to say that the essays bear no relationship to the 'real' historical world of early eighteenth-century England," he explains, "but that the essays' relationship to the real is mediated through the performative force – linguistic, discursive and representational – by which the papers aim to transform the world in which they circulate."[81] The result is a fresh understanding of these periodicals and their rhetorical-cultural strategies, and a subtle and sophisticated critique of the Habermasian notion of a public sphere fostered partly by such writings.

It is possible to direct such rhetorical analysis to texts and utterances still further removed from the sphere of the literary, and closer to the contemporary world.

We can begin outside of literature and indeed outside of formal or academic disciplines by considering how New Formalist analysis might help
to illuminate the political rhetoric with which we are deluged every day.
The term "rhetoric," of course, is popularly used in a variety of ways. At
times, it means the deceptiveness and empty language of those we don't
like or trust, as in "That's just rhetoric." Here, the term is shorthand for
vacuous promises, hyperbolic attacks, gaseous inflation – in short, language used to deceive, with little concern for honesty or truth. At other
times, "rhetoric" – still a negative term – seems to mean any concerted
or discoverable attention to style at all, the implication being that virtually any figure of speech, patterning of sound, stylistic emphasis, or
other verbal strategy betrays a deviation from the artless, unrhetorical,
straightforward prose that we should expect from speakers and writers of
upright character. In this second definition, it is less the uses to which
rhetoric may be put that are the problem than the intrinsically shady
nature of rhetoric as such.

But those who express this distrust of verbal ornament or rhetorical patterning rarely ask what would happen if we tried to avoid them
entirely: just speak the truth, go beyond style and rhetoric to a region of
pure meaning uncontaminated by linguistic artifice of any kind. Does
such a region exist, and what language would we use to describe it?
Here is Mario Cuomo, delivering the 1984 Democratic National Convention Keynote Address. In order to succeed, says the Governor, rallying
his party,

> we must answer our opponent's polished and appealing rhetoric with
> a more telling reasonableness and rationality. We must win this case
> on the merits. We must get the American public to look past the
> glitter, beyond the showmanship to the reality, the hard substance of
> things. And we'll do it not so much with speeches that sound good as
> with speeches that are good and sound; not so much with speeches
> that will bring people to their feet as with speeches that will bring
> people to their senses.[82]

Whatever else this stirring rejection of rhetoric may be, it is richly
rhetorical. It develops an opposition between Republican superficiality
and Democratic substance, in part by making massive use of the rhetorical pattern of antithesis: "rhetoric" vs. "reasonableness and rationality,"
"glitter" and "showmanship" vs. "reality" and "the hard substance of
things," "speeches that sound good" vs. "speeches that are good and
sound," and so on. There is also the artful placement of the short

second sentence, with its mostly monosyllabic words, to emphasize no-nonsense directness, and to evoke the idealized impartiality of the legal system. And there is the way the repetition of "we must" at the beginning of clauses and sentences (the figure called anaphora) contributes to the cumulative weight of Democratic imperatives. The final sentence of this excerpt, moreover, doesn't just develop a stirring antithesis. It also catches the Democratic reversal of the Republican program in the figure called chiasmus, in which elements are arranged symmetrically, ABBA, like a rhetorical butterfly, or like a progression that undoes itself. This is the pattern that "sound^A good^B ... good^B and sound^A" falls into. "Sound" and "good," of course, have different meanings and are different parts of speech when they are repeated here, and this repetition-with-a-difference is another rhetorical figure, called ploce. Something similar happens with the two different senses – one literal, one figurative – of the repeated "bring" in the final words of the excerpt: "bring people to their feet ... bring people to their senses." These devices contrast the opponents' flashy rhetoric with the home team's reasonableness and realism.

What are we to conclude from the fact that Cuomo's rejection of rhetoric is expressed in language that is intensely rhetorical? Not, I think, that the passage is dishonest. For one thing, it doesn't attempt to conceal its rhetorical effects; they are right there on the surface. For another, no matter what stylistic choices the Governor or his speechwriters might have made, contradictions like those we have noted could scarcely have been avoided in a speech condemning speechifying, though they might have been muted. Rhetoric is inescapable; it comes with the verbal territory. In consequence, even the argument that we should go "beyond rhetoric," like every other argument conducted in language, will have to display the structurings – grammatical, stylistic, rhetorical – that can't be separated from language any more than size, shape, and color can be separated from any actual barn or bumblebee or babushka. If Cuomo's speech is inconsistent, it is inescapably so. When we speak and write, then, the question is not what game we will play, but how we will play it. Rhetoric is the only game in town. Politically, we might understand this moment in the speech as one that discloses the similarities as much as the differences between Democrats and Republicans, and that requires us to look beyond the naive opposition of a rhetorical versus a non-rhetorical language to those differences of policy, values, and history that allow voters to make a significant choice between the two parties – something we cannot do so long as we think the goal is to choose the party without rhetoric over the party with rhetoric. From this perspective, passages like the excerpt we have been analyzing may be a means of educating citizens in the crucial choice between the "hard substance" of two different value systems and philosophies of governance. Close reading of a New Formalist kind can help us see where the important choices are, and where they are not.

It can also help us to grasp and absorb the conceptual content of informative writing, academic or popular, even if we are not always aware that it is doing so. Jonathan Miller's *The Body in Question*, which was written to accompany his television series of the same name, is an exploration of medicine, physiology, and in particular the semiotics of the human body: of the ways we lend meaning to the body and read significance there. It argues that the body is culturally encoded – that we don't just "know" its meanings immediately or intuitively but learn to read them within an elaborate, shared scheme of interpretation. Here is a paragraph making that point, among others:

> Although our experience of our body is so vague and muddy, our mind does everything it can to intensify the images with which it is supplied – like the computers which sharpen the pictures sent from distant planets. In the absence of any immediate knowledge of our own insides, most of us have improvised an imaginary picture in the hope of explaining the occasional feelings which escape into consciousness. Our mind, it seems, prefers a picture of some sort to having to live through the chaos of sensations that would otherwise seem absurd.[83]

This is a lucid passage, making its point with helpful concreteness, but its richly figurative language is not merely ornamental, or simply pleasurable to read. Rather, it suggests a number of things about the experiences Miller describes that the passage does not explicitly state. Our experience, the text's figurative language tells us, is not perspicuous – it is metaphorically identified with "muddy" water (presumably); our mind is personified, has a life of its own, "prefers" a picture to a chaos of sensations; but it is also compared by means of simile to a computer that works to intensify images; some of our feelings can "escape" (like a prisoner? an animal? a slip of the tongue?). And not only are the sensations that we experience chaotic and thus difficult to understand, they are also, in some figurative sense, unimaginably remote – as alien to us as are the "distant planets" whose crisp visibility depends on computer enhancement. These are nuances of Miller's argument that only close textual attention will fully register.

Miller's language of visibility – real pictures, imaginary pictures, images – is of course also metaphoric, for he is writing about intellectual understanding rather than visual sensation. As I have said, one of his principal arguments concerns the fact that we know our bodies not by direct sensory experience but by a complex mental interpretation of bodily information.[84] Why, then, all the visual imagery, the pervasive vocabulary of pictures and seeing? And why is it that the written text of *The Body in Question* shares its space with numerous illustrations of varied shape and size? On just the two pages (42–3) to which the book opens when we read the passage above, for example, four pictures occupy a significant amount of space and seem to crowd and compete with rather than merely supplement the written text. Two of the illustrations focus on camouflage (one of a snake rendered virtually invisible by its setting, one of the snake in sharp relief against the background of the white page); a third is of Houdon's bust of Voltaire; and the fourth reproduces Salvador Dali's *trompe l'oeil* painting in which a depiction of Houdon's bust unpredictably gives way to visual details of a slave market, whence the painting's title: "Slavemarket with the disappearing bust of Voltaire."[85]

We can begin by noting that several of these illustrations concern visual phenomena that are not simply "given" to perception. To find the snake in the wild, we need to read or decode the patterns and colors of its skin, which resemble those of its surroundings. To find the bust of Voltaire in Dali's painting, we need to reinterpret the heads and clothing of two pictured women as Voltaire's eyes, cheekbones, nose, mouth, chin, and jaw. These illustrations, that is, need to be read or interpreted rather than simply viewed; mere sensory input prior to the mind's interpretive activity will not allow us to "see" what is there. But the same is true of Miller's written text as well. To understand letters and words, we need to interpret shapes on the page and construe them into letters, words, and meanings – just as, at another level, we construe instances of figurative language. To find the snake, or Voltaire, we must look at the illustrations in a certain way, interpreting them into meaning. And to understand our bodies, argues Miller, we must construe the vague, muddy, and chaotic sensations we experience into some sort of "picture" or idea or concept that will provide intelligibility and meaningfulness. Thus, Miller's figurative language and numerous illustrations powerfully generalize his argument about the way we understand our body, since it is also the way we understand his written text as well as the book's numerous visual illustrations.

The effect is to illustrate – implicitly as well as explicitly – the impossibility of an unmediated grasp of reality by breaking down the conventional conceptual barrier between objects we know through intellectual interpretation (texts, mathematical formulae, chemical equations, etc.) and objects that we allegedly know through direct sensuous apprehension (the faces of other humans, works of visual art, our own bodies). As a result, the body becomes a cultural object in need of interpretation and not just a physical entity given to the senses. The process by which we come to know the physical world and our own bodies is structurally analogous to the process by which we come to know Miller's argument about the way we come to know the physical world and our bodies. His prose may make some of its claims directly, but it also performs them – and many others – by means of textual strategies like those I have tried to describe. This is to say that what we take away from that text by attending only to its overt, paraphrasable content is only part of what the text delivers by mobilizing its linguistic and semiotic elements in a way that is apprehensible by close reading of a formalist kind.

vii Formalist analysis of non-literary texts: popular history

Close reading can also illuminate linguistic features that reveal an author's methodological assumptions, or explain a book's appeal to its audience, or both. Barbara W. Tuchman's *A Distant Mirror: The Calamitous 14th Century*, was greeted with high praise and energetic sales by general readers in the late 1970s, though with considerable skepticism by academics – especially professional medievalists.[86] The premise of its title – that fourteenth-century European culture offers a mirror in which modern readers can discern the forms of their own time – is evidently winning and evidently problematic, but it is the book's details at the level of language and style that I want to focus on briefly. Two instances of two sequential paragraphs, from the book's fourth chapter and from the Epilogue that follows its 27th chapter, reveal patterns of style that construct particular notions of agency and causation, among other things, raising questions about the proper objects of historical analysis, the level at which to analyze them, and the relation of past to present. This long book also achieves a measure of graspable unity and of biographical interest by viewing a century of history through the life of a single person: "I have chosen a particular person's life as the vehicle of my narrative," says Tuchman. In addition to narrowing the field to "a manageable area," and providing "human interest," she writes that her choice imposes upon the historian "enforced obedience to reality," because she is "required to follow the circumstances and the sequence of an actual medieval life, lead where they will."[87] It is, of course, naive or disingenuous or merely fanciful to think that a biographical focus ensures veracity or freedom from bias. After all, individual lives, too, must be interpreted. Moreover, such a focus gives extraordinary prominence not just to "a particular person's life" but also to the "particular person" as the most salient unit of history (a Marxist would say that it fetishizes the individual) – a choice with powerful methodological consequences that are connected to the stylistic features I want to explore.

Here are the two two-paragraph sequences (the numbering is mine):

1

The defeat of French chivalry and of the supposedly most powerful sovereign in Europe started a train of reactions that were to grow more serious with time. Although it did not bring down the French monarchy nor bring it to terms, it did cause a crisis of confidence in the royal government, and a general resentment when the king once more had to resort to extraordinary taxation. From this date, too, began an erosion of belief in the nobles' performance of their function.

Philip had neither the instinct for rule possessed by Philip the Fair and St. Louis, nor councillors capable of reforming the military and financial customs to meet the new dangers that had come upon them. The provincial estates whose consent was required for new taxes were reluctant, like most representative bodies, to recognize crisis until it was underfoot. Given an inadequate and obsolete system, the King had to devise substitutes like the sales tax – called *maltôte* because it was so hated – or the equally unpopular salt tax; or else he fell back on devaluing the coinage. In disruption of prices, rents, debts, and credit, the effect of this subterfuge for taxation was regularly disastrous. "And in the year 1343 Philip of Valois made 15 deniers worth three," wrote one chronicler in sufficient comment.[88]

2

In the next fifty years, the forces set in motion during the 14th century played themselves out, some of them in exaggerated form like human failings in old age. After a heavy recurrence in the last year of the old century, the Black Death disappeared, but war and brigandage were renewed, the cult of death grew more extreme, the struggle to end the schism and reform the abuses of the Church more desperate. Depopulation reached its lowest point in a society already weakened both physically and morally.

In France, Jean de Nevers, who had succeeded his father as Duke of Burgundy in 1404, turned assassin, precipitating a train of evils. In 1407 he employed a gang of toughs to murder his rival Louis d'Orléans in the streets of Paris. As Louis was returning to his hotel after dark, he was set upon by hired killers who cut off his left hand holding the reins, dragged him from his mule, hacked him to death with swords, axes, and wooden clubs, and left his body in the gutter while his mounted escort, which never seems to have been much use on these occasions, fled.[89]

These sequences embody, in a sense, the central formula of Tuchman's book, and the clear pattern they display is repeated in a variety of ways throughout the volume. What is at first most striking is how similar the first paragraphs in each sequence are, how similar the second are, and how sharply the first paragraphs differ from the second. These differences are stylistic and rhetorical, but such textual phenomena articulate contrasting historiographical perspectives, radically different ways of understanding the past and representing it in writing. The principal agents in both first paragraphs are large, anonymous forces, massively impersonal and even inhuman, though at times personified as a single, seemingly sentient being ("the struggle to end the schism and reform the abuses of the Church [grew] more desperate"). Elsewhere, agency is elided altogether: "From this date, too, began an erosion of belief..." In such a perspective, there are few or no individual human agents: no desperate strugglers, just a desperate struggle; no human believers, just belief that erodes spontaneously – indeed, almost no human causes or agents at all.

There is also a nearly diagrammatic clarity in the operation of historical forces: no ambiguity, no complexity, no obscurity, and only untroubled assurance on the part of the authorial perspective depicting them. In such a world, forces "played themselves out," "war and brigandage were renewed," the "Black Death disappeared," a "defeat...started a train of reactions" and "cause[d] a crisis of confidence...and a general resentment." Few qualifying (as opposed to descriptive) adjectives, few qualifications at all, no division of opinion, no historical ambiguity or opacity to contend with. The actors here are not persons but simple and understandable forces, diseases, defeats, and we are left to infer who, exactly, renewed the war and brigandage, whose belief eroded, who felt resentment. But that is only if we insist on retaining our conventional belief in human agency. If we simply read what the passages are saying, we find that forces "play ... themselves out," war and brigandage renew themselves, defeats start trains of reactions, and so on. Either the human agents that performed many of these actions are not named, then, or the chief historical actions in this period were not performed by humans at all but by vast and obscure "forces": historical currents, struggles, declines, defeats. Tracts of historical time even come to look like the humans they have displaced, as when "forces" that have "played themselves out" do so "in exaggerated form like human failings in old age."

The second paragraph in each sequence shifts to a dramatically different rhetoric, and a dramatically different representation of historical persons and events. There is a sudden turn to particularized human agency, to individuals and groups who have names, social positions, traits, emotions, abilities, and failings. They possess interiority, and they perform actions that are concretely detailed even at the microlevel. There are Philip, Philip the Fair, St. Louis, King Louis, Jean de Nevers and his father (both Dukes of Burgundy at different times). There are councillors, estates, gangs of toughs, hired killers – even another historian/chronicler whom Tuchman allows to speak in his own, immediate voice. Here, things happen because individuals and their acts are causative forces: "Jean de Nevers ... turned assassin, precipitating a train of evils." The King "had to devise substitutes like the sales tax," or "he fell back on devaluing the coinage" – a "subterfuge for taxation" that was "disastrous." In this view, things and actions are precisely specified, not evoked in abstract and featureless clarity: "salt tax," "deniers" (medieval French coins), "the streets of Paris," the precisely named "*maltôte*." Times of day – indeed, of a single day – are differentiated ("after dark"); we learn about Louis' "left hand holding the reins," and about "swords, axes, and wooden clubs" with which he is "hacked ... to death" (though perhaps not with the wooden clubs) and then left "in the gutter."

However distant the mirror, these are individuals like us, acting on recognizable human motives – and specified in familiar detail as to body, mind, setting, and actions. More cozily still, readers are implicitly invoked as the audience of a human drama, not as observers of massive historical spectacle; we are called upon as tacit assenters to general human truths and traits that presume our agreement and stress our kinship and continuity – with the twentieth-century historian and with the inhabitants of fourteenth-century France as well. When the historian notes that "The provincial estates whose consent was required for new taxes were reluctant, *like most representative bodies*, to recognize crisis until it was underfoot," she presumably appeals to readers' own widespread skepticism about governmental action and inaction. Something similar takes place when she remarks that Louis' "mounted escort, *which never seems to have been much use on these occasions*, fled." In both instances, writer and reader join in a clear-eyed and perhaps smilingly rueful recognition of timeless and universal human frailty.[90]

On the one hand, then, a map or grid of forces – lucid, perspicuous, abstract, ineluctable. Here, historian and reader hover above like airplane passengers perceiving the distinct and inevitable patterns of farm and field, land and water, from an immense and clarifying height – a height from which no individuals are visible. On the other hand, a close-up view of individual persons, human actions, human hearts, human failings and fears, human changeability ("turned assassin"). These human actors perform in a gritty and detailed world of vivid concreteness, where they confront problems and attempt to solve them. There are, then, two distinct rhetorics here, and two corresponding conceptions of the past and how to understand it – indeed, two different modes of knowing. But can they coexist, especially in the compressed and dramatic space of two-paragraph units, and can history-writing move from one conception to the other as easily as these second paragraphs follow from the first? Both modes supply readerly gratification, of course. The first does so by providing a sense of mastery, and of the knowability of history. It places us in a position of powerful understanding that allows us to see through complexity, ambiguity, intricate detail, and a welter of seemingly unrelated facts – to see through all of these and grasp, instead, the lucent outlines of "the calamitous 14th century." The second gratifies us with human interest, the opportunity for human identification, an invitation to assume continuity of human motives and values across the divides of space, time, and linguistic and cultural difference. It may be called "distant," but the fourteenth century seen thus is indeed a mirror, and what we see when we peer into it is ourselves.

But gratification is only one pertinent dimension of the juxtapositions and contrasts that Tuchman's rhetorical strategy creates. We must also consider what each mode of apprehension omits. The first leaves out complexity, ambiguity, a sense of the historian's own investments and inescapably mediating presence, the role of particulars, especially particular individuals, and their interaction with larger forces. And it leaves out the distance and dimness of much of the past, the conjunction of illumination and darkness in any given historical moment or scene as it presents itself to the interpreting consciousness, however scholarly and astute. This is to say that the first approach entirely omits the *problem* of knowing the past, and of interpreting it. Which leads us to the second mode, for what it, too, leaves out (though in a different way) is historical difference: the fact that the past (other eras, cultures, nations, geographical regions, and their inhabitants) is not just a mirror to our present but also Other in important and inescapable ways. What is erased is a sense of the past as something that must be read, that is, interpreted – encouraged to allow its otherness to complicate, exceed, alter, and even defy the structure of expectations, prejudice, ideology, and assumption that we bring to it.

When the lovable and illiterate Joe Gargery, in Dickens' *Great Expectations*, announces to Pip that he is "uncommon fond of reading," he means, in effect, that he is capable of finding in the text only what he already knows and has – in this case, what he already is. Taking up the letter that Pip has laboriously written to him, Joe says, "Why, here's a J,...and a O equal to anythink! Here's a J and a O, Pip, and a J-O, Joe."[91] To read this way, to find in the texts we read – or in the pasts we study – only what we already know and are, is to peer into a mirror that is exactly – one wants to say "calamitously" – not distant enough. I have already noted one of the ways this insufficient distance emerges in Tuchman's "second" paragraphs: in their very modern assumption that the most significant agents are particular human individuals and groups. Such a view plays down forces like ideology, geography, climate, economics, class, gender, race, and much else. In doing so, it enshrines individual agency along with the assumption that human nature is unchanging across space, time, or culture, and that the historian's objects are nothing more than different historical manifestations of a Human Nature universal in every important particular.

One could try, of course, to see the two perspectives as complementary, somewhat like long or "establishing" shots and close-ups in film. The first provides a view of an entire scene in broad outline, from the outside, and the second takes the viewer into the finer detail of experience seen and lived from the inside, or at least at closer range – *la vie particularisée*. But even in film, what the two kinds of shot provide is not really "the same thing" shown at different scales or magnifications.

If a photographic portrait of an attractive nude model is followed by a photograph of some skin cells of the same model taken through a microscope, much more is changed than scale or perspective. For one thing, the sequence of photographs transforms the body from an aesthetic – perhaps an erotic – entity to a medical or cytological entity. (This claim can be tested by trying to imagine someone not floridly abnormal carrying around a picture of the microscopically viewed cells and sharing them with another admirer of that particular model, or using them as a masturbatory aid.). The different scales create different things, just as an actuarial table about farmers or schizophrenics or teenage male drivers projects a different reality than does acquaintance with any particular farmer or schizophrenic or teenage male driver. And in any case, the objections I have tried to describe are not mainly problems of scale but of historiographical assumption. To become aware of these problems through close reading, to understand the text as an object of New Formalist analysis as well as a representation of the fourteenth or any other century, is to begin reading critically as well as appreciatively, and thus to use formalist concerns and analyses as tools to understand historical texts and perhaps to produce better history and better historiography. As Cohen remarks, "a historically aware formal analysis may be applied not only to the various social practices and discourses that make up our sense of history, but to the discourse of history itself" – past or present.[92] Formalist analysis allows us to enter critically into the discourse of the discipline of history, and to demonstrate with pertinence and precision that what we see and know depends on how we see and understand – and how we write and read.

viii   Formalist analysis of non-literary texts: economics/sociology/satire

The last text I want to look at is an excerpt from Chapter 3, "Conspicuous Leisure," of Thorstein Veblen's *The Theory of the Leisure Class*. It is a text likeliest to be assigned in an American Studies or Cultural Studies course, though it may make an appearance in Economics or Sociology syllabi as well. It is a dramatic example of the way a singular vision of economics, social structure, and cultural symbolism – a vision at once illuminating, exact, and satiric – is shaped by remarkable verbal details that reward stylistic no less than conceptual analysis: stylistic analysis that is *also* conceptual analysis unavailable to a non-textual approach. To read Veblen's text carefully, with attention to its language and not just its paraphrasable content, is to grasp far more precisely and completely its conception of social behavior and social identity. Here is the passage (one of many that might have served equally well):

> Abstention from labour is not only a honorific or meritorious act, but it presently comes to be a requisite of decency. The insistence on property as the basis of reputability is very naive and very imperious during the early stages of the accumulation of wealth. Abstention from labour is the conventional evidence of wealth and is therefore the conventional mark of social standing; and this insistence on the meritoriousness of wealth leads to a more strenuous insistence on leisure. *Nota notae est nota rei ipsius.* [A sign of a sign is a sign of the thing itself.] According to well-established laws of human nature, prescription presently seizes upon this conventional evidence of wealth and fixes it in men's habits of thought as something that is in itself substantially meritorious and ennobling; while productive labour at the same time and by a like process becomes in a double sense intrinsically unworthy. Prescription ends by making labour not only disreputable in the eyes of the community, but morally impossible to the noble, freeborn man, and incompatible with a worthy life.

This tabu on labour has a further consequence in the industrial differentiation of classes. As the population increases in density and the predatory group grows into a settled industrial community, the constituted authorities and the customs governing ownership gain in scope and consistency. It then presently becomes impracticable to accumulate wealth by simple seizure, and, in logical consistency, acquisition by industry is equally impossible for high-minded and impecunious men. The alternative open to them is beggary or privation. Wherever the canon of conspicuous leisure has a chance undisturbed to work out its tendency, there will therefore emerge a secondary, and in a sense spurious, leisure class – abjectly poor and living a precarious life of want and discomfort, but morally unable to stoop to gainful pursuits. The decayed gentleman and the lady who has seen better days are by no means unfamiliar phenomena even now. This pervading sense of the indignity of the slightest manual labour is familiar to all civilised peoples, as well as to peoples of a less advanced pecuniary culture. In persons of delicate sensibility, who have long been habituated to gentle manners, the sense of the shamefulness of manual labour may become so strong that, at a critical juncture, it will even set aside the instinct of self-preservation. So, for instance, we are told of certain Polynesian chiefs, who, under the stress of good form, preferred to starve rather than carry their food to their mouths with their own hands. It is true, this conduct may have been due, at least in part, to an excessive sanctity or tabu attaching to the chief's person. The tabu would have been communicated by the contact of his hands, and so would have made anything touched by him unfit for human food. But the tabu is itself a derivative of the unworthiness or moral incompatibility of labour; so that even when construed in this sense the conduct of the Polynesian chiefs is truer to the canon of honorific leisure than would at first appear. A better illustration, or at least a more unmistakable one, is afforded by a certain king of France who is said to have lost his life through an excess of moral stamina in the observance of good form. In the absence of the functionary whose office it was to shift his master's seat, the king sat uncomplaining before the fire and suffered his royal person to be toasted beyond recovery. But in so doing he saved his Most Christian Majesty from menial contamination.

Summum crede nefas animam praeferre pudori,

Et propter vitam vivendi perdere causas.

[Believe it the worst of sins to purchase life with dishonor,

And, in order to live, to lose all reason for living.][93]

How might an attentive undergraduate paraphrase this passage if an instructor were to ask, "What is Veblen saying here?" Perhaps this way:

Veblen says that wealth is a sign of your social standing, and that not having to work shows that you're wealthy. So even if you're poor, you can *pretend* that you have money – and thus a high place in society – by not working, and by making it obvious that you're not working and don't want or need to work.

This is a pretty good discussion-launching summary.

The one curious note, though, is the hypothetical student's use of "you." It sounds overly personal, even intimate, in this context, and the reason it does is not far to seek. There is no "you" in Veblen's passage and, except for the Polynesian chief and the French king, there are scarcely any individuals at all. When one does appear, "the noble, freeborn man," for example, he is a typical rather than an individual figure (like "the decayed gentleman" a little further on), and he is neither the principal agent nor the grammatical subject of the sentence. The student's "you" – an individual who does things, who wants to create certain impressions, and whose point of view the student paraphrases – is entirely foreign to the world of Veblen's discourse. In that world, individuals recede into the background. As in Tuchman, though to utterly different effect, the foreground is dominated by universal forces – usually represented by abstract nouns – that are both the grammatical subjects of Veblen's sentences and the authentic agents of the social scene he depicts. "Abstention," "insistence," "prescription," "tabu," "the canon of conspicuous leisure" – such forces, often personified, are the real "characters" in Veblen's drama.

For some readers, this demotion of the individual in favor of abstract social forces is precisely what is wrong with the social sciences, and Veblen's prose is just another symptom of the Pretty Pass to which Spencer, Durkheim, and the others have brought us. Those readers would be quite wrong, but they could certainly marshal a lot of stylistic evidence to argue that Veblen's discourse is nearly that of sociology itself, or of the social sciences generally. The bill of indictment might include:

1. Nominalization, especially the use of abstract nouns as subjects of sentences where good style would require a human agent and the finite, active verb from which the noun had been made.
2. A high frequency of abstract, Latinate diction, generating considerable stylistic elevation and pomposity.
3. Over-reliance on forms of "to be."
4. Passive constructions, with their muting or effacement of agency.
5. Excessive personification, and thus promiscuous reification, of abstractions ("prescription...seizes upon this evidence...").
6. A vocabulary of causality that mechanizes human behavior and describes it in terms of quasi-scientific necessity: "a further consequence"; "the predatory group grows"; "by a like process"; "a chance undisturbed to work out its tendency"; "well-established laws of human nature." This sense of rigid causality is reinforced by the pervasive interconnectedness of forces that Veblen's hypotaxis often suggests.
7. Vague management of the vocabulary of morality (by "moral," Veblen seems often to mean far less than he ought to).
8. Inconsistent management of levels of diction: "his royal person," for example, clashes ludicrously with "toasted."

These features of style are undoubtedly present in the passage, but they do not demonstrate either that Veblen writes badly or that his social-scientific abstraction and neutrality thoughtlessly dehumanize individual men and women. It would be truer to say that Veblen is not neutral at all – that his prose is filled with attitudes, judgments, assessments, and evaluations; that these are frequently ironic (comically or grimly, at times both); and that the "dehumanization" his prose projects is not the result of a methodological stance but of a particular vision of human nature. Finding that human beings *operate as though* they lacked individual wills and authentic personal values, Veblen found almost ready to hand the perfect style for symbolizing – and satirizing – this surrender of selfhood: the cool distance of his idiosyncratic version of the language of social science. But this style becomes, in Veblen's hands, an ironic mirror reflecting our actual vacuity, not that of the social sciences as a discipline. Unlike more conventional social scientists, Veblen has not "abstracted from" a rich and multiform human reality in order to isolate trends and laws and group tendencies. In his ironic vision, that is simply all there is.

Perhaps this detached and acerbic vision of humanity – as a "predatory group" beset by one "tabu" or another – is what led one disciple of Veblen's to term him a visitor "from another world" and to assert that "no other such emancipator of the mind from the subtle tyranny of circumstance has been known in social science, and no other such enlarger of the realm of inquiry."[94] From an interpretive and appreciative perspective, our list of Veblen's prose "faults" can be rewritten as a repertoire of rhetorical and stylistic means to certain ends:

1. Nominalization: a stylistic means of withdrawing agency from persons and their actions and of ascribing it to large, abstract forces.
2. Abstract, Latinate diction (at times, pompous): a reinforcement of nominalization, and one source of a detached, ironic tone. This tone is mock-heroic, at times, to designate petty figures caught up in grand processes they scarcely understand: processes which, for all their scope, are neither dignified, nor moral, nor even in the best interests of individuals.
3. Reliance on forms of "to be" and on passive constructions: a way of minimizing human agency, and of insisting on the ineluctability or static intransigence of social forces and structures – of that which "just is."

4, 5. Passive constructions and personification: a displacement of human agency from the humans who have surrendered it to the real agents of human experience in society.

6. A vocabulary of rigid causality and of scientific necessity: in effect, a stylistic index of human predictability. If you could set your watch by Kant's strolls, you can found an entire scientific discipline on the unvarying behavior of people in societies, Veblen implies.

7. Vague management of moral terms: a stylistic mirror of the human tendency to term "moral" whatever is expedient for social advancement. Such ironic redefinition of morality is common in Veblen. Government and war, he argues in another passage, are indeed carried on for pecuniary gain, but "it is gain obtained by the honourable method of seizure and conversion. These occupations are of the nature of predatory, not productive, employment" and – this is Veblen's point – that's why they count as "honourable."

8. Clashes of diction: part of a pervasive mock-heroic strategy which sets human pretensions to dignity, intelligence, and free will against the actual mechanisms of mundane human behavior.

Much more could be said about Veblen's prose: about the comic irony in calling "abstention from labour" an "act"; about the parallelism, antithesis, and chiasmus that provide syntactic analogues to the structures that lock individuals into patterns, as in the third sentence of the second paragraph:

$$
\begin{array}{cccc}
A & B & B & A
\end{array}
$$

"impracticable ... seizure ... industry ... impossible";

about the play with audience – and the witty redefinition of "civilised" – implied in his claim that "This pervading sense of the indignity of manual labour is familiar to all civilised peoples"; about the use of the present tense to suggest that certain actions are timeless, unvarying, and irresistible. Enough has been said, however, to show that the paraphrase with which we began is both correct and hopelessly inadequate. It is inadequate because it looks "through" Veblen's language to the meaning that allegedly lies behind it, instead of looking "at" that language in order to receive the rich range and nuance of the meanings the language performs as well as states.[95] Only attention to style and language generally can begin to make available the full range of meaning in Veblen's prose, in part because an essential part of that meaning is Veblen's attitude toward the phenomena he analyzes, and this attitude is created largely through stylistic means. Since this meaning embodies an entire vision of human nature in society, it is at least as pertinent to the sociologist or the economist as it is to the literary critic. The meanings generated by this style, that is, are not aesthetic frills but essential features of one classic text in the discourse of the social sciences – and meanings that only formalist analysis can disclose.

ix   Formalist analysis: rhetorics of science and mathematics

These examples, taken from political oratory, semiotics and the history of medicine, medieval history, and a hybrid of economics, sociology, and satire, could be extended into discourses still further afield from the humanities and the social sciences. The past quarter century has seen numerous studies of the rhetoric of the social sciences, and of the sciences as well: studies seeking to explore and delineate the aims, procedures, methodological assumptions, criteria of validity, and verbal and rhetorical strategies that shape modes of language and modes of knowing across a wide range of disciplines. In doing so, such studies restore to visibility the textual dimension of the fields they investigate and render the documents of those fields susceptible to close reading, to formalist analysis: analysis of their rhetorical situations (speaker, audience, implied context, etc.), their defining grammatical and figurative strategies, their deployment of the persuasive and epistemological dimensions of graphs, illustrations, formulae, and other visual and symbolic elements, and so on. Close reading can foreground such pointed and ideologically fraught elisions of human perspective, agency, and point of view as are made possible by the non-agential passive voice ("The mixture was then placed in a centrifuge." "A decision was taken to bomb the nursery school."); the ostensible non-authoredness of most equations in chemistry, physics, or mathematics; and the rhetoric of transparency generally, the illusion of phenomena seemingly "given" – as though the result of no interpretation or diagnosis. In each case, and many others, the discipline's rhetoric shapes what it will know, how it knows it, how it judges what it knows, and how it seeks to persuade or to win assent. This is true of the humanities, the social sciences, and the sciences. Indeed, there is no reason to exclude even the seemingly non-textual and non-rhetorical discipline of mathematics.

As Michael Barany has argued in an illuminating essay, the rhetoric of most mathematical discourse rests on the implicit assumption of a quasi-Platonic realm of truth and objectivity, free of both material circumstance and human constructedness, whose meanings it is the

mathematician's job to transmit or translate (*not* interpret) for the purpose of enlarging the store of mathematical knowledge. The first thing
a New Formalist might notice, therefore, is the powerful decontextual-
ization performed by mathematical rhetoric. Of both formal logic and
mathematics, Barany writes:

> In the production of a proof or the assertion of a logical proposition,
> it is easy to overlook the circumstances of creation and address which
> make the proof or proposition possible ....Indeed, a central proposi-
> tion behind the purity of logic is that its truth is utterly independent
> of the time and place in which it is conceived and enunciated. If
> mathematical objects and mathematical truths pre-exist in a Platonic
> realm of ideal truth, then they have no need for exposition in order
> to exist, and so there is a vested interest for the logical paradigm in
> the suppression of the actual acts of generation and transmission of
> mathematics.[96]

For Wittgenstein and some others, the mathematician "is an inven-
tor, not a discoverer," but as Barany says, "Wittgenstein's viewpoint...remains rare in the common imagination of mathematics,
where Platonism continues to provide the basic viewpoint for contextu-
alizing mathematical 'discovery' and ideation."[97] Context, that is, "can
be hidden away until needed," so mathematicians characteristically "tell
a story of mathematics ripped from its context."[98] The rhetoric that performs this ripping is of course the language of the freestanding, the
independent, the atemporal, the nonhuman, the non-constructed, the
discovered rather than invented or constructed. Put differently, math's
characteristic "grammar of enunciation fabricates a sense of disembodiment which makes it possible to believe there would be math without
mathematicians, or even without humans."[99]

This sense of disembodiment takes a variety of particular textual
forms. One is the rhetorical effort to render the speaker – an inescapable
back-formation of virtually every instance of discourse – invisible, even
non-existent, by means of "a pronominal disjunction, often through
a shifting use of the first person plural." This strategy "creates a space
within which enunciation can be imagined without a speaker," or with
a "speaker" conceived at most as a kind of translator – a translator not
of a prior speaker's discourse but of the authorless and non-contingent
realm of meaning that is mathematics itself. Like a sibyl who is not
the originator or even the interpreter of a more authoritative discourse
but merely an opening through which that discourse may pass into

the world of men and women, the mathematical "speaker" is a rhetorical construct in which "identity is abstracted from communication."[100]
A similar rhetorical sleight of hand evaporates the audience as well:

> Often, textbooks will give the reader token mention in an introduc-
> tion or preface, and frequently there is a statement that the reader
> will have a "certain mathematical maturity," which is to say that the
> reader has been socialized to accept the Platonic order of the produc-
> tion of mathematical truth embraced by the logical paradigm.... The
> mathematical speaker can be said to have confused address with com-
> munication in presenting a proof as though its truth was pre-given
> and independent of the audience's comprehension or assent.[101]

Context, discursive or textual identity, speaker, audience: an arsenal of
rhetorical strategies – the rhetoric of textual effacement, one might term
it – obscures these entities in much mathematical as well as scientific
discourse.

   This effacement extends even to narrative, whose authentic temporality is, in mathematical writing, generally displaced by the artificial and
atemporal sequences of logic.[102]

> The archetypal mathematical paper begins with a short expository
> motivation, states definitions, gives one or more examples or con-
> structions, states a theorem, states and proves several supporting
> lemmas, proves the main theorem, and closes with some applica-
> tions or open problems. This representation of the proof completely
> obscures its production.... By telling a narrative more in line with
> the logical paradigm of orderly discovery of mathematical truth than
> with the actual heuristic principles involved in the production of the
> proof, a mathematician or logician projects the former heuristic in
> place of the latter. *A rupture in mathematical thought is transformed into
> continuity by the narrative re-imagining of history.*[103]

If such a transformation is a kind of metaphoric substitution or
identification – historical continuity *is* logical sequence – metaphors
and other figures of speech are also prevalent, if not always obvious,
in mathematical discourse. Logical operations stand in for sequences of
human reasoning; metaphors – material and other – render accessible
the immaterial abstractions of the world of numbers ("three cubed is
twenty-seven"); and a demonstration that the area of a given triangle
whose base is 8" and whose height is 7" is 28 square inches is both a

singular assertion of fact and a synecdochic promise that this triangle may stand for any other, the area of any and all being calculable by the formula $A = \frac{1}{2}$ bh. In Barany's words,

> At the heart of the problem of definition in mathematics is the role and function of metaphor. Metaphors operate on many levels in the mathematical sign system. The rules of symbolic logic function as metaphoric substitutes for supposedly basic human logical intellect. Any commerce in ideal objects is bound to use metaphoric devices to represent and break apart details and structures of inaccessible generalities. Most proofs, and especially geometric proofs, make extensive use of synecdoche in treating general classes of related mathematical objects. Finally, because math must claim access to infinite classes of objects, all proofs and operations must be defined through the use of metaphor, where corresponding operations on related objects are performed "in the same manner" as those for a few sample objects.[104]

Observations such as these are not an "exposé" of the sneaky metaphoricity of a discipline associated in the popular imagination – and often, in the ideology of mathematics itself – with cool and pellucid rationality. They simply affirm the textual character of mathematical discourse, its rhetoric, and thus its susceptibility to analysis of a formalist kind.[105] If the example with which we began –Cuomo's rejection of "polished and appealing rhetoric" in favor of "a more telling reasonableness and rationality" – ends up demonstrating that there is no discourse of reasonableness and rationality without a rhetoric of *some* sort (whether "polished and appealing" or not), the discussion of mathematics with which we close simply seeks to extend that discursive given to symbol systems not obviously poetic, literary, or even principally linguistic. One could go further still, to the rhetoric of visual arts and cultural signs, the rhetoric of fashion or gesture or gender, and well beyond, but this is principally an essay in New Formalist analysis of texts, those we term literary but also those we do not, and the rhetoric of mathematics can serve as one, admittedly artificial, limit of that undertaking.

4
Textual Infatuation, True Infatuation

i Introduction: wholes and parts

In order to really know a literary text, or a loved person, one must risk a sustained raptnesss of attention that transgresses the boundaries of the moderate and seemly, of common sense. This chapter's principal aims, therefore, are twofold. The first is to rethink and rehabilitate two forms of intensive scrutiny that regularly draw skepticism and even scorn: what is called "overreading" in literary criticism, and what is termed "infatuation" in romantic and affectional life. In both spheres, I argue, a particular kind of attention, even hyperattentiveness, enables forms of knowing both valuable and legitimate (that is, objective). The second, related aim is to question traditional allegiance to the concepts of wholeness, unity, and generality in literary criticism – not in order to reject them, but to liberate the minute attention to parts that is inhibited by what Adorno calls "this passing-on and being unable to linger, this tacit assent to the primacy of the general over the particular."[1] I explore and advocate a conscious, New Formalist fetishizing of parts – of textual elements – to a point at which the whole they constitute recedes almost to vanishing, or is bracketed almost to the point of annihilation. Such an effort does not represent an ultimate denigration of textual or other artistic wholes, but it enables a realization of individual elements that would otherwise be impossible – a realization that can redeem both the charge of critical overreading and that of romantic infatuation.

Aristotle says in the *Metaphysics* that "When we say what [a thing] is, we do not say 'white' or 'hot' or 'three cubits long,' but 'a man' or 'a god'" (Book Z [vii]).[2] We designate the being or identity of the thing, not its attributes or conditions – in an older idiom, its substance, not its accidents. Similarly, when we designate a thing, we do not name one or more of its parts but choose a term labeling what it is as an entirety or a whole – not a steering wheel or a stamen or a stanza but an automobile, or a flower, or a poem. This implicit terminological insistence on essential identity and on wholeness plays an obvious role in literary critical notions such as generic and formal identity (lyric, epic, or dramatic; sonnet or elegy or epyllion), and in ideas of unity – whether "organic" or not – from Plato to Coleridge to Brooks and Warren. In some cases, in the history of criticism, the attempt to demonstrate a work's wholeness and unity has been an important – at times, a dominant – goal of critical analysis, often in polemical refutation of prior charges of disunity or incoherence. In others, it has been an honorific byproduct or corollary of such analysis: this work has such and such interesting and significant themes, patterns, implications for our lives, and by the way, since it is an excellent work, it also displays significant unity. And in still other cases, such as the preceding chapters, if unity plays a role, it is largely as a regulative assumption rather than a quality to be demonstrated: an assumption enabling analyses whose principal goals frequently have little or nothing to do with questions of unity and wholeness.[3] Geoffrey Hartman's essay, "The Voice of the Shuttle: Language from the Point of View of Literature," focuses critically, as Philip E. Lewis says, "upon the sometimes sacrosanct concept of unity. Nothing in the elemental structure of literary speech authorizes the designation of unity as a primary value. In art as in life, what counts is first and foremost the pursuit of the possibilities that disunification opens up, including subsequently that of achieving a unity which overlays disunity and embellishes its form."[4]

Yet even in this last and least insistent form, the shadow of the whole can still prove constraining; at least, it can still reinforce the notion that the critic's *final* concern is with the artwork as a whole. Yet in interpretive essays focused on questions of language and poetics, such as Hartman's remarkable "The Voice of the Shuttle," which moves between close reading and speculative poetics, or Jonathan Culler's penetrating exploration of "Apostrophe," and even in many powerful essays more resolutely focused on analysis of a single work, attention to the entire text or to the question of wholeness is frequently muted, vestigial, or absent entirely.[5] When such questions do appear prominently, they are regularly less compelling than other dimensions of the studies and seem rarely to be integral parts of the analysis and argument; they function almost as symbolic or quasi-phatic gestures, establishing the writer's degree of literary critical or academic socialization and serving to assure readers that the intensity and sharpness of focus required for detailed analytical investigation have not entirely blinded the investigator to the larger picture. Against this background, I propose to state – perhaps even to overstate – the case for minutely attentive New Formalist analysis: for dedicated – even fervent – attention to individual textual particulars.

ii Doing without organic unity: John Crowe Ransom (and others)

If we seek a New Critical precedent for such an emphasis, the work of Cleanth Brooks is probably not the place to look. However detailed Brooks' analyses of paradox or irony or linguistic registers or vocabularies, his allegiance is finally to the poem (or prose text) as a whole: the poem is a "pattern of resolved stresses" that "attains its unity by establishing meaningful relationships among its apparently discordant elements."[6] There are tensions and stresses among parts, but they are resolved; elements are discordant, but only apparently so. Eliot had formulated a conception of the "ideal order" formed by all existing works of art – an order that is slightly altered by the appearance of each new work in such a way that "the whole existing order must be, if ever so slightly, altered; and so the relations, proportions, values of each work of art toward the whole are readjusted."[7] This is a vision of literary history as a perpetually readjusting organic unity. Brooks conceives of the individual poem in an analogous way. Novel or discordant or seemingly disruptive elements acquire their proper place in a system of relations that they simultaneously re-order; such elements are temporary wanderers on their way to a home they will both enter and alter.

Far less committed to the notion of a text as unified, systematic, and organically whole is the New Critical theory of John Crowe Ransom. Brooks and Ransom share a number of critical and cultural values, including the importance of detailed analysis, the value of poetry as a concrete force resisting the abstractions of science and the simplifications of propaganda – "man cannot consider life merely in abstract and quantitative terms, such as pure science dictates" – and as a stabilizing and rendering of the concrete external world.[8] The poem, says Brooks, "if it be a true poem[,] is a simulacrum of reality."[9] But they part ways on several issues. For one thing, Brooks did not contribute to the 1930 volume of essays, *I'll Take My Stand: The South and the Agrarian Tradition*, to which Ransom offered an essay, as did Robert Penn Warren and Allen Tate. In his contribution, Tate voices a concern that aligns itself more closely with the ontological dimensions of Ransom's theory of poetry than with Brooks'. Indeed, unlikely as it may seem, the critique of industrialism, scientific and other instrumental discourses, abstraction, the interchangeability of concrete objects, and the erosion of personhood voiced by Ransom and Tate in a nostalgic look back at the agrarian South chimes powerfully, if incompletely, with the very differently based critiques of Max Horkheimer and Theodor Adorno in their joint volume, *Dialectic of Enlightenment*, and of Adorno in his *Minima Moralia*.[10]

Here, for example, is Tate, defending a particular mode of Southern religion as against the ontological impoverishments he associates with the rise of industrial society. "Abstraction," he declares,

> is the death of religion, no less than the death of anything else. Religion, when it directs its attention to the horse cropping the blue-grass on the lawn, is concerned with the whole horse, and not with (1) that part of him which he has in common with other horses, or that more general part which he shares with other quadrupeds or with the more general vertebrates; and not with (2) that power of the horse which he shares with horsepower in general, of pushing or pulling another object. Religion pretends to place before us the horse as he is.[11]

The reduction of the individual "horse cropping the blue-grass on the lawn" to its generic equinity, or its commonality with all quadrupeds, or its force-value in horsepower or ergs or foot-pounds has a counterpart in the more secular vision of Adorno. His vocabulary of reification, relations of production, appropriation, fungibility, and the qualitative and the quantitative reflects an analysis shaped by Marxist critique rather than Southern agrarianism, yet the overlap is noteworthy.[12] Next to Tate's horse, we can put Adorno's vision of the fate of the individual, turned by society "back into precisely what the developmental law of society, the principle of the self, had opposed: mere examples of the species, identical to one another through isolation within the compulsively controlled collectivity."[13] This abstraction of the individual also appears in more narrowly economic terms: "In this country there is no difference between a person and that person's economic fate ... They know themselves as nothing else ... 'I am a failure,' says the American – and that is that."[14] More tartly still: "Animism had endowed things with souls; industrialism makes souls into things."[15]

Like the New Critics generally, Tate does not employ Adorno and Horkheimer's economic and political vocabulary, or most of their post-Hegelian and Marxist conceptual apparatus, but what all three share with Ransom is distress at the felt ontological fragility of the world's particulars – including the self – under the dominion of science and industrialism. Ransom's "fundamental interest," in the words of Douglas Mao, lies "in protecting the concrete particular from the onslaught of abstracting generalization."[16] Natural particulars, threatened by "science's violence" and "will to mastery," are defended by art, "which counters the will to mastery by promoting contemplation of the particular for its own sake."[17] In his significantly titled *The World's Body*, Ransom develops a post-Kantian position on contemplation "under … the form of art" – a knowing of the object "for its own sake," and an ability to conceive it "as having its own existence" rather than existing for another's possession, use, or exploitation.[18]

To know the object in this way, schooled by the study of poetry, is for Ransom to attain "a new kind of knowledge" set in "a new world."[19] Elsewhere, he elaborates this quasi-utopian scenario:

> The critic should regard the poem as nothing short of a desperate ontological or metaphysical manœuvre…. The poet perpetuates in his poem an order of existence which in actual life is constantly crumbling beneath his touch. His poem celebrates the object which is real, individual, and qualitatively infinite. He knows that his practical interests will reduce this living object to a mere utility, and that his sciences will disintegrate it for their convenience into their respective abstracts. The poet wishes to defend his object's existence against its enemies, and the critic wishes to know what he is doing, and how.[20]

And in another formulation:

> The true poetry … wants to realize the world, to see it better. Poetry is the kind of knowledge by which we must know what we have arranged that we shall not know otherwise.[21]

With that last aphoristic generalization, the redemptive claims of this theory of poetry promise to undo not simply the impositions of scientific thinking and discourse but perhaps those of ideology and hegemony as well.

How does poetry manage to accomplish this feat of ontological redemption, to recover a "denser and more refractory original world" and to leave us "looking, marvelling, and revelling in" that world's "thick *dinglich* substance"?[22] Most often by honoring the individuality, particularity, and unappropriated thereness of the objects it represents, and by consisting of verbal structures that are not mere signs or indices or depictions of the objects represented but symbols instinct with the represented reality: the fully realized "verbal image" or "verbal icon," in Wimsatt's terms, that "somehow shares the properties of, or resembles, the objects which it denotes."[23] Moreover, Ransom conceives of poetry as "directing the attention to particulars, heterogeneous elements that the poem's logical argument or prose sense cannot fully absorb."[24] A poem's structure is thus twofold – and twofold in an irreducible and internally heterogeneous way. One element is "the prose core," its logical or semantic structure; the other is "the differentia, residue, or tissue" – phonetic, metrical, other – "which keeps the object poetical or entire" by supplying a "tissue of irrelevance" that the logical structure cannot subdue.[25] The logical or prose or semantic dimension Ransom terms "structure," reserving the term "texture" for the recalcitrant, unassimilable dimension.

One of Ransom's several explanations of this relationship distinguishes between illustrations and images. Illustrations are pictures or images or instances that are perfectly subdued to the discourse they illustrate, and do not extend in their meaning or import beyond the concepts they concretize and render; they remain "transparent" and "everywhere translatable into idea."[26] Whether an "illustration" in this sense is even possible is a real question, at least in linguistic discourse. And even at the extremes of abstraction, as in mathematical or logical notation, one might still wonder if a plus sign is always *entirely* subdued to the additive function or, additionally and "irrelevantly," capable of momentarily evoking a tilted "x," or a quartered pizza, or the crosshairs of a rifle scope. Images, on the other hand, are not purely illustrative but have an "adventitious" or unsubduable dimension that exceeds the illustrative function. And not just images. Meter functions as irrelevant texture (Ransom derides the notion that every detail of meter is perfectly expressive – "illustrative" – of some aspect of the prose structure or logical sense), and so does a text's phonetic dimension.[27] But meaning, too, can generate textural elements:

> Tinkering with the words loosens up the logic, introducing periphrases, ellipses, inaccuracies, and, what is much more valuable, importations . . . . so a texture of meaning is established with respect to the structure; and nothing is so remarkable in poetry as this. It is the thing that particularly qualifies a discourse as being poetic; it is its differentia.[28]

In sharp contrast to Brooks' "pattern of resolved stresses," then, Ransom gives us a verbal structure fundamentally at odds with itself, and a poem that, in the divided and heterogeneous character of its existence, offers "a kind of knowledge which is radically or ontologically distinct" from scientific knowledge, a knowledge that can "recover the denser and more refractory original world which we know loosely through our perceptions and memories."[29] This knowledge is the product not of poetic unity or wholeness but, on the contrary, of textual particulars that refuse to be subdued to an encompassing or overarching whole.

iii Refractory parts and fetishized wholes

In contrast to the main emphases of Brooks, then, who by and large subdues parts to whole, stresses to resolution, conflicting voices to coherent drama, Ransom offers contemporary criticism a New Critical model emphasizing dissonance, heterogeneity, and excess – the "residuary tissue" of poetic texture that resists assimilation to the whole.[30] Ransom is far from blind to questions of unity, but he characteristically emphasizes the variety of elements to be unified and he distrusts unities too easily achieved. Speaking of Ben Jonson and dramatic unity, for example, he notes that a drama "has *human situations*, and it has *characters*, who make *speeches*."[31] Thus, despite "the remarkable unity of a Jonson play,…the structural materials" make us "feel that we are in for a vast degree of heterogeneity."[32]

Even if New Formalism refuses Ransom's particular ontological commitments, then, and his conception of poetry as a means to renew the particulars of the world's body, he provides a conceptualization of the part–whole relationship that not only differs sharply from the organic unity that has achieved normative status in accounts of the New Criticism but may even sensitize us to latent and often overlooked dimensions of that standard New Critical position. Early in *The Well Wrought Urn*, for example, Brooks contrasts the tendency of science to "stabilize terms" and "freeze them into strict denotations" with poetry's "disruptive" linguistic practice in which "terms are continually modifying each other, and thus violating their dictionary meanings."[33] In this opening chapter, Brooks is introducing the idea that "the language of poetry is the language of paradox," which he will go on to illustrate in a reading of Donne's "Canonization" that works toward a "union," a "fusion," a Coleridgean welding together of "the discordant and the contradictory" that is peculiar to Donne's poem but also characteristic of the poetic undertaking – the "creative imagination" – itself.[34]

But before reaching that vision of achieved unity, Brooks not only introduces terms like "disruptive" and "violating," but also has recourse to this complex and striking image: "The poet must work by analogies, but the metaphors do not lie in the same plane or fit neatly edge to edge. There is a continual tilting of the planes; necessary overlappings, discrepancies, contradictions."[35] The imagery suggests an indefeasible discord of planes disrupted by tilting, boundaries violated by overlappings, harmony and univocality vexed by discrepancy and contradiction. Citing this and other passages from *The Well Wrought Urn*, Wolfson has shrewdly remarked that "If the dominant and subordinate clauses in some of these alertly tortured sentences were inverted, Brooks' poetics of unity would release a deconstructive difference."[36] The moral to draw from such passages, I think, is not that Brooks' project is incoherent or that New Criticism was a direct precursor of deconstruction, but that implicit within all but the most primitive, un-nuanced, and perhaps unthinkable conceptions of unity and wholeness is a counterforce of heterogeneity, self-contestation, and individuated particularity: a moment of inertial singularity that any unifying impulse must encounter. The part–whole relationship is thus inescapably dialectical, and as Brooks himself repeatedly suggests, any meaningful assertion of wholeness and unity will derive much of its strength and significance from the freedom allowed to isolable particulars before these are comprehended in the whole.

From this perspective, the refractory particularity that Ransom terms "texture" is, if not an ontological stumbling block to structure, an element essential to the latter's non-triviality – for Ransom, but also, in a different way, for Brooks. If the whole subsumes those elements and gives them a context, a network of relationships, and a significance that they do not have alone, the elements give the whole its depth and complexity, its dynamic tensions and significative chiaroscuro, in part because their subsumption in that whole is inevitably incomplete. Croce claims, in his *Aesthetic*, that when the artist incorporates individual elements into an artistic unity, it is like putting "formless pieces of bronze and choicest statuettes" into a crucible, where those "statuettes must be melted just like the pieces of bronze before there can be a new statue."[37] But as Wimsatt points out, "this analogy may not in fact read so smoothly. Do the conceptual materials (the old saws, catch words, and the like) which one finds in a poem really melt out of sight? Or don't they have to retain their form and meaning in order to operate poetically at all?"[38] The incorporated element is never a mere cipher, assigned an entirely new meaning and being by the artwork as a whole. Its identity or *haecceitas* – its "thisness" – is transformed, certainly, but it remains recognizable as *this* transformed element rather than another, and rather than no element at all. If Tate's "horse cropping the blue-grass on the lawn" were part of a painted scene, it would enter into, alter, and be altered by its relationship to other elements of the scene and to the scene as a whole. But even as an element integral to and transformed by the entire composition, it would not be a zebra, and it would not be nothing.

Croce's assertion is an aesthetic claim, but its larger context is a powerful bias in Western thought, extending from Plato (at least) to the present, that favors wholes over parts – "the primacy of the general over the particular," in Adorno's words.[39] This bias, or predisposition, or tradition governs a great deal of aesthetic discourse, ancient and modern. Writing about criticism and poetry (the latter metaphorically compared to female beauty), Alexander Pope admonishes, "Tis not a *Lip*, or *Eye*, we Beauty call,/But the joint Force and full *Result* of all."[40] Elsewhere, turning to the universe and to human knowledge, he warns, " 'Tis but a part we see, and not a whole."[41] This valorizing of the whole no doubt also reflects metaphysical investments in the idea of a whole and unified cosmos or uni-verse, and is likely grounded in an evolutionary preference for conceiving of the human body – and the personhood it represents – as one or another sort of unity rather than an aggregate of disparate parts. Insistent erotic interest in isolated parts of the body, after all, attracts names like "perversion," or "fetishism," or "objectification" – or even (metaphoric) "dismemberment" – from the psychological community and popular culture alike. Even the pathos of Lacan's "mirror stage," in which the child's ego is constituted as both absurdly idealized and forever ungraspable – "The ego is human being's mental illness," he remarks – reveals a primordial and even potentially tragic inability to resist the idea of wholeness.[42]

There is also the overwhelming dominance of maxims and admonitions stressing the need to free one's attention from the partial and minute and attend instead to totalities of one or another kind. We are taught from childhood that the whole is greater than (even) the sum of its parts; that we should try to see the big picture, or take the large view; that we must beware of losing the forest for the trees; that we should avoid getting mired in details. If the devil is in those details, it is true that – in another version of the maxim – so is God; but this is one of the few part/whole apothegms to be regularly reversed. In fact, the weight of tradition favoring wholes over parts becomes clear from the gentle *frisson* produced by inverting some of these admonitions: the sum of the parts is greater than the whole; don't let the big picture blind you to the details; take small, detailed views; don't lose the trees – or the tree – for the forest; don't let the whole blur the details.[43] Nor is the issue simply one of scale, for there is often the suggestion that the parts, taken alone, display a kind of metaphysical as well as aesthetic or conceptual inadequacy, that energetic attention to parts is not just narrow but in some sense unfair or morally suspect. Thus with "perversions" of erotic attention that foreground breasts or buttocks, biceps or beards, we can group Pope's suggestion that elements of the workings of the universe are not only lesser than the whole, but perhaps in need of the whole to redeem them: "All partial Evil, universal Good."[44]

In interpretive practice, as in literary or aesthetic theory, announced concern for the whole artwork is still normative, but that concern often pales since the work of explication and the teaching of close reading require surprisingly patient attention to the individual elements of a text: words, sounds, allusions, rhythms, speech registers, specialized vocabularies, etymologies, figuration, and so on. Jane Gallop argues for the salutary effects of this kind of attention:

> The difference between close reading and the way most people read most of the time is that, whereas it is generally agreed that it is the big picture that matters, close reading emphasizes small details. We have been trained to read a book globally: that is, to think of the book as a whole, identify its main idea, and understand all of its parts as fitting together to make up that whole. Close reading, on the other hand, is a technique for letting the whole book, the main argument, the global picture fade into the background. When we close read, we zero in on details but we do not immediately fit those details into our idea of the whole book. Instead we try to understand the details themselves as much as possible, to derive as much meaning as we can from them. The reason for this is that the detail is the best possible safeguard against projection. It is the main idea or the general shape which is most likely to correspond to our preconceptions about the book. But we cannot so easily predict the details. So by concentrating on the details, we disrupt our projection; we are forced to see what is really there.[45]

When, for example, we come upon the opening words of "The Poet's Final Instructions" by John Berryman – "Dog-tired, suisired," – we cannot situate them in the poem's formal or significative wholeness without considering them also as elements, as temporarily isolable parts or components.[46] There is the slangy, singsong canine comparison, conveying animal and existential fatigue, a sense of diminishment or giving out – perhaps, in this poet of multiple voices and *personae*, a suggestion of dramatic role-playing as in "It's a dog's life." In that dramatic context, "-tired" may even remind us of "tiring-room," an Elizabethan phrase for the dressing room of a stage where costumes and makeup helped transform actors into characters.[47] The next word, "suisired," unfolds into the suggestion of suicide, perhaps with anger ("ire") near its center – whether the speaker's own or his father's, the latter central to a number of *Dream Songs*. But Berryman's coinage "suisired" also suggests, *via* its Latin roots, a siring or fathering or begetting of oneself, making self-creation and self-destruction into an oxymoronic unity, a kind of double exposure. This link echoes other Berryman poems like Dream Song No. 31, with its humorous auto-patronymic, "Henry Hankovitch" – Henry, son of Hank. But given the speaker's regular tendency to represent himself as a fallen figure, the word also recalls the despairing rebelliousness of Milton's Satan, who pretends to Abdiel that the rebel angels were the authors of their own being:

> "That we were form'd then, say'st thou? And the work
> Of secondary hands, by task transferred
> From Father to his Son? Strange point and new!
> Doctrine which we would know whence learnt. Who saw
> When this creation was? Remember'st thou
> Thy making, while the Maker gave thee being?
> *We know no time when we were not as now;*
> *Know none before us, self-begot, self-raised*
> *By our own quick'ning power* ...."[48]

Explicative activity like this is standard fare in the literature classroom, and in the indispensable exegetical work from which critical arguments are constructed. Its frequency and necessity can remind us that, most of the time, the critic's construing of a text into meaningful wholeness is not even thinkable without a minute and recursive attention to parts that constitutes the majority of the work of interpretation.[49]

iv   Overreading and infatuation

Any whole text is a part also, whether of a larger structure like a sonnet sequence or single volume of poems, or an author's body of work, or a genre, or a literary movement or period or particular culture. Here, too, especially in works of literary history and of cultural criticism, vigorous subordination of part to whole is routine, largely because the work of those disciplines is traditionally the discerning of patterns and the formulation of generalizations. Of course, individual texts are almost always permitted to exert some counter-pressure of specificity and idiosyncrasy that keeps them from being mere "illustrations," in Ransom's sense: examples that are "everywhere translatable into idea," illuminating the category they represent with no surplus of meaning or significance.[50] Despite that counter-pressure, however, a principal imperative of generic, historical, and cultural studies – reinforced by the traditional valuing of wholeness and totality – is to make discernible a whole of which any individual work is by definition only a part, and this act of generalization inescapably entails the muting – even erasure – of many particulars. At the very least, a responsible New Formalism can ensure that such muting is a conscious and methodologically entailed procedure, not a simple ignoring or suppression of textual features that complicate easy generalizations.

But this is a very limited task indeed. In the face of regular pressures to assimilate the elements of a text to an overarching unity, to submit whole texts to the generalizations of genre study and of historical and cultural analysis, and indeed to surrender the category of form entirely so as to enable a more fluent discourse resting on paraphrase, content analysis, and the identifying of ideological, political, and theoretical themes, formalism needs to reaffirm and refocus attention on the refractory particulars of texts. Against this background, then, and with the awareness that the concepts of unity and wholeness will reassert themselves before very long, I want to experiment with a kind of reverse discrimination, a partiality to the partial, one aim of which is to dramatize the sort of attention, even raptness, that often animates formalist attention to minute textual particulars – to parts.[51] As Culler remarks in a discussion of interpretation and overinterpretation, "I suspect that a little paranoia is essential to the just appreciation of things."[52]

Such attention is a kind of textual counterpart to the experience of infatuation in romantic and affectional life, and suffers a similar stigma of partiality and wrongheadedness. In the common understanding, infatuation is an idealizing, a fetishizing, a hypercathexis: an uncritical adoration that is unable or unwilling to admit negative perceptions of its object. The word shares a Latin root with "fatuous," after all. The infatuated person dwells on seemingly minor or undistinguished traits and features, finding them remarkable sources of meaning, significance, and satisfaction. And indeed, one hermeneutic counterpart of such infatuation appears in some deconstructive uses of etymology, in which every identifiable source, nuance, root, branch, and proto-form is taken to "inhabit" a given word while the delimiting effects of any particular context for the word are largely ignored. J. Hillis Miller calls such simultaneous interpenetration of all discoverable meanings in a given word's history an "inexorable law."[53] Claims like this are perhaps what lead Richard Strier to assert – understandably but erroneously – that "a way of reading that sees all semantic possibilities as actual in every context, without regard for what Empson called 'situations,'" is "fundamental to both New Critical and deconstructive poetics."[54] In the present context, however, it is not the idealizing or evaluative dimension of infatuation that is pertinent but the intensity and minuteness of focus and receptivity – a romantic counterpart to what students sometimes term "reading too much into the text." And just as I am frequently skeptical of that last phrase (though not because I think overreading is impossible), I hope to engage in a modest rehabilitation not just of rapt attention to the elements of a text but of the phenomenon of infatuation itself.

If Adorno's critique of abstraction resonates with the very different critiques of Tate and Ransom, his exploration of particularity also recalls their concern with the particulars of the world's body and with the individuality of concrete objects. Much as science for Tate and Ransom dissolves any particular horse into one abstract generality or another, we have seen that society for Adorno reduces particular individuals to "mere examples of the species, identical to one another through isolation within the compulsively controlled collectivity."[55] But his defense of the particular is far from simple. It rests on a critique of Hegelian totalities into which particular contradictory entities are sublated (both annulled and conserved), becoming parts of a larger whole. It is less Hegel himself than the work of the English Hegelians, and of John Dewey, that comes in for the brunt of Adorno's criticism, because they align dialectic with "a sense of proportion, a way of putting things in their correct perspective, plain but obdurate common sense."[56]

What is wrong with proportion, common sense, the large view and the big picture? After all, Adorno concedes, common sense "shares with the dialectic a freedom from dogma, narrow-mindedness and prejudice."[57] The problem is that common sense is a matter of the generally agreed-on, which means that the large and measured view it encourages is likely to lack passion, originality, and evidence of critical or contrary thinking. In fact, "The sense of proportion entails a total obligation to think in terms of the established measures and values."[58] Unlike genuinely dialectical thinking, the large view recommended by common sense harmonizes readily with what is most commonly thought and believed; it is large, but also conventional and therefore respectable. In contrast, genuine dialectic, at its best and most original, sets itself against common sense and widespread belief and appears as a form of passionate unreason until its conflict with what is generally accepted produces a new version of the reasonable and true. For Adorno, "the value of a thought is measured by its distance from the continuity of the familiar."[59] Great thinkers of the past had to "prejudice and falsify the [received] image of the world in order to shake off falsehood and prejudice"; the duty of the authentic dialectician is thus to help the "fool's truth" of authentic and individual thought "to attain its own reasons" – reasons without which "it will certainly succumb to the abyss of the sickness implacably dictated by the healthy common sense of the rest."[60] The project of the genuine discoverer is not to tell the whole truth but to insist passionately on those partial truths that will compel the agonistic but salutary transformation of the current whole truth into something truer.

Such a position helps to clarify the special role that particularity and "partiality" play in Adorno's thinking about art, a role underscored by some of his pithier remarks. Here are the opening words of Simon Jarvis' critical introduction: "Why read Adorno today? Many people probably first encounter Adorno through one of the small group of aphorisms for which he has become famous . . . 'The splinter in your eye is the best magnifying glass.' 'The whole is the false.' "[61] Adorno provocatively reverses a traditional scheme of values, including the priority of whole over part, and wittily reinterprets the visual obstructions of Matthew 7:3 ("And why beholdest thou the mote that is in thy brother's eye, but considerest not the beam that is in thine own eye?") as instruments of more intense seeing. For Jarvis, the ambition of Adorno's aesthetic theory, which is built on such values, is that

> it offers to give a philosophically stringent account of art and of aesthetic judgement and experience. Yet it hopes to do this without losing its immersion in the minutest details of works of art themselves. Indeed, on Adorno's account it can only do this if it does not sacrifice such immersion.[62]

Adorno's championing of the particular and the partial as against the general and the whole, along with his insistence on the unfamiliarity and seeming error of the "fool's truth" the jester is licensed to speak to power, are closely linked to his conception of the difference between knowledge and possession. As Mao puts it, in spite of the absence of much direct interchange between Continental philosophy and Anglo-American criticism in the early part of the century, the Frankfurt School and the New Critics clearly share an intense anxiety about subjectivity's predatory relation toward the object, an anxiety explicitly anti-Hegelian in orientation and grounded in a profound mistrust of the transformations of life occurring in the age of the commodity.[63]

Thus Adorno remarks, for example, that when a love object has become "wholly a possession, the loved person is no longer really looked at... [S]uch possessiveness loses its hold on the object precisely through turning it into an object."[64] In knowledge or in love, the grasp of possession annihilates the being of the object. This can be understood in more than one way. The object itself may be displaced by the satisfaction of possessing it, its ownness giving way to its ownedness, so to speak. Or ownership (literal or figurative) may condemn the object to share the status of possession with other possessions, and thus to surrender its uniqueness to comparability and exchangeability, at which point it becomes, in effect, one commodity among others. Possessiveness, therefore, not only "loses its hold on its object" but also, in a further irony, "forfeits the person whom it debases to 'mine.' "[65]

v Particularity and hermeneutic surprise

From the interpretive or epistemological perspective rather than the affectional-economic, there is another way of considering the relation between knowledge and possession. The possessive reduction of the unique object to one among other exchangeable and comparable objects implies, in the realm of knowledge, a system of similarities, comparabilities, and adequations that links possession with conventional apprehension. The more firmly the object is grasped, the more it looks like other objects and like conventional conceptions of itself. The grasp of possession immobilizes the object, so to speak, and keeps it from disclosing the unique and unsuspected features that distinguish it – features that its freedom and mobility would have allowed it to display. A single pinned butterfly, part of an antiquated museum collection arranged in neat rows and columns, is most readily apprehensible as one among many similar objects, or as a way-station on the road toward abstract butterflyness – not as the unique object it is. Possession, objectification, instrumentality, generality, abstractness, the big picture, common sense – these are different but related forces serving to obscure the objects they claim to reveal. Beneath the familiar and comfortable knownness of ideology, common sense, and "established measures and values," they bury the surprising truths of those objects.[66]

The idea of surprise is important to Adorno's account of truth and *doxa* but also, more particularly, to the critical interpretation of texts. Surprise operates in this latter context not principally as an emotional experience, pleasurable or unpleasurable, but as a methodological or epistemological investment: the possibility that further discovery may inhabit relative settledness of interpretation – may inhabit even the very heart of certainty. This is not to say that New Formalist analysis, or any other kind of analysis, will usher us into the presence of naked otherness, beyond all cultural assumptions and human forms of knowing. But it is to point to a strategy of reading that, in its openness to what formal structures may disclose, encourages those structures to lead us beyond the obvious and familiar, the merely semantic or thematic, the conventionally generic – beyond the insights of an ostensibly open-ended investigation that actually "knows everything beforehand."[67] In one sense, of course, this is a "strategy" pertinent to any inquiry whatsoever – scarcely more than a recommendation to keep an open mind. As Richard Strier sensibly remarks, "By resisting our totalizing impulses and acknowledging where texts offer resistance to us, we gain the possibility of surprise."[68] But the linkage between occasions for surprise and the investigation of specifically *formal* features of a text is more specific, and more particular to the discipline of criticism.

Although even the semantic import of a word or phrase is not something we apprehend immediately, it often seems as though we do because processing the range of a word's dictionary meanings is extremely rapid and conventional – in everyday life, and even in a variety of literary contexts. There are, of course, numerous moments in which the semantic dimension withholds itself and provides a kind of double take, an initial apprehension of the unexceptional followed by a recognition that there is more there than meets the eye. Such withholding frequently occurs through the agency of the pun. Consider these lines from Hart Crane's *The Bridge*:

> How many dawns, chill from his rippling rest
> The seagull's wings shall dip and pivot him,
> Shedding white rings of tumult, building high
> Over the chained bay waters Liberty –

> Then, with inviolate curve, forsake our eyes
> As apparitional as sails that cross
> Some page of figures to be filed away;
> – Till elevators drop us from our day.[69]

It may take some time for us to think about the colors of dawn and thus to hear in that fifth line "within violet curve" as well as "with inviolate curve," the visible words forsaking our eyes as gull and sails forsake the page of figures. Similarly, when Browning's duke hypothetically imagines rebuking his last duchess for her behavior, and adds parenthetically, "and if she let/Herself be lessoned so, nor plainly set/Her wits to yours, forsooth, and made excuse," we may not immediately hear that there is a humiliation in being thus instructed, that to be thus "lessoned" may also entail being "lessened," diminished.

Yet pun is a figure of speech, a formal structure, and not simply a semantic instance. When we encounter formal patterns still further from the purely semantic, their import recedes from immediacy, in part because their range of significance is not largely prescribed beforehand as the sense of both "lesson" and "lessen" is.[70] Except in the vaguest and most general way ("alliteration links words by sound in order to suggest similarity, difference, or another relation between their meanings"), we do not know the meaning of a formal pattern until we have interpreted it in the individual instance. Alliteration, rhyme, hypotaxis, chiasmus, metaphor, and the rest can only signify after being interpreted in themselves and in the particular textual system of which they form a part. Thus there is something distinctly non-immediate about the meanings they carry, since there is almost always a considerable gap between the identification of a figure of speech, say, and an account of how it functions in this or that text. In that sense, the structure of "surprise" is built into the act of interpretation because something different and additionally meaningful emerges from whatever givenness may first seem to attach to a formal feature. This structure of surprise can serve as a model for the larger enterprise of interpretation, since no reading is ever final, however conclusive it may feel at the moment of its realization by the critic. To adapt Jarvis' paraphrase of Adorno, "Works of art do not *assure* us of anything." Rather, "they hold open the possibility of new experience."[71]

The relation of expectation (or knownness) and surprise can be thought of in a variety of ways. T. S. Eliot describes a related phenomenon in the experience of reading. "You don't really criticize any author to whom you have never surrendered yourself," he writes.

Even just the bewildering minute counts; you have to give yourself
up, and then recover yourself, and the third moment is having something to say, before you have wholly forgotten both surrender and
recovery. Of course the self recovered is never the same as the self
before it was given.[72]

Eliot's is a traditional vocabulary of readerly surrender to a text or
author, emphasizing the possibility of acquiring new experience before
one is quite sure what that experience is. As he writes in his essay on
Dante, "genuine poetry can communicate before it is understood."[73]
Both that surrender and that faith in communication acknowledge a
horizon beyond which readerly understanding may advance but which
it has not yet reached – a horizon where the capacity for surprise and
the as yet undisclosed character of what will surprise us meet.

   Central to the New Formalist undertaking, that is to say, is the possibility of surprise as a sustained hermeneutic expectation and a faith in
the significative potential of forms – an attitude caught in these playfully
ambiguous lines of Kevin Davies:

> These cheesy little hypertexts
> are going to get better.
> I don't know
> how *much* better, but *we'll see*.[74]

On the one hand, the lines express confidence that future writers will
supply better versions of the genre "cheesy little hypertexts." But the
deictic immediacy of "these" also implies that these very texts – the
ones before us right now – are going to get better as we read them in
ways that *make* them better. And this process is endless. Like an actual
hypertext, as Catherine Burroughs has remarked, each interpreted poem
generates another on the trajectory toward the ever-receding horizon of
interpretation.[75] The only way toward that horizon leads through formal
analysis. "To read past or through this formal work," as Ellen Rooney
says, "is not to misread but to dismiss reading as such. In such a process,
all of our texts are reduced to banalities, that is, to the already known."[76]

vi   Singularity, realization, and Adorno's "sabbath eyes"

The ideas of surprise (or discovery), formal analysis, non-possessiveness,
and the singularity of any particular text connect in several ways with
Adorno's exploration of parts and partiality. For one thing, Rooney's

distinction between formally grounded reading and the mere produc-tion of "the already known" can remind us that the relation of formal features to the overall meaning of a text is something like the relation of parts to whole in Adorno's aesthetic theory. What Adorno terms "this passing-on and being unable to linger, this tacit assent to the primacy of the general over the particular," also describes the impatience of many readers to justify their analysis of textual particulars by moving quickly to a thematic paraphrase of the text as a whole. Moreover, "lingering" is a somewhat restrained term for the activity of minute concentration on particularity that Adorno regularly endorses, and that I want to inflect in the direction of New Formalist analysis. It is more like a conscious and non-pathological fetishizing of parts – a kind of Vaihingerian heuristic fiction in which we adopt what "appear to be consciously false assump-tions . . . but which are intentionally thus formed in order to overcome difficulties of thought . . . and reach the goal . . . by roundabout ways and bypaths."[77]

This temporary muting of wholeness and of context(s) in order to bring to the object of analysis a maximally heightened attention recalls what Jarvis terms the "immersion in the minutest details of works of art" that for Adorno was the condition of arriving at "a philosophically stringent account of art and of aesthetic judgement and experience."[78] In the case of New Formalist interpretation, such immersion attempts to free the object from its encrusted familiarity, its interpretive history, its customariness – from what I. A. Richards calls "stock responses" and Adorno "ready-made judgments."[79] It attempts this in order to bring each textual element – and finally, the text – into fullest being, to help it to a fulfillment of form and meaning: to *realize* it as a theater director realizes a play's text by interpreting it into stage life and existence. The goal is to allow text and critic to produce between them a significant encounter, inevitably historically shaped, that will prove critically, tex-tually, and culturally enriching. Maximally heightened attention in the service of maximal realization.[80]

To attend to one or another textual element in this way can, of course, seem unfair, partial in both senses, even if the tacit promise to ultimately reinsert or recontextualize the interpreted element is always penum-brally present. Adorno himself calls such attention a form of injustice, though he clearly regards it as ultimately a salutary practice:

> One might almost say that truth itself depends on the tempo, the patience and perseverance of lingering with the particular: what passes beyond it [the particular] without having first entirely lost

itself, what proceeds to judge without having first been guilty of *the injustice of contemplation*, loses itself at last in emptiness.[81]

Elsewhere, he finds the general in the particular rather than the reverse, and finds it there only by resolutely not looking elsewhere: "Knowledge can only widen horizons by abiding so insistently with the particular that its isolation is dispelled."[82] Or, "The universality of beauty can communicate itself to the subject in no other way than in obsession with the particular."[83] The link between an intent focus on particularity and the possibility of an authentic grasp of the general or universal – the belief, in Roger Foster's words, that "The route to the truth about the social totality must go through the experiencing subject, in the strong sense that it is in the core of what is most 'subjective' that the interpretive key for unlocking the objective world is to be found" – appears in negative form in this mordant remark from earlier in Adorno's text: "the individual as individual, in *representing* the species of man, has lost the autonomy through which he might *realize* the species."[84]

What is true of the particular's relation to the general is also true of a whole artwork's relation to the galaxy of other artworks. Indeed, Adorno's language here intensifies. Speaking of the persistent effort to evaluate, rank, and thus compare artworks, despite their "noncomparability," he insists that the works themselves "refuse to be compared." Instead, "they want to annihilate each other, … each the mortal enemy of each."[85] He elaborates:

> For if the Idea of beauty appears only in dispersed form among many works, each one nevertheless aims uncompromisingly to express the whole of beauty, claims it in its singularity, and can never admit its dispersal without annulling itself. Beauty … manifests itself not in the synthesis of all works … but only as a physical reality: in the downfall of art itself. This downfall is the goal of every work of art, in that it seeks to bring death to all others.[86]

This *agon* between artworks doubtless expresses the "desire" of art, in Adorno's view, to reach a point at which it can bring itself to an end as no longer necessary because the truth of the world has become adequate and art's critical function is no longer required – a function that is performed on the world, but also on other artworks: "The truth content of artworks is fused with their critical content. That is why works are also critics of one another."[87] And doubtless, despite his insistence that "works refuse to be compared," the very *agon* that Adorno envisions requires – if not comparability – something short of absolute mutual alterity if there is to be conflict at all. Linguistic usage itself suggests as much. A military battle is an "engagement"; even bitter and irreconcilable enemies "join" battle. And indeed, *agon* in the sense of "combat" derives from a Greek word for a gathering or assembly, a shared location – like the site of public games – where such combat can take place.[88] And yet, Adorno not only insists on the particularity and non-comparability of works of art; he also studiously interweaves the vocabularies of the particular and the singular with the vocabularies of *agon* and annihilation.

This mingling of vocabularies suggests, I think, that a work's incomparable singularity and particularity are somehow closely linked with its toxicity to other, competing works. Thus, instead of happily taking its place in an array or culture-museum of similar objects ("Like many Modernist monologues, *The Love Song of J. Alfred Prufrock . . .*"), each work really wants to claim such a degree of singularity, of non-comparability and non-fungibility, that it in effect creates an aura in which other works are unable to survive, as human organisms cannot survive on a planet with an atmosphere of pure methane. The implicit claims of any given work, its particularities of form and meaning, the ideas of beauty and much more that it tacitly endorses and exemplifies, far from being "harmonizable" with other works and their singularities, actually wish to seize all the territory, invalidate every other work, and thereby also undo the very idea of comparability.

This is not a rivalry of Bloomian so-called Strong Poets but of the artworks themselves. It entails imagining that, say, *The Dunciad,* "Tintern Abbey," and "My Last Duchess" are each so singularly and particularly what they are that any one of them is in some sense the denial, the artistic or ontological assassin, of the others. Each threatens to annihilate the others not so much out of competition in the traditional sense but because each so thoroughly exudes and enacts its own singularity that it leaves no place for the others to be – even, perhaps, to be thinkable. To the New Formalist critic, that singularity can only become fully visible when a text is sedulously, if provisionally, abstracted from the galaxy of other texts that surround it. As soon as one says, for example, that Pope's and Browning's poems are in some sense both satires, or that the speakers of "Tintern Abbey" and "My Last Duchess" both invoke the past, the truth of the comparisons is bought at the expense of the particular identity of each work. A text entered into or inhabited so assiduously, even obsessively, forestalls – or at least postpones – not only the particular-subsuming claims of Hegelian or other wholes but even the simple and reasonable fairness of a remark like "Surely there are *other* good dramatic monologues by Browning."

Paradoxically, a benign, even fetishistic, attention to the part(s) is the condition of fullest textual realization of the whole – even though concern with the whole must be muted, bracketed, temporarily obscured if the part is to get its full interpretive and significative due. It might seem that a mechanism of idealization is at work, threatening to enshrine this chiasmus or allusion, or that pattern of metaphors or apostrophes or verb tenses, as an impossibly rich bearer of impossibly valuable meanings. But that is not the case. Such heightened attention as I am describing does not also entail an attribution of goodness or even a conferring of value at all. Even if one shares Walter J. Ong's belief – that "[a]nything that bids for attention in an act of contemplation is a surrogate for a person. In proportion as the work of art is capable of being taken in full seriousness, it moves further and further along an asymptote to the curve of personality." – it is imperative to note that Ong doesn't say the work of art approaches the status of a good or admirable or even pleasant personality.[89] He is paying it an ontological tribute, not one of approval or admiration. Admittedly, both romantic or other forms of idealization and the heightened textual attention I associate with New Formalist criticism are in some sense "not normal" – unjust, in Adorno's vocabulary. But they are qualitatively different in the kind of homage they pay to their respective objects. Idealization insists on the rarity, superiority, and excellence (all comparative terms) of its object; heightened textual attention insists on its *haecceitas* or thisness, its ontological and significative particularity and density.

In the sphere of love rather than textuality, Troy A. Jollimore offers a similar distinction. "Loving a person," he argues, "constitutes a specifically *moral* way of seeing, insofar as it is an attempt to recognize a person in her full individuality and involves a kind of generous attention."[90] To "recognize...full individuality" and to pay "generous attention" amounts to trying to realize the being and actuality of the object, but not necessarily idealizing or even approving. When Jollimore turns to works of art, he is perhaps more explicit, saying that such an effort "does not guarantee that we will end up liking the work..."[91] Adorno's notion of "sabbath eyes" illuminates the concept of generous attention from a different perspective. Here is a central passage:

> In so far as the existent is accepted, in its one-sidedness, for what it is, its one-sidedness is comprehended as its being [or its "essence"], and reconciled. The eyes that lose themselves to the one and only beauty

are sabbath eyes. They save in their object something of the calm of its day of creation.[92]

To see with sabbath eyes is to see the particularity of "the existent," and to see it in virtual isolation – in its one-sidedness understood as its being.[93] Again, such seeing or attention brings to the object a patient realization and an affirmation that are not the same as an evaluative liking or admiration, though this affirmation, as Harold Schweizer notes, echoes the approval expressed in the account of creation in Genesis:

> The sabbath eyes not only attend to the object in its essential justifi-cation, the sabbath eyes also survey the work of creation at the end of the Creator's week, on the threshold of time.... What the sabbath eyes see is "good" – for they see as if with the Creator's eyes at the beginning of time. "And God saw that it was good" we read at the end of each day in the Book of Genesis. Likewise, the sabbath eyes that rest on their object attend to the completeness and justness and legit-imacy of that object.... The aesthetic acknowledgment is, or reveals, the day of the creation of the object, that is to say its singularity and particularity.[94]

Schweizer's vocabulary avoids simple appreciation or admiration and instead builds on a more ontological set of terms: "justification," but also "completeness," "justness," "legitimacy," "singularity," "particular-ity." For a text or other cultural object, of course, an essential dimension of its being is its significative or semiotic potential, the range of meaning and kinds of meaning that only a diligent "lingering with the particular" can realize.

vii   Textual infatuation, true infatuation

Let's explore a little further this specialized mode of infatuation that does not so much idealize as painstakingly realize its object. Here is another key sentence from the "sabbath eyes" section of *Minima Moralia*. The gaze capable of attaining beauty, says Adorno, must cultivate indif-ference, even contempt, for anything outside the object on which it focuses, for "it is only infatuation, the unjust disregard for the claims of every existing thing, that does justice to what exists."[95] Perhaps the best context for thinking about such infatuation is not the traditional valorization of "an evenhanded account" but something like the adver-sary system of justice. Here, the prosecution and defense each offer an intentionally one-sided argument, though presumably conducted with some respect for the truth, and a third party (judge, jury) is required to make an impartial assessment of the competing arguments in order to render a decision. A variation on this process is the Roman Catholic procedure for beatification and canonization, in which the Devil's Advocate is charged to make the most energetic and persuasive case possible against the candidate – presumably, in order to ensure as rigorous an examination of the facts as possible and thus to indemnify the conferring of sainthood against as much error or inattention or laxity as possible.[96]

If the adversary process of law operates under the binary innocence/guilt, and that of canonization under that of sanctity/impurity, a New Formalist adaptation of the sabbath eyes perspective is governed by oppositions such as generality/particularity, or inattention/attention, or dismissal/realization. This is as true in the romantic-affectional sphere as in the textual. And just as Adorno insists on the inappropriateness (to say no more) of a comparative evaluative perspective – "the non-comparability of works of art"[97] – so is it with human objects of love or adoration. "What matters," writes Jollimore,

> is not that one's beloved is unique, but that one's way of seeing picks him out *uniquely*, which means making him the subject of a special level of attention that is not directed toward others, and appreciating his value as a human individual in a way that does not involve a neutral comparison of his various valuable properties with those of other individuals – not even with individuals whom one might have come to love instead had circumstances been different.[98]

Thus when a long-married man says something like, "In my eyes, Marge is the only woman in the world," he is claiming not that he has discovered the sole and unique love object possible for him in the habitable world, nor that Marge is objectively the best woman in the world and thus simply a rational choice as a love object, but that his way of seeing her is not comparative at all – even though, if pressed, he could probably answer questions about whether Marge is more or less philosophical than Nancy, more or less witty than Gloria, more or less charitable than Annette. The particular combination of attention and investment that one brings to the object – call it "cognition through cathexis" – is not a matter of ranking relative to others, nor of cool and skeptical detachment, nor of projection – wishful or otherwise. Indeed, what is "bestowed" on the object, in Jollimore's words, "is not the value itself – again, presumably that was there all along – but rather the sort of close, generous, and imaginative attention that allows valuable features of this sort fully to reveal themselves."[99]

Clearly, we are speaking of more than one mode of infatuation. The first or traditional notion – the one relying on the link with "fatuous" – understands infatuation as a combination of obsession, idealization, and uncritical admiration. It is incontestably comparative and evaluative, and it seeks both to aggrandize the object and to attach the self powerfully to it. In fact, given the significant role that projection can play in such idealization, it is not clear that aggrandizement and attachment can be very sharply distinguished. The blindness or bedazzlement of this form of infatuation – blindness both to the actuality of the principal object and to much besides that object – is caught in the word translated as "infatuation" in the Adorno passage quoted a little earlier: "infatuation, the unjust disregard for the claims of every existing thing." The original German sentence is, "Und es ist einzig die *Verblendung*, das ungerechte Verschließen des Blicks gegen den Anspruch, den alles Daseiende erhebt, wodurch dem Daseienden Gerechtigkeit widerfährt."[100] The word "Verblendung," in common parlance, signifies blindness, dazzlement, delusion – in short, garden-variety infatuation.

In the context of Adorno's sentence, however, it is clear that he is commandeering its traditional semantic charge so as to take it in quite another direction, much as we have seen him transform a Biblical reproof into a redefinition of proper sight, or insight: "The splinter in your eye is the best magnifying glass."[101] Here we move toward a second mode of infatuation, far from the beaten track of the first – a mode that begins to approach the form of knowledge named in Jollimore's title: *Love's Vision*. Jollimore is writing about love, not infatuation, yet his account of the epistemic modalities of love has significant overlaps with the essential characteristics of this second form of infatuation. There is his central claim "not merely that love alters one's way of seeing but that love itself *is*, in large part, a way of seeing – a way of seeing one's beloved, and also a way of seeing the world"; his defense of emotionally invested seeing and knowing as against a widespread and infrequently questioned norm of cool analytic distance or "disinterested concern"; his linking of "love's vision" with a full and generous realization of the object – indeed, he terms it "a specifically *moral* way of seeing, insofar as it is an attempt to recognize a person in her full individuality and involves a kind of generous attention"; and his extending of such attention to cultural objects and artworks like literary texts since

> What is necessary for appreciating most poetry is precisely *not* a state of detachment but a state of engagement. Being open and engaged in the relevant sense is a matter of...approaching the work as if one already believed that there is something of value to be obtained – or, at the very least, as if one already believes it likely that this is so.[102]

This last is not so much a positive presumption of the work's meaning or significance or value as a way to head off the sort of dismissive pre-judgment that would foreclose the possibility of discovering what the work actually has to offer. The heuristic fiction that the work carries meaning and value can always be countered by the work's finally failing to match up to such expectations, after sustained attention and analysis. The "generous attention" Jollimore describes is an ethical as well as an interpretive stance since – in the realm of persons – it remains open to the full realization of the object. But much the same is true of literary texts and other artworks as well. Along with Miller's idea of an ethics of reading – "the moral necessity to submit in one way or another...to...the power of the words of the text over the mind and words of the reader" – there is a second ethical imperative: to allow the text to perform or accomplish itself maximally so that the power of which Miller speaks can reach readers in the fullest, most nuanced, and most profoundly realized fashion.[103]

This second sort of hyperattentive realization – whether of persons or of texts – has been termed "true infatuation," a phrase that wittily and economically attempts to cross the divide between the conventionally opposed categories of "true love" and "mere infatuation." It is not a simple reversal of binary values, elevating infatuation over love, nor exactly a deconstruction of that binary. Like Adorno's at times dizzying revisions of conventional relations between general and particular, or just and unjust ("it is only infatuation, the unjust disregard for the claims of every existing thing, that does justice to what exists"), "true infatuation" calls attention at once to the limitations of the conventionally privileged concept, and to the hidden powers of the conventionally inferior one, and thus troubles the tidiness of the opposition between them. As a coinage and a solecism, the phrase detaches itself from both common usage and a normative hierarchy of value in attempting to name an as-yet-emergent category – a category important to the development of a contemporary critical practice such as New Formalism, and secondarily to a contemporary erotics.[104]

viii   Wholeness, paraphrase, and "the injustice of contemplation"

The argument, then, is that there is a cognitive gain or hermeneutic payoff in the effort to cultivate a benign form of infatuation enabled by an insistence on moving from parts to wholes as slowly as one reasonably can. In both textual and romantic forms of infatuation, moreover, a form of hypertrophied attention can enable a fuller – and truer – realization of the "object" than would otherwise be possible. In a sense, I have tried to rehabilitate two parallel modes of unseemly attentiveness and absorption – overreading and infatuation – by dividing each internally into a fantasmatic or ungrounded and a realistic or grounded ("true") form of interpretation. Most narrowly, this means situating New Formalist critical attention in a larger interpretive, epistemological, and ethical context concerned not with comparisons and evaluative hierarchies but with an apprehension of otherness patient and inventive enough to be adequate to its object.

But there is no reason, in principle, to limit context to the formalist interpretation of texts and the epistemic dimension of romantic infatuation. That juxtaposition suggests a much more general claim about knowledge, interpretation, analysis, and the realization of objects of attention, a claim that can extend to virtually any field of investigation in which sharpness of focus on the object at hand, and the strategic deferral of concern with larger contexts or "the big picture," make for productive ventures of knowing. The scientific and social valorization of what is termed "basic research," for example – research that seeks to expand or refine knowledge without concern for practical applications or goals beyond the improvement of knowledge itself – points to another, extensive area in which not being concerned with what the object might be good for, or what contexts it might be placed in, enables valuable investigation precisely *because* that investigation is not conducted within a holistically or teleologically limiting frame of conceptualization and interpretation.[105] Whether the "object" is a person, a text, a physical phenomenon undergoing scientific scrutiny, a complex of persons, objects, and events subject to legal or criminal or medical investigation, or something else entirely, the common thread involves patient attention to that object in the interests of enabling its fullest realization.

The pertinent distinction can also be formulated as a contrast between the act of interpreting and an achieved interpretation. To envision the whole one is studying is to proceed from interpreting to an interpretation, from poring over textual or other phenomena to coming to a decision about their significance – in short, it is to move from the object to its meaning. If the text or the interpreter allows this movement to be made facilely or quickly, the character of the object tends to dissolve in what it is taken to signify – in its paraphrase or name or label. As Roland Barthes remarks in *The Responsibility of Forms*, "form is what is *between* the thing and its name, form is what delays the name."[106] Without such a salutary "between" or delay, we are likely to have the meaning but miss the experience (to misquote Eliot). "Perhaps," says Angela Leighton,

> it is the way we write our critical paraphrases that needs reformulation. It may be that we should ask, not "what is the poem about?" but "how is the poem discovering?" In other words, how does the poem reorganize the very ways in which we might discover it? How does literature take us on a pilgrimage of paraphrase? – an invitation to a voyage of thinking which may give us nothing very much to take away as final thoughts, as final meaning, but which sets us constantly re-hearing, re-discovering, re-making the sense. So paraphrase as a noun, a "what are your poems about?" may be a heresy. But paraphrasing, as a verb or participle, attending to how a poem goes about its business, might still offer a way to think about the activity we call literary interpretation.[107]

The New Formalist analysis I am describing, then, works to keep a text textual, a verbal phenomenon or unfolding rather than a fixed repository of meaning, whether for a short or a long time. Derek Attridge proposes "that we think of the literary text not as an object possessing meaning or meanings but as an *act of signification*," a remark that may recall Adorno's assertion that the crux of a (philosophic) text "is what happened in it, not a thesis or a position, the texture, not the deductive or inductive course of one-track minds."[108]

This is not to contend that interpretation of a particular text should never cease lest it lose its dynamic object to the abstractness of static meaning, but it is to venture several more limited claims. First, the meaning of a whole text – as that meaning is given verbal formulation by a reader or critic – is not just a thematic formulation that replaces the act of interpreting but also, however accurate on its own terms, an impoverishment of the text it characterizes. It is an impoverishment because it is inevitably a reduction of the work's complexity – "Robert Frost's 'The Most of It' is about the fortuitous glimpsing of the otherness that lies beyond the customary boundary of human consciousness" – as well as a translation of it into the mode of thematic paraphrase. And it is at times a methodological impoverishment because, traditionally as well as rhetorically, it can imply that such thematic paraphrase is the end toward which interpretation strives, or ought to strive, instead of a springboard to – or a reminder of – an adequate act of interpretation. For these reasons, a summary statement of the whole meaning of a text is not a particularly important interpretive goal, though it may be a short-hand essential for mnemonic, classificatory, or other purposes, and for channeling critical analysis of a particular text in a fresh direction.

Second, it is probably not a good idea to separate a text too sharply from a statement or paraphrase of its meaning. Like an athletic team's name or logo on a uniform, a paraphrase is a kind of shorthand allusion, a gesture toward an object that it can indicate but not fully capture or embody. Beyond its usefulness in processes such as sorting or distinguishing or aligning, such a statement functions as a kind of promissory note that is formally distinct from but necessarily connected to what it designates. Thus a thematic paraphrase like the bald account of Frost's "The Most of It" offered above, beyond its possible role in efforts of classification and summary, is perhaps most useful as one half of a stereoscopic vision that simultaneously considers the poem itself. The paraphrase functions as a trigger or stimulus whose secondary purpose is to characterize the object (here, the poem) in a certain way but whose primary function is to evoke the text of the poem itself, the verbal object. The resulting juxtaposition of two texts of differing rhetorical and ontological status, each in some sense a necessary accompaniment of the other, can recall Kant's remark that "neither concepts without an intuition corresponding to them in some way nor intuition without concepts can yield any real knowledge ... *Thoughts without contents are empty, intuitions without concepts are blind.*"[109] Thus if a paraphrase of a whole text is considerably less significant than the patient realization of its parts, that paraphrase is nonetheless indispensable, serving the role of "concept" to the actual interpreted text's "intuitions."

And here, of course, we come up against one of the limits of the sort of textual infatuation I have been describing: the potential triviality of an endless and underconceptualized attending to parts. Put another way, however assiduously attention to the textual whole is deferred, it must be reinvoked at some point or – perhaps more important – allowed to remain, penumbrally and *almost* invisibly, at the margins of the focused analysis from which it has been all but banished.[110] Completely uncentered atomistic analysis cannot serve as the basis for a critical stance – New Formalist or otherwise. We must at last experience a return of the (not repressed but) suspended concern with the whole, if only so that we can grasp what thing – and what kind of thing – this text is as opposed to other texts. Of course, there can be many characterizations of the "whole" of any given single text. Wimsatt's paraphrase of Aristotle, cited earlier, is pertinent here: "If a thing is a thing at all, it's a certain *kind* of thing." In fact, a single text of any complexity may plausibly be construed as many kinds of thing, whether those construals take the form of thematic paraphrase, or traditional generic classification, or the inferring of a singular, individualized textual identity such as Donoghue proposes when he urges "concern for the particularity of form in every work of art."[111] What we cannot have is a textual whole that is no kind of whole, any more than we can have a textual whole that is purely an aggregate of unrelated parts.

Thus if the analysis of textual elements constitutes the majority of the work of interpretation, that fact does not finally obviate the need for some meaningful sense of textual unity, textual wholeness. There is a real – though limited – place in New Formalisms for active concern with the whole, the general, the paraphrasable, and for the idea of the "whole text" or unity as a regulative fiction – something that can inaugurate and thus govern analysis but that is held in abeyance and subordinated to the multiform realization of the parts that constitute it. How that unity is to be approached, however, is a central methodological question. Adorno's admonition concerning the truth of a desirable wholeness, and the paradox of interpretive justice through injustice, can stand as a fitting and monitory conclusion to this discussion:

> One might almost say that truth itself depends on the tempo, the patience and perseverance of lingering with the particular: what passes beyond it [the particular] without having first entirely lost itself, what proceeds to judge without having first been guilty of the injustice of contemplation, loses itself at last in emptiness.[112]

However this imperative is negotiated in any given instance of critical practice, the central interpretive work of fully realizing the elements of those wholes is a mode of textual infatuation and an essential feature of the New Formalisms I have attempted to describe, theorize, illustrate, and advocate.

Coda: New Formalisms

As noted in the Introduction, the label "New Formalism" in this study (like "New Formalist") has no connection with the movement in American poetry of the same name – a movement Susan Wolfson tartly characterizes as "a Reagan-80s school of American poetry, with a formalist agenda that was reactionary, politically and poetically."[1] The possibility of mistakenly allying current formalist criticism with that poetic school is only one of Wolfson's objections to the term. Like some other critics, she also hears in "New Formalism" the implication that attention to form had virtually disappeared from criticism until bravely resurrected by a few contemporary stalwarts. But in fact, as she notes, there have never *not* been literary students attentive to form, however marginalized they may have been – or been made to feel – by such phenomena as the rise of politically engaged, largely thematic critical writing, particularly during the 1980s and after. From this perspective, a label like "New Formalist" obliquely denigrates those who have been practicing formalism all along. Yet it is nonetheless the case that a number of modern critical trends or schools, quite different from one another, may arguably claim the label "formalist": Russian Formalism, the art criticism of Roger Fry, the French tradition of *explication de texte*, New Criticism, Deconstruction, New Historicism (at times), and more. In consequence, it seems reasonable to understand "New Formalism" and "New Formalist" as distinguishing descriptive labels rather than self-congratulatory rallying cries, and that is how I have used them here.

For some other critics, a label like "New Formalism" implies a degree of methodological unity, or a theoretical consensus, or a doctrinaire rigidity, or a defined repertoire of interpretive "moves" that the diversity and heterogeneity of actual New Formalist critical practice do not support. Yet one of the distinguishing features of formalist critical efforts after the New Criticism has been precisely their willingness to ally an unwavering methodological commitment – what Hartman terms a method "of revealing the human content of art by a study of its formal properties" – with the diverse emphases, concerns, modes of analysis, and investments of a broad array of critical schools, many of them scarcely formalist at all.[2] As this study has tried to demonstrate, those alliances have linked New Formalisms, in various ways and configurations, to deconstruction, New (and older) Historicism, ideological criticism, Jamesonian and other Marxisms, colonial and postcolonial studies, contemporary aesthetics, queer theory, ecocriticism, and more. Typically, New Formalists have attempted neither to subsume those disciplines and their attendant commitments in a quasi-imperialist master discourse of formalism, nor to dutifully offer up New Formalist readings to them – to provide, for example, mere "raw materials that can be manufactured into the goods of political analysis," as Dubrow puts it.[3] Rather, they have explored and adapted the assumptions, concerns, and interpretive strategies of those schools while maintaining a primary commitment to what Garrett Stewart terms "the formalist imperative" – namely, "to read what is written as a form (and formation) of meaning."[4] It is not, then, internal homogeneity or the dogged replication of a few foundational interpretive moves that authorizes the use of "New Formalist" and "New Formalism" as useful labels but persistent fidelity to something like Stewart's very general "formalist imperative" combined with an exploration of a broad range of specific critical procedures and interests.

Among the most important things that New Formalism brings to those largely non-formalist practices – and not always in the same way – is a salutary resistance of the impulse to move too hastily from text to context, or from readerly present to textual and cultural history, or from work to world, or from work to self (the reader or humanity in general), or from literary study to political praxis and activism. Michael P. Clark finds such haste, for example, in "the new cultural criticism," which "identified literary analysis with political action to such an extent that the critic was portrayed as the modern avatar of Sir Philip Sidney's soldier-poet."[5] Peter Brooks seeks resistance to identifications like these in a stringent self-discipline, a "self-imposition of the formalist *askesis*," and asserts that "this alone can assure the critic that the act of interpretation has been submitted to an otherness," a formal and textual otherness that inhibits easy assimilation of the text either to the desires of the self or the structures of the world, simple identification or naive application.[6] Whether allied with contemporary aesthetics, ideology critique, gender studies, ecocriticism, or other forms of interpretation, the formalist imperative or *askesis* resists the slide from textual analysis and respect for forms either to a text-dissolving fixation on content and reference or, alternatively, to a frequently fantasmatic identification of textual or cultural analysis with the readerly psyche or with political activism and other modes of real-world activity.

New Formalisms enact such resistance in a variety of ways, but in each case, they work to maintain distinctions between work and world, the textual and the historical. They may do so by sheer attention to the textual and linguistic surface of the work, insisting on its mediation and on the need to look *at* the language we are tempted to look *through* – more precisely, on the need to look *at* the language of the text in order to see the world it gives us rather than a projected world produced by eliding that language. Or they may re-theorize the operations of reference to avoid ignoring the textual generation or construction of what is presented as a pre-existent reality. Or they may understand the reading process as an activity not of simple identification or simple repudiation but a provisional entertainment of attitudes, postures, ways of feeling and thinking, virtual selves that can allow readers to enlarge their possible ways of being rather than – or before – committing themselves to existential actualities.

This last process is related to what Frye has called the construction of "possible models of human experience" through the "power of detachment in the imagination," a detachment made available because, in the study of literature, "things are removed just out of reach of belief and action."[7] Such detachment is exactly not the unworldly, "purely aesthetic," history-denying, and politically conservative or quietist stance so often misattributed to New Critical and other formalist undertakings by critics who take literature and criticism to be direct calls to political action or, worse, forms of political action themselves. It is, rather, an effort to avoid sacrificing the work to the world, or the reverse – an effort to value and respect what Clark terms "the unique vision literature affords for readers able to tell the difference between the work and the world, and able to read *what the work tells us* about the world in that difference."[8] For the text to bear on the world, it must remain distinct from – rather than merged with – that world. St. Augustine expresses this relationship between reality and representation by making use of the vocabulary of truth (reality) and falseness (representation). He finds it "marvelous" that

> things are in certain aspects true, by this very thing that they are in certain aspects false, and that for their quality of truth this alone avails them, that they are false in another regard.... How would a

picture, for instance, be a true picture, unless it were a false horse? or how could there be in a mirror a true image of a man, if it were not a false man? Wherefore, if it avails some things that they be somewhat false in order that they be somewhat true; why do we so greatly dread falsity, and seek truth as the greatest good?[9]

A text cannot represent the world unless it is not the world – unless, that is, it is a text; its work of representation depends on its refusal to be the object of representation. Similarly, its capacity to mean depends precisely on its ontological difference from those meanings it may support and enable. A text without meanings is unintelligible, but – equally – a meaning without a text is inconceivable. One reductive but not inaccurate way of describing the principal task of New Formalist criticism, then, is to say that it insists on the textual identity of texts. Early in this study, I cited Paul Valéry's contention that "A bad poem is one that vanishes into meaning."[10] It may be appropriate to conclude by extending Valéry's remark from poetry to literary criticism, for if New Formalism has a single guiding motto, it is that only an adequately formalist criticism can keep a poem – or any text – from thus vanishing.

Notes

Introduction

1. The quotation first appeared in Paul de Man, "Semiology and Rhetoric," *Diacritics*, 3:3 (Autumn, 1973), 27, and then in *Allegories of Reading: Figural Language in Rousseau, Nietzsche, Rilke, and Proust* (New Haven and London: Yale Univ. Press, 1979), 3.
2. W. J. T. Mitchell, "The Commitment to Form; Or, Still Crazy after All These Years," *PMLA* 118:2 (Mar., 2003), 323.
3. Caroline Levine, "Scaled Up, Writ Small: A Response to Carolyn Dever and Herbert F. Tucker," *Victorian Studies*, 49:1 (autumn 2006), 100.
4. Heather Dubrow, "Foreword" to Verena Theile and Linda Tredennick, eds., *New Formalisms and Literary Theory* (Basingstoke, England: Palgrave Macmillan, 2013), vii, ix.
5. Herbert F. Tucker, "Tactical Formalism: A Response to Caroline Levine," *Victorian Studies*, 49:1 (autumn 2006), 86.
6. Ellen Rooney, "Form and Contentment," in *Reading for Form*, ed. Susan J. Wolfson and Marshall Brown (Seattle and London: Univ. of Washington Press, 2006), 37, 8.
7. Marjorie Levinson, "What Is New Formalism?" *PMLA*, 122 (2007), 561. The embedded quotation is from Mark David Rasmussen, "Introduction: New Formalisms," in *Renaissance Literature and Its Formal Engagements*, ed. Mark David Rasmussen (New York: Palgrave, 2002), 1.
8. Richard Strier, "How Formalism Became a Dirty Word, and Why We Can't Do Without It" in ed. Rasmussen, *Renaissance Literature and Its Formal Engagements*, 213. And compare Stephen Cohen, "Between Form and Culture: New Historicism and the promise of a Historical Formalism," in ed. Rasmussen, 33: "new historicism ... has been less successful at theorizing ... the *transformation visited upon extraliterary materials* before they are recirculated by performance or publication to act upon the culture at large," my emphasis.
9. Rooney, "Form and Contentment," 34, 35.
10. The terms "New Formalism," "New Formalist," and the like, in the context of the present study, have no connection with the late twentieth-century movement in American poetry usually called "New Formalism." For the latter, see Roland Greene, editor in chief, *The Princeton Encyclopedia of Poetry and Poetics*, 4th ed. (Princeton and Oxford: Princeton University Press, 2012, s.v. "New Formalism."
11. Samuel Otter, "An Aesthetics in All Things," *Representations*, 104:1 (Fall 2008), 116.
12. Hartman, "Beyond Formalism," 45.
13. Frye, *Anatomy of Criticism*, 345–6.

14. Hans Vaihinger, *The Philosophy of "As If,"* trans. C. K. Ogden, 2d. ed. (London: Routledge & Kegan Paul, 1935).
15. Charles Altieri, "What Theory Can Learn from New Directions in Contemporary American Poetry," *New Literary History*, 43:1 (Winter 2012), 85.
16. William J. Spurlin, "Afterword: An Interview with Cleanth Brooks," in *The New Criticism and Contemporary Literary Theory*, ed. William J. Spurlin and Michael Fischer (New York: Garland, 1995), 367–8.
17. See Michael Fried, *Roger Fry's Formalism*, 6–7, 11. http://www.tannerlectures.utah.edu/lectures/documents/volume24/fried_2001.pdf
18. See Cleanth Brooks and Robert Penn Warren, *Understanding Poetry: An Anthology for College Students*, rev. ed. (New York: Henry Holt and Co., 1953), 686–7, s.v. "form."
19. Barbara Johnson, *The Critical Difference: Essays in the Contemporary Rhetoric of Reading* (Baltimore: Johns Hopkins Univ. Press, 1980), 5; Alan Liu, "The Power of Formalism: The New Historicism," *ELH* 56:4 (1989), 721–71.
20. Geoffrey Hartman, *Beyond Formalism: Literary Essays 1958–1970* (New Haven and London: Yale UP, 1970), 42.
21. Denis Donoghue, *Walter Pater: Lover of Strange Souls* (N.Y.: Knopf, 1995), 288. Donoghue, *Speaking of Beauty* (New Haven & London Yale UP, 2003), 121. Both cited in Angela Leighton, *On Form: Poetry, Aestheticism, and the Legacy of a Word* (Oxford & New York: OUP, 2007), 23.
22. Ellen Rooney, "Form and Contentment," in *Reading for Form*, ed. Susan J. Wolfson and Marshall Brown (Seattle and London: Univ. of Washington Press, 2006), 46.
23. Angela Leighton, *On Form: Poetry, Aestheticism, and the Legacy of a Word* (Oxford & New York: OUP, 2007), 18. Focillon's book first appeared as *Vie des Formes* (Paris: Ernst Leroux, 1934).
24. Among the figures sometimes identified as New Critics (apart from Brooks, Warren, Ransom, Tate, and Wimsatt) – several with fairly tenuous links to the undertaking – are René Wellek, Yvor Winters, R. P. Blackmur, F. R. Leavis, and Kenneth Burke.
25. Robert Kaufman, "Everybody Hates Kant: Blakean Formalism and the Symmetries of Laura Moriarty," *MLQ* 61:1 (March 2000), 147–8, 155.
26. Theodor Adorno, *Minima Moralia: Reflections from Damaged Life*, tr. E. F. N. Jephcott (London & New York: Verso, 2005), 77.
27. Susan Wolfson, *Formal Charges: The Shaping of Poetry in British Romanticism* (Stanford: Stanford UP, 1997), 3, 30.
28. The vast majority of the literary analyses in this book focus on poetry, mainly because of the sharp focus and economy of exposition that a short poem makes possible. In principle, though, the critical assumptions, methods, and "moves" employed are largely applicable to long poems, to drama, to fiction, and to other forms of literary prose as well.
29. See Michael Barany, "Mathematical Ideality and the Practice of Translation," and "The Proof is in the Putting: Testimony, Belief, and Why Mathematicians Make Bad Witnesses," unpublished papers, used by kind permission of the author. See also Michael Barany and Donald MacKenzie, "Chalk: Materials and Concepts in Mathematics Research," under revision for *New Representation in Scientific Practice*, Catelijne Coopmans, Michael Lynch, Janet Vertesi, and Steve Woolgar, eds. (forthcoming, MIT Press).

30. Adorno, *Minima Moralia*, 74.
31. John Crowe Ransom, *The New Criticism* (Norfolk, CT: New Directions, 1941), 281.
32. William K. Wimsatt, Jr. and Cleanth Brooks, *Literary Criticism: A Short History* (New York: Knopf, 1957), 507.
33. Douglas Mao, "The New Critics and the Text-Object," *ELH* 63.1 (1996), 231.
34. Simon Jarvis, *Adorno: A Critical Introduction* (Cambridge: Polity Press, 1998), 91.
35. Troy A. Jollimore, *Love's Vision* (Princeton: Princeton Univ. Press, 2011)
36. Jonathan Culler, "In Defence of Overinterpretation," in Umberto Eco, with Richard Rorty, Jonathan Culler, Christine Brooke-Rose, ed. Stefan Collini, *Interpretation and Overinterpretation* (Cambridge: Cambridge Univ. Press, 1992), 113. Eco's remark about the rights of interpreters appears on p. 23 of the same volume.
37. Ibid., 122–3, emphasis on second phrase mine.
38. I hesitate slightly at the word "wonder," in Culler's formulation, as I do at Colin Davis' endorsement of Emmanuel Levinas' linking of "excess of research" and an "infinite reading" with "adoration" in the case of Talmudic interpretation. Such words venture too near the traditional delusional overtones of "overreading" and "infatuation." See Colin Davis, *Critical Excess: Overreading in Derrida, Deleuze, Levinas, Žižek and Cavell* (Stanford: Stanford Univ. Press, 2010), 186. Frye's remark is from the essay "On Value-Judgements," in *The Stubborn Structure: Essays on Criticism and Society* (Ithaca, N.Y.: Cornell University Press, 1970), p. 70.
39. Adorno, *Minima Moralia*, p. 77.
40. It is difficult to know how to take Terry Eagleton's 2007 venture into close reading, *How to Read a Poem* (Oxford: Blackwell, 2007). At least as surprising as this inveterate historicizer and paraphraser's defense of the verbal medium is the fact that the majority of his analyses and critical strategies derive not from the evolving formalisms of the past twenty – or fifty – years but from the vocabulary and assumptions of the early years of the New Criticism in England and America.

1   Method, Meaning, New Formalism

1. *Stephen H. Daniel*, http://philosophy.tamu.edu/~sdaniel/Notes/epi-kant.html
2. Nelson Goodman, *Ways of Worldmaking* (Indianapolis: Hackett, 1978), x.
3. Stanley Fish, *Is There a Text in This Class? The Authority of Interpretive Communities* (Cambridge, MA & London: Harvard Univ. Press, 1980), 322. See also the stimulating discussion in John M. Ellis, *The Theory of Literary Criticism: A Logical Analysis* (Berkeley & Los Angeles: Univ. of California Press, 1974), esp. Ch. 2, "The Definition of Literature" (24–53).
4. Fish, 326.
5. Thomas S. Kuhn, *The Structure of Scientific Revolutions* (Chicago: Univ. of Chicago Press, 1962), 5 *et passim*.
6. Cleanth Brooks, *The Well Wrought Urn: Studies in the Structure of Poetry* (New York: Harcourt, 1947), 203.

7. For reasons of space and brevity, the analyses in the present study focus mostly on poems, and short poems at that. The principles and practical interpretive "moves" employed, however, apply equally to longer poems, to stories and novels, and to virtually any other genre. As Garrett Stewart remarks of J. Hillis Miller's "commitment to reading fiction and poetry alongside each other," "nothing beyond large-scale formal or structural considerations – nothing in consciousness and nothing in figuration – privileges one genre over another." Garrett Stewart, "Staying Powers," *MLQ* 54:2, 298.

8. David Lodge, *Language of Fiction: Essays in Criticism and Verbal Analysis of the English Novel* (N.Y.: Columbia UP, 1966), 78.

9. Steven Knapp has attempted to recuperate and modify the notion of a distinctive literary language by arguing that "literary interest" is created by "analogical structures" that give a work its "peculiarly literary status." Such a formulation, as Jonathan Culler says, allows us "to locate the distinctive features of literature not in particular qualities of language or framings of language but in the staging of agency and in the relation to otherness into which readers of literature are brought." More particularly, Culler notes that Knapp focuses on problems of agency outside a work that also appear within it. Phrasing it as a question, Culler paraphrases Knapp: "[I]s what the author is doing in writing a poem analogous to what happens in the poem?" Knapp's argument is finally, in my view, reducible to a mode of reading that looks for or creates such analogies rather than simply finding them in "literary" texts. And though Culler terms such a view as mine "patently unsatisfying," it's hard to see what – except nostalgia for intrinsic literariness – allows Knapp's intricate evasion of the social constructedness of the literary to offer a solider satisfaction. See Steven Knapp, *Literary Interest: The Limits of Anti-Formalism* (Cambridge, MA, and London: Harvard UP, 1993), 3, and Jonathan Culler, *The Literary in Theory* (Stanford: Stanford UP, 2007), 33, 27, 26.

10. Susan Sontag, *Against Interpretation and Other Essays* (New York: Farrar, Straus, and Giroux, 1966), 12. Sontag's argument is complicated somewhat by her (finally, anti-interpretive and anti-intellectual) assumption that "interpretation" presupposes the transparency of a work of art and should be opposed by a *non*-interpretive focus on the sensory apprehension of the work: "In place of a hermeneutics we need an erotics of art" (Ibid., 14).

11. Walter J. Ong, S. J., "The Jinnee in the Well-Wrought Urn," *Essays in Criticism* IV (July 1954), 319. See also Kenneth Burke, "Implicit in Poetic Organization *per se* There Is the Assertion of an Identity," *The Philosophy of Literary Form: Studies in Symbolic Action*, revised ed. (New York: Random House, 1957), 34.

12. Jane Gallop, "The Ethics of Reading: Close Encounters," *Journal of Curriculum Theorizing*, 16:3 (2000), 12.

13. Marjorie Levinson, unpublished talk delivered at Cornell University's School of Criticism and Theory, August 2007, p. 19. I am grateful for the author's permission to cite from this text, and for her stimulating conversation about critical theory.

14. Geoffrey Hartman, *Criticism in the Wilderness: The Study of Literature Today* (New Haven and London: Yale UP, 1980), 173, my emphasis. The passage cited is from the chapter "The Work of Reading" (161–88), which shrewdly

explores the labor of reading as a discipline resisting the easy assimilation of texts to "meaning." See also Gallop, "Ethics of Reading," 10:

> Whereas in reading our own writing, we merely fail to see our own inadequate expression, in reading the writing of others, our failure is much more serious: we read our own ideas in place of what the other person has written. There's a technical term for this: it's called projection. Rather than read what the other person has actually written, we project onto the page what we think he would have written.

> It's amazing how much reading is really projection. In fact, I would say that most of the time most people read not what is in front of them but what they expect to find in front of them.

15. Theodor Adorno, *Negative Dialectics*, trans. E. B. Ashton (New York: Continuum, 1973), 33. Cited in Jonathan Culler, *The Literary in Theory* (Stanford: Stanford UP, 2007), 38. On p. 39, Culler invokes the still harsher language of Paul de Man, for whom the readerly confirmation of "sense and meaning" comes about only "through the violent positings of the aesthetic and of understanding."
16. Paul Valéry to Philip Guston, quoted in Dore Ashton, *A Critical Study of Philip Guston* (Berkeley and Los Angeles: University of California Press, 1976), 132.
17. Henri Focillon, *The Life of Forms in Art*, trans. Charles B. Hogan and George Kubler (New York: Zone Books, 1992), 96, 95.
18. Geoffrey Hartman, *Beyond Formalism: Literary Essays 1958–1970* (New Haven and London: Yale UP, 1970), 53–4, my emphasis.
19. Also pertinent here is Frank Kermode's argument in *The Genesis of Secrecy: On the Interpretation of Narrative* (Cambridge: Harvard Univ. Press, 1979).
20. Douglas Mao, "The New Critics and the Text-Object," *ELH* 63.1 (1996), 19.
21. Ibid., 25.
22. Ibid., 25.
23. *The Letters of W. B. Yeats*, ed. Allan Wade (London: Rupert Hart-Davis, 1954), 922.
24. John Stuart Mill, "What is Poetry?" in M. H. Abrams and Stephen Greenblatt, *The Norton Anthology of English Literature*, 7th edition, vol. 2, 1143.
25. Northrop Frye, *Anatomy of Criticism: Four Essays* (Princeton: Princeton UP, 1957), 5.
26. Frye, 12.
27. Archibald MacLeish, "Ars Poetica," in *Collected Poems 1917–1982* (Boston: Houghton Mifflin, 1985), 106–7.
28. See Joel Weinsheimer's pertinent and interesting discussion of Gadamer's distinction between sign and symbol, a discussion that takes MacLeish's poem in a different but related direction. Joel Weinsheimer, *Philosophical Hermeneutics and Literary Theory* (New Haven & London: Yale UP, 1991), 90–1. Best and Marcus seem to simplify this issue when they describe a form of "surface reading" that

> assumes that texts can reveal their own truths because texts mediate themselves; what we think theory brings to texts (form, structure, meaning) is already present in them. Description sees no need to translate the

text into a theoretical or historical metalanguage in order to make the text meaningful. The purpose of criticism is thus a relatively modest one: to indicate what the text says about itself.

See Stephen Best and Sharon Marcus, "Surface Reading: An Introduction," *Representations*, 108:1 (Fall 2009), 11.

29. W. H. Auden, "Squares and Oblongs," reprinted in Charles Feidelson, Jr., and Richard Ellmann, ed., *The Modern Tradition: Backgrounds of Modern Literature* (New York: Oxford UP, 1965), 209.

30. Wilbur Marshall Urban, *Language and Reality: The Philosophy of Language and the Principles of Symbolism* (New York: Macmillan, 1939), 262. Cited in Brooks, *Urn*, 199.

31. Brooks, *Urn*, 74. Against such antiformalist claims as Merleau-Ponty's, for instance, that "It is certainly right to condemn formalism, but it is ordinarily forgotten that its error is not that it esteems form too much, but that it esteems it so little that it detaches it from meaning," we can put Brooks' formalist complaint that

> The dualism of form and content ... puts a stop to criticism by compelling us to locate the poetry in the truth of the statement made by the poem or contained in the poem (actually, a paraphrase of the poem, not the poem itself); or, to locate the poetry in the 'form' conceived as a kind of container, a sort of beautified envelope.

Maurice Merleau-Ponty, *Signs*, trans. Richard C. McCleary (Evanston: Northwestern UP, 1964), 11; Brooks, *Urn*, 226.

32. Mao, 13.

33. Lodge, *Language of Fiction*, 62. This topic is elaborated below under the concept of back-formation.

34. R. P. Blackmur, rev. of Norman Macleod, *Horizons of Death*, in *Poetry*, 46:2 (May 1935), 108. My emphasis.

35. More accurately, "language, among other symbolic forms," since Cassirer treats myth, art, religion, and science, as well as language.

36. On the link with Romantic ideas of symbolism, see William K. Wimsatt, Jr., and Cleanth Brooks, *Literary Criticism: A Short History* (New York: Knopf, 1957), 497–8, 584, 700–03.

37. Ernst Cassirer, *Language and Myth*, trans. Susanne K. Langer (New York: Harper & Brothers, 1946), 8, my emphasis. The sentence immediately following the quoted passage is: "The question as to what reality is apart from these forms, and what are its independent attributes, becomes irrelevant here."

38. Walter Benn Michaels, "Saving the Text: Reference and Belief," *MLN*, 93:5 (December 1978), 780.

39. Ernst Cassirer, *The Philosophy of Symbolic Forms, Volume Two: Mythical Thought*, trans. Ralph Manheim (New Haven and London: Yale UP, 1955), 25–6.

40. See Caroline Levine, "Strategic Formalism: Toward a New Method in Cultural Studies," *Victorian Studies*, summer 2006, 631.

41. Cleanth Brooks, *Historical Evidence and the Reading of Seventeenth-Century Poetry* (Columbia, Mo., and London: University of Missouri Press, 1991), 52.

42. Frank Lentricchia, Preface to *Close Reading: The Reader*, ed. Frank Lentricchia and Andrew Dubois (Durham, NC: Duke University Press, 2003), ix.

43. Jonathan Culler, "The Closeness of Close Reading," *ADFL Bulletin* 41:3 (2011), 11. See also Richard A. Lanham, "*At* and *Through*: The Opaque Style and Its Uses," in *Literacy and the Survival of Humanism* (New Haven and London: Yale UP, 1983), 58–86.

44. *Boswell's Life of Johnson, together with Boswell's Journal of a Tour to the Hebrides and Johnson's Diary of a Journey into North Wales*, ed. George Birkbeck Hill, and revised by L. F. Powell. 2nd ed. (Oxford: Clarendon Press, 1964–1971), V.79, my emphasis.

45. Brooks, *Urn*, 212–13.

46. Brooks, *Urn*, 213–14, 222–3.

47. Walter Benjamin, "Theses on the Philosophy of History," VII, in Fredric Jameson, *The Political Unconscious* (Ithaca, N.Y.: Cornell UP, 1981), 281; Jameson, 299.

48. Ellis, 179.

49. Marjorie Levinson, unpublished talk, School of Criticism and Theory, Cornell University, summer 2012, 10, used by kind permission of the author.

50. Frye, *Anatomy*, 24. By "tropical," Frye means criticism that is "primarily concerned with the contemporary reader" rather than with the history of a text or of its readership (*Anatomy*, 21).

51. Stephen Cohen, ed., *Shakespeare and Historical Formalism* (Aldershot, England: Ashgate, 2007), 3.

52. SJ, *Rambler* No. 60, on biography.

53. Mao, 3, 24.

54. Weinsheimer, *Philosophical Hermeneutics and Literary Theory*, 37–8.

55. See note 36, above.

56. Weinsheimer, 149.

57. Gadamer, *Truth and Method*, 289, quoted in Weinsheimer, 135.

58. Frye, *Anatomy*, 345.

59. Ibid., 345–6.

60. Kenneth Burke, *The Philosophy of Literary Form* (New York: Vintage, 1957), 253–62. By this phrase, however, Burke does not mean what he terms "easy consolation," such as is supplied by "inspirational literature" (258). Here is an example of what he does mean:

   > A work like *Madame Bovary* (or its homely American translation, *Babbitt*) is the strategic naming of a situation. It singles out a pattern of experience that is sufficiently representative of our social structure, that recurs sufficiently often *mutatis mutandis* for people to "need a word for it" and to adopt an attitude towards it (259).

   In a sense, Burke is viewing literary works here as templates or rehearsals or virtual attitudinal mappings that will allow readers to make sense of and negotiate similar real-life situations. See also Marielle Macé, "Ways of Reading, Modes of Being," *New Literary History*, 2013, 44: 213–229.

61. Geoffrey Hartman, "Beyond Formalism," *MLN*, 81:5 (Dec. 1966), 545.

62. T. S. Eliot, "Tradition and the Individual Talent," in Frank Kermode, ed., *Selected Prose of T. S. Eliot* (San Diego, New York, London: Harvest Books, 1975), 38–9.

63. Cf. Mao's thoughtful discussion of New Critical assumptions that the poem is both "an object" and a shareable "experience" (23). Ong makes a related point in very different language, though both are grappling with the double relation of distance and nearness between reader and text. Here is Ong:

> The assertion that in works of art it is the object itself which counts...must be made with great honesty, which means with circumspection and humility. Not only the truth of the situation but its awkwardness, as well, must be faced. This awkwardness derives from the fact that...each work of art is not only an object but a kind of surrogate for a person.
>
> Jinnee (319)

Finally, Kenneth Burke: "Implicit in poetic organization *per se* there is the assertion of an identity" (*The Philosophy of Literary Form*, 3d. ed. (Berkeley: Univ. of California Press, 1984), 39).

64. Richard A. Lanham, "*At* and *Through*: The Opaque Style and Its Uses," in *Literacy and the Survival of Humanism* (New Haven and London: Yale UP, 1983), 58–86. Stephen Best and Sharon Marcus link the "at"/"through" distinction with their defense of "Surface Reading" in Stephen Best and Sharon Marcus, "Surface Reading: An Introduction," *Representations*, 108:1 (Fall 2009), 9: "A surface is what insists on being looked *at* rather than what we must train ourselves to see *through*." They urge a "willed, sustained proximity to the text" (10).

65. M. H. Abrams, "Art-as-Such: The Sociology of Modern Aesthetics," in *Doing Things with Texts: Essays in Criticism and Critical Theory* (N.Y. and London: W. W. Norton, 1989), 139–41, 148–9, 157–8, and especially 153–6.

66. Samuel Johnson, "Preface to The Plays of William Shakespeare," *Samuel Johnson: Selected Poetry and Prose*, ed. Frank Brady and W. K. Wimsatt (Berkeley and Los Angeles, London: Univ. of California Press, 1977), 312.

67. I allude to two of the famous illustrations of Gestalt psychology that attempt to portray visual ambiguity: the faces/vase, and the duck/rabbit.

Such double consciousness on the part of the actor rather than the audience is, interestingly, a central feature of the eighteenth-century acting theories of Diderot (*Paradoxe sur le Comédien*, written early 1770s) and Boswell (*On the Profession of a Player*, pub. 1770).

68. And of course, it is formalist analysis that will put into play the details and nuances of the text, strengthening and deepening an already strong approval or disapproval, or qualifying approval or disapproval with the counter-energies of a discovered complexity or richness or dividedness in the text.

69. Derek Attridge, "Literary Form and the Demands of Politics: Otherness in J. M. Coetzee's *Age of Iron*," in George Levine, ed., *Aesthetics and Ideology* (New Brunswick, NJ: Rutgers University Press, 1994), 248.
70. Northrop Frye, *The Educated Imagination* (Bloomington and London: Indiana UP, 1964), 76–8.
71. Bernard Sharratt, *Reading Relations* (Brighton: Harvester Press, 1982), 9–34, 93–107, 125.
72. Ibid., p. 33.
73. T. S. Eliot, "The Use of Poetry and the Use of Criticism," and "Dante," in Frank Kermode, ed., *Selected Prose of T. S. Eliot* (San Diego, New York, London: Harvest Books, 1975), 85, 221.
74. Brooks, *Urn*, 69, 102, 212. Warren is of course referring to the role of the "devil's advocate" in the process of canonization. Additionally, it should be noted that his use of "proves" mobilizes the older sense of the word – "tests, submits to a test" – rather than the more recent sense of "demonstrates the truth or existence" of something.
75. See above, note 17. For a different formulation of Hartman's point, see Walter J. Ong, "Wit and Mystery: A Revaluation in Mediaeval Hymnody," *Speculum* XXI (July 1947), 326–7.
76. Robert Kaufman "Everybody Hates Kant: Blakean Formalism and the Symmetries of Laura Moriarty," *MLQ*, 6:1 (March 2000), 141.
77. Knapp, 101, 139.
78. Culler, *The Literary in Theory*, 33.
79. Charles Altieri, "Taking Lyrics Literally: Teaching Poetry in a Prose Culture." *New Literary History* 32 Spring (2001), 262, 287. Quoted in Levinson, "What Is New Formalism? (Long Version)", 6, 9, http://sitemaker.umich.edu/pmla_article/home
80. Levinson, "Long Version," 8–10. Percy B. Shelley, *A Defence of Poetry*, par. 37, http://www.bartleby.com/27/23.html
81. And this is to consider only the solitary reader alone with the text. There is also the reader as part of a reading community, actual (classroom, conference, conversation, etc.) or virtual (as when we think of ourselves as making one in a body of readers, past, present, or both). In such cases, the "trying on" or readerly role playing we perform has a social or communal dimension. That is to say, one of the selves we are when reading is a social self. See Ong, "Jinnee," 312, for some interesting remarks on this dimension of reading. On the question of the reader's desire for or possessiveness toward the text, compare Ong's discussion of readerly expectations that the text be responsive in turn: "Plenary attention, serious and protracted and repeated, ... involves love, and the question is whether it can be carried on, or how far it can be carried on, without some suggestion of reciprocity" (Ong, "Jinnee," 314).
82. Emile Benveniste, *Problems in General Linguistics*, trans. Mary E. Meek (Coral Gables: Univ. of Miami Press, 1971), 46. Cited in Weinsheimer, 90.
83. Peter Brooks, "Aesthetics and Ideology – What Happened to Poetics?" in George Levine, *Aesthetics and Ideology*, 165. And see the related (and generalizable) claim by Derek Attridge that the "formal singularity" of J. M. Coetzee's writing "is bound up with the capacity of his work to engage with – to stage, confront, apprehend, explore – *otherness*, and in this

engagement it broaches the most fundamental and widely significant issues involved in any consideration of ethics and politics." Attridge makes this claim in his essay "Literary Form and the Demands of Politics: Otherness in J. M. Coetzee's *Age of Iron*," in Levine, *Aesthetics and Ideology*, 244.

84. Even "to make it kingly," in one entertaining alternative etymology. See OED, s.v. *"realize," v. 1.*: "1611 FLORIO, *Realizzáre, to reallize or make Kingly.*"

85. As of several other modes of post-New Critical interpretation.

86. Roman Jakobson, "Closing Statement: Linguistics and Poetics," in *Style in Language*, ed. Thomas A. Sebeok (Cambridge, MA: MIT Press, 1960), 350–77. Page references will appear in parentheses in the body of my text.

87. Nelson Goodman, *Ways of Worldmaking* (Indianapolis: Hackett, 1978), 69. These pages of my argument adapt a few pages of a talk, " 'Exemplification' and 'The Poetic Function of Language': Nelson Goodman and Roman Jakobson," that I gave as part of the Cornell University English Colloquium, 3 November 2006.

88. Jakobson, 356. Recall that "message" here does not refer to content or meaning but to the verbal artifact itself. German *Einstellung* means "stance," "attitude," "focus."

89. If we (1) align the axis of selection with readerly distance, the sort of distance that permits us to look at a textual element as "possible," as one of many that might have been selected in its place; and if we (2) align the axis of combination with readerly nearness to or investment in the text, because the text's unfolding syntax is what permits us to discover in it a narrative or attitude or another sort of representation that, as Frye contends, can draw us into its orbit of seeming actuality; then we can (3) rewrite Jakobson's selection/combination dyad as the complex readerly doubleness that I have compared to a metaphor (above, 67–9). Perspective from the point of view of "selection," and perspective from the point of view of "combination," then, allow Jakobson's account of poetic textuality and a neoformalist account of the reader's relation to the text to be inter-translatable.

90. Compare the formulation of Jan Mukarovsky, in "Poetic Designation and the Aesthetic Function of Language," in *The Word and Verbal Art*, ed. John Burbank and Peter Steiner (New Haven and London: Yale UP, 1977), 66: "Our attitude toward the utterance in question will…completely change when it is conceived as a poetic quotation [instead of an everyday communicative message]. The focal point of our attention will immediately become its relation to the surrounding [verbal] contexture, even if it is only an assumed one."

91. Robert Frost, "Education by Poetry," *Selected Prose of Robert Frost*, ed. Hyde Cox and Edward Connery Lathem (New York: Collier Books, 1968), 37, 38. Frost wittily implies, I think, that if he had made metaphor "the whole of thinking," he would thereby have created a metaphor ("thinking is metaphor") that does *not* "break down at some point" – something he regards (as do I) as an impossibility.

92. Ibid., 37.

93. See above, p. 7. I have removed Burke's original italics.

94. Hans Vaihinger, *The Philosophy of "As If,"* trans. C. K. Ogden. 2nd ed. (London: Routledge & Kegan Paul, 1935), xlvi–xlvii, 18. With Vaihinger's "roundabout ways and bypaths," compare W. H. Auden, "Our Bias": "When

have we not preferred some going round/To going straight to where we are?" (13–14). And see Frank Kermode, *The Sense of an Ending: Studies in the Theory of Fiction* (New York: Oxford UP, 1967), 39: "Fictions can degenerate into myths whenever they are not consciously held to be fictive … Myths call for absolute, fictions for conditional assent."

95. J. Hillis Miller, *The Linguistic Moment: From Wordsworth to Stevens* (Princeton: Princeton UP, 1985), 26. Barry Stampfel pursues connections between Vaihinger and Wolfgang Iser, Frank Kermode, and J. Hillis Miller, among others, in "Hans Vaihinger's Ghostly Presence in Contemporary Literary Studies," *Criticism*, vol. 40, summer 1998, 437–54. Online at: http://findarticles.com/p/articles/mi_m2220/is_n3_v40/ai_21182132

2 Old and New Formalisms

1. John McIntyre and Miranda Hickman, eds., *Rereading the New Criticism* (Columbus: Ohio State University Press, 2012), 233.

2. William K. Wimsatt, Jr., and Cleanth Brooks, *Literary Criticism: A Short History* (New York: Knopf, 1957), 32. It may seem tempting to enlist Horace as a minor member of this tradition. Although, in the opening lines of the *Ars Poetica*, he is primarily concerned to ridicule indecorous minglings of genre, there is a sense in which he, too, keeps alive something like a holistic sense of unity:

> Imagine a painter who wanted to combine a horse's neck with a human head, and then clothe a miscellaneous collection of limbs with various kinds of feathers, so that what started out at the top as a beautiful woman ended in a hideously ugly fish. If you were invited, as friends, to the private view, could you help laughing? Let me tell you … a book whose different features are made up at random like a sick man's dreams, with no unified form to have a head or a tail, is exactly like that picture … In short, let it be what you will, but let it be simple and unified.

in Horace, *Ars Poetica*, trans. D. A. Russell, in *The Norton Anthology of Theory and Criticism*, Vincent B. Leitch, general editor (New York and London: Norton, 2001), 124. But in addition to being principally concerned with the decorum of genres, Horace here – at least when viewed as a theorist rather than a poet – intimates a conception of unity that is not so much tensional or dialectical as a matter of consistency and uniformity: "simplex et unum."

3. Plotinus, *Ennead* I.vi.8, trans. Stephen MacKenna, 5 vols. (London: Faber and Faber, 1917–30). Cited in Wimsatt and Brooks, *Short History*, 114. Cf. St. Augustine: "Any beautiful object … is more worthy of praise in its totality than in any one of its parts. So great is the power of integrity and unity that what pleases us as a part pleases much more in a unified whole." *De Genesi Contra Manichaeos*, I.xxi. Cited in Wimsatt and Brooks, *Short History*, 123.

4. This is part of a well known paragraph in Chapter 14 of *Biographia Literaria*, ed. James Engell and W. Jackson Bate (Princeton: Princeton UP, 1983), II.16.

On Coleridge's debt to Plotinus, and even to Augustine, see Wimsatt and Brooks, *Short History*, 653.

5. We should also recall the work of the English critic Christopher Caudwell, who before his early death produced a considerable body of work in a Marxist vein, most notably *Illusion and Reality: A Study of the Sources of Poetry* (1937).

6. John Crowe Ransom, *The World's Body* (New York and London: Charles Scribner's Sons, 1938), 335.

7. Alvin Kernan, *In Plato's Cave* (New Haven and London: Yale UP, 1999), 34.

8. Ransom, *World's Body*, 173.

9. On structure and texture, see, for example, Ransom, *The New Criticism* (Norfolk, CT: New Directions, 1941), 279–80.

10. As Wimsatt says: "The concern for the poem as an objective thing is the special highlight of the classicism of Eliot" (Wimsatt and Brooks, *Short History*, 676).

11. Doing so, of course, does not get us from assertion to demonstration in the evaluative realm, but it at least reflects a *desire* for grounds in evaluation rather than a confident reliance on Delphic voicings of "taste."

12. T. S. Eliot, "The Metaphysical Poets" (1921), in *Selected Prose*, 64. The "dissociation of sensibility" is discussed on 64–5.

13. Ibid., 63, 67.

14. Samuel Johnson, "Life of Cowley," in M. H. Abrams *et al.* eds., *The Norton Anthology of English Literature*, 7th ed. (New York and London: Norton, 2000), I:2737; Eliot, *Selected Prose*, 61.

15. See above, p. 60 and n. 75.

16. Eliot, *Selected Prose*, 170.

17. Cleanth Brooks, "Empson's Criticism," *Accent* 4 (summer 1944), 208.

18. John Paul Russo, *I. A. Richards: His Life and Work* (Baltimore: Johns Hopkins UP, 1989), 523.

19. C. K. Ogden, I. A. Richards, James Wood, *The Foundations of Aesthetics*, 2nd ed. (N.Y.: International Publishers, 1925), 75, 78.

20. I. A. Richards, *Practical Criticism: A Study of Literary Judgment*, 1929 (San Diego, New York, London: Harcourt Brace, 1966), 177.

21. Ibid., 292, 314, 316.

22. Cf. Russo, *Life and Work*, 216: "In his practical criticism Richards had a microscopic eye ... No detail at first glance seemed too minor ... "

23. Ibid., 277–8.

24. Russo, *Life and Work*, 232: "Richards introduced the terms *tone* and *speaker* to criticism." On coherence *versus* correspondence, cf. Walter J. Ong, S. J., "From Rhetorical Culture to New Criticism: The Poem as a Closed Field," in *The Possibilities of Order: Cleanth Brooks and His Work*, ed. Lewis P. Simpson (Baton Rouge: Louisiana State UP, 1976), 157: "The poem, in other words, is what it is because of its interior economy, not because of the way it ties in at specific points with 'life' or with anything else."

25. Richards, *Practical Criticism*, 17–170. The book was first published in 1929.

26. Cited in John Haffenden, *William Empson: Among the Mandarins* (Oxford and New York: Oxford UP, 2005), 207.

27. William Empson, *Seven Types of Ambiguity*, 1930 (New York: New Directions, 1966), 256.

28. Wimsatt and Brooks, *Short History*, 638.
29. Empson, *Seven Types*, x, 2, xv, 3, 1. The tendency to describe ambiguity as a textual phenomenon at some times, and as a matter of readers' reactions at other times, is a feature of Empson's writing.
30. Ibid., 192.
31. Ibid., 192, 195, my emphasis on "then."
32. "The logical laws of thought do not apply in the id, and this is true above all of the law of contradiction. Contradictory impulses exist side by side, without cancelling each other out or diminishing each other ... There is nothing in the id that could be compared with negation." Sigmund Freud, *New Introductory Lectures on Psycho-analysis*, trans. James Strachey (New York and London: Norton, 1990), 92.
33. Ibid., 194.
34. Empson, *Seven Types*, 192.
35. "Almost never," because Brooks' language at times pays a deeper than ordinary tribute to the conflicts and heterogeneities of poetic language: "The poet must work by analogies, but the metaphors do not lie in the same plane or fit neatly edge to edge. There is a continual tilting of the planes; necessary overlappings, discrepancies, contradictions" (*Urn*, 9–10).
36. "Wit in the *Essay on Criticism*," in William Empson, *The Structure of Complex Words* (Ann Arbor: Univ. of Michigan Press, 1967), 92. The essay first appeared in *Hudson Review* 2 (1950): 559–77.
37. See above, p. 88, n. 132.
38. René Wellek and Austin Warren, *Theory of Literature*, 3rd. edition (New York: Harcourt Brace, 1956), 139.
39. Ransom, *New Criticism*.
40. Among the others cited – some with fairly tenuous links to the New Criticism – are Wellek, Yvor Winters, R. P. Blackmur, F. R. Leavis, and Kenneth Burke.
41. M. H. Abrams, "The Transformation of English Studies: 1930–1995," *Daedalus*, 126: 1 (winter 1997), 109, 111.
42. Ibid., 108–9.
43. William J. Spurlin, "Afterword: An Interview with Cleanth Brooks," in *The New Criticism and Contemporary Literary Theory*, ed. William J. Spurlin and Michael Fischer (New York: Garland, 1995), 366.
44. Spurlin, "Afterword," 367–8.
45. John Henry Cardinal Newman, *The Idea of a University*, ed. Martin J. Svaglic (New York: Holt, Rinehart, Winston, 1964), 219, 208.
46. Newman, 215.
47. Spurlin, "Afterword," 368, my emphasis.
48. Cleanth Brooks, "My Credo – The Formalist Critics," in Spurlin and Fischer, 45. The essay first appeared in *Kenyon Review* 13 (Winter 1951), 72–81.
49. Brooks, "My Credo," 48.
50. Ibid., 53.
51. Frye, *Anatomy*, 20.
52. Ibid., 23.
53. Wimsatt, *Verbal Icon*, 235. My emphasis. Cf. Wellek and Warren, *Theory of Literature*, 250.

54. Cf. Brooks, in Spurlin, "Afterword: An Interview with Cleanth Brooks," 373: "The reader's role is a very important one; it is to realize the work, to find a meaning, an experience, a judgment."
55. Wellek and Warren, *Theory of Literature*, 146.
56. Frye, *Anatomy*, 25.
57. Ibid., 24.
58. Dubrow's phrase and her role in New Formalist Renaissance studies are discussed in the introduction to *Renaissance Literature and its Formal Engagements*, ed. Mark David Rasmussen (New York: Palgrave, 2002), 4.
59. Douglas Bruster, "Shakespeare and the Composite Text," in Rasmussen, 44.
60. Heather Dubrow, "The Politics of Aesthetics: Recuperating Formalism and the Country House Poem," in Rasmussen, 85.
61. Mary Poovey, "The Model System of Contemporary Literary Criticism," *Critical Inquiry* 27 (Spring 2001), 410, 432.
62. Rasmussen, 7.
63. Ellen Rooney, "Form and Contentment," in *Reading for Form*, ed. Susan J. Wolfson and Marshall Brown (Seattle and London: Univ. of Washington Press, 2006), 33–4. Rooney's essay was first published in 2000.
64. See the fuller discussion of intention below, pp. 88–92.
65. See above, pp. 77–8 and n. 105.
66. Thus, Interpretation actively uses the text in certain ways and produces certain kinds of meaning to the exclusion of others. The difference between this New Formalist position and that of the New Criticism lies in the denial of an intrinsic appropriateness of this sort of analysis to certain kinds of text, and in a refusal to label other sorts of interpretive strategy and the meanings they produce as illegitimate, or inappropriate to a "literary text." New Formalisms recognize that formalist criticism is not criticism *tout court*, even though the success of the New Criticism, as William Cain has argued, ensured that for a time formalism would enjoy just such an elevation to the generic, to the status of what Kuhn calls "normal science." For a particularly direct statement of this view, see William E. Cain, *The Crisis in Criticism: Theory, Literature, and Reform in English Studies* (Baltimore: Johns Hopkins Univ. Press, 1984), 105.
67. Stefano Rosso, "An Interview with Paul de Man," cited in de Man, *The Resistance to Theory*, foreword by Wlad Godzich (Minneapolis: Univ. of Minnesota Press, 1986), 118.
68. Caroline Levine, "Strategic Formalism: Toward a New Method in Cultural Studies," *Victorian Studies*, Summer 2006, 634–5.
69. Frye, *Anatomy*, 16.
70. Wimsatt and Beardsley, "The Intentional Fallacy," in *The Verbal Icon*, 12.
71. Poovey, "The Model System of Contemporary Literary Criticism," 416.
72. Eric Savoy, "Restraining Order," *ECS: English Studies in Canada*, 29:1–2 (March/June 2003), 79. On catachresis, see Barbara Johnson, *A World of Difference* (Baltimore and London: Johns Hopkins University Press, 1987), 53: Catachreses are "figures for which no literal, proper term can be substituted... 'figures of abuse,' figurative substitutes for a literal term that does not exist."
73. Ibid., 81, 80.

74. Eric Savoy, "Subjunctive Biography," *The Henry James Review*, 27:3 (Fall 2006), p. 249. And see Stephen Best and Sharon Marcus, "Surface Reading: An Introduction," *Representations*, 108:1 (Fall 2009), 1–21.

75. Dana Phillips, "Ecocriticism, Literary Theory, and the Truth of Ecology," *New Literary History*, 30:3 (Summer, 1999), 589–90. See also Phillips' more recent *The Truth of Ecology: Nature, Culture, and Literature in America* (Oxford: Oxford University Press, 2003).

76. Sarah Ensor, "Spinster Ecology: Rachel Carson, Sarah Orne Jewett, and Nonreproductive Futurity," *American Literature*, 84:2 (2012), 410, 419, 431n.4.

77. Debra Fried, "Andromeda Unbound: Gender and Genre in Millay's Sonnets," *Twentieth- Century Literature* 32:1 (Spring 1986), 17.

78. Fried, "The Stanza: Echo Chambers," Erik Martiny, ed., *A Companion to Poetic Genre* (Oxford: Wiley-Blackwell, 2012), 53.

79. Stephen Cohen, ed., *Shakespeare and Historical Formalism* (Aldershot, England: Ashgate, 2007), 14.

80. Levine, "Strategic Formalism," 626.

81. Susan Wolfson, *Formal Charges: The Shaping of Poetry in British Romanticism* (Stanford: Stanford UP, 1997), 3. And compare Stephen Cohen, "Between Form and Culture: New Historicism and the promise of a Historical Formalism," in Rasmussen, ed., 33: "A historical formalism is, in short, not a return to but a remedy for formalist essentialism, a theory of literature as both a measure and a means of historical change."

82. Ibid., 21 (my emphasis), 30.

83. Ibid., 232.

84. Culler, *The Literary in Theory*, 9. On symptomatic reading, in general and in its particular Jamesonian incarnation, see also Stephen Best and Sharon Marcus, "Surface Reading: An Introduction," *Representations*, 108:1 (Fall 2009), 3, 5.

85. Dubrow, "The Politics of Aesthetics," in Rasmussen, 85. On the same page, she argues that "the assumption that formalism may once again become respectable simply because it can serve the needs of . . . historical and political criticism . . . relegates the formal to a secondary, supplementary role that neglects the depth and the range of its contributions to style and meaning."

86. Robert Kaufman, "On Susan J. Wolfson's Formal Charges: The Shaping of Poetry in British Romanticism." *Romantic Circles Reviews* 4:1 (2001): 25 pars. 15 Jan. 2001, par. 1. http:/www.rc.umd.edu/reviews/wolfson.html

87. Kaufman, "Everybody Hates Kant: Blakean Formalism and the Symmetries of Laura Moriarty," *MLQ*, 6:1 (March 2000), 131–55.

88. Jonathan Loesberg, "Cultural Studies, Victorian Studies, and Formalism," *Victorian Literature and Culture*, 27:2 (1999), 544.

89. Ibid.

90. Mary Janell Metzger, "Teaching Shakespeare and the Uses of Historical Formalism," in Cohen, ed., *Shakespeare and Historical Formalism*, 207. See the fascinating linkage of figuration and ideology in Dickens's *Dombey and Son* in Garrett Stewart, "The Foreign Offices of British Fiction," *MLQ* 61:1 (March 2000), 181–206.

91. Marjorie Levinson, unpublished talk, School of Criticism and Theory, Cornell University, summer 2012, p. 11, used by kind permission of the author. My emphasis.

92. Ibid., 7.

93. Hannah Ginsborg, "Kant's Aesthetics and Teleology," *Stanford Encyclopedia of Philosophy*, §2. http://plato.stanford.edu/entries/kant-aesthetics/

94. Ibid., §2.1.

95. Ibid., §2.8.

96. Charles Altieri, *The Particulars of Rapture: An Aesthetic of the Affects* (Ithaca and London: Cornell UP, 2003), 1.

97. Ibid.

98. Ibid., 4–5.

99. Where? When? For whom? Scarry's claims make Eliot's argument about a "dissociation of sensibility" look positively airtight.

100. Elaine Scarry, *On Beauty and Being Just* (Princeton: Princeton UP, 1999), 85, 84, my emphasis. If anyone doubts the potentially uncritical intensity of what Levinson terms the contemporary wish to "re-enchant the object," Scarry's is the book to read. For a critical account of Scarry's book, see Denis Dutton, "Mad about Flowers: Elaine Scarry on Beauty," *Philosophy and Literature* 24 (2000): 249–60. http://denisdutton.com/scarry_review.htm

101. On logic: Scarry argues that to pursue something is to want to be or partake of that something: "If one pursues goodness, one hopes in doing so to make oneself good," etc. That is, there is "continuity between the external object and the person who is dedicated to it." Not so with beauty; in fact, "most people who pursue beauty have no interest in becoming themselves beautiful." This makes beauty a seemingly singular case, she says, since it thus differs from other versions of continuity between object and pursuer. "[C]ould one," she asks, "pursue truth if one had no interest in becoming knowledgeable?" But according to her own logic, the pursuer of truth should wish to become *true*, not *knowledgeable*. This slip is an indication of the way analogy and causality or entailment blur continually for Scarry. See Scarry, 87–8, 97.

102. Ibid., 62, 7.

103. Dubrow, "The Politics of Aesthetics," 68–70, 85.

104. Kaufman, "Everybody Hates Kant," 131.

105. Ibid., 133.

106. Ibid., 147–8.

107. Ibid., 155.

108. Angela Leighton, *On Form: Poetry, Aestheticism, and the Legacy of a Word* (Oxford and N.Y.: Oxford University Press, 2007), 27.

109. Ibid., 135, my emphasis.

110. Henri Focillon, *The Life of Forms in Art*, trans. Charles B. Hogan and George Kubler (New York: Zone Books, 1992), 124, 33.

111. Marshall Sahlins, *Culture and Practical Reason* (Chicago: Univ. of Chicago Press, 1976).

112. Sahlins, viii, 214, 130.

113. Compare the discussion of Cassirer in Ch. 1, above. Pertinent, too, in a different mode (recall Kaufman's evocation of Blake) are these lines from Yeats's "The Tower": "Death and life were not/Till man made up the

whole,/Made lock, stock and barrel/Out of his bitter soul, Aye, sun and moon and star, all…" Richard J. Finneran, ed., *W. B. Yeats: The Poems. A New Edition* (N.Y.: Macmillan, 1983), 198.
114. Whether conceptually, imaginatively, or – as for Sahlins – symbolically.
115. Here is a somewhat different formulation from Kaufman, "On Susan J. Wolfson's *Formal Charges*," par. 19:

> The aesthetic, while looking like conceptual-objective, useful, content-determined thought or activity, only 'looks like' them. Aesthetic thought-experience in some way precedes conceptual-objective, content-and-use-oriented thought; in that sense, the aesthetic is formal because, rather than being determined by, it provides the form for conceptual, 'objective' thought or cognition. Aesthetic thought-experience remains 'free' (at least, relative to more properly conceptual thought) from pre-existent concepts or cognitive rules. In the Kantian lexicon, this makes the aesthetic a site of 'reflective' rather than 'determinate' judgment. The aesthetic, then, serves as mold or frame for the construction of 'cognition in general,' as Kant puts it.

116. Alexander Pope, "Epigram. Engraved on the Collar of a Dog which I gave to his Royal Highness," John Butt, ed., *The Poems of Alexander Pope* (New Haven & London: Yale Univ. Press, 1963), 826.
117. Denis Donoghue, *Walter Pater: Lover of Strange Souls* (N.Y.: Knopf, 1995), 288. Donoghue, *Speaking of Beauty* (New Haven & London Yale UP, 2003), 121. Both cited in Leighton, *On Form*, 23.
118. Nor should we overlook Kaufman's next sentence: "By the same token, the formal gets to be formal only by its momentary, experimental coincidence with the material." Kaufman, "Everybody Hates Kant," 135. Compare Leighton, *On Form: Poetry, Aestheticism, and the Legacy of a Word* (Oxford & New York: OUP, 2007), 2: "It is as if there were something unfinished, even unformed, about form. It hangs on its other half, needing that support or relief."
119. Douglas Bruster, "The Materiality of Shakespearean Form," in Stephen Cohen, ed., *Shakespeare and Historical Formalism*, 36.
120. Wolfson, *Formal Charges*, 30.
121. Brooks in Spurlin, "Afterword," 366.
122. Cited in Leighton, *On Form*, 1, my emphasis. The original – Paul Valéry, "Léonard et les Philosophes," in *Morceaux Choisis* (Paris: Gallimard, 1930), 106 – is somewhat different: "La philosophe ne conçoit pas facilement que l'artiste passe presque indifféremment de la forme au contenu et du contenu à la forme; qu'une forme lui vienne avant le sens qu'il lui donnera, ni que l'idée d'une forme soit l'égale pour lui de l'idée qui demande une forme." Valéry's chiastic structures here enact the inseparability he speaks of.
123. Levinson, "What is New Formalism? Long Version," p. 28. Available online at http://sitemaker.umich.edu/pmla_article. The shorter version of the essay, "What is New Formalism?" is in *PMLA*, 122 (2007): 558–569. Ellen Rooney, "Form and Contentment," in *Reading for Form*, ed. Susan J. Wolfson and Marshall Brown (Seattle and London: University of Washington Press, 2006), 33–4. Rooney's essay is a particularly astute and forceful account of the cost of failing to attend to form. "The loss of the *work* of form should be

the focus of our concern," she writes, because "the extinction of an entire range of modes of formal analysis has eroded our ability to read *every genre of text* – literary texts, nonliterary texts, and the social text itself" (34, 35). Fish, 13.

124. Fish, 13. See also 331.
125. These are my examples, not Fish's.
126. Leighton, *On Form*, 18. Focillon's book first appeared as *Vie des Formes* in 1934.
127. Wimsatt and Beardsley, "The Intentional Fallacy," in *The Verbal Icon*, 3, 5.
128. Though not usually the weight of the volume it appears in, the history of the typeface in which it is printed, the marital histories or dietary preferences of compositor or proofreader, etc. The quotation is from Kenneth Burke, *The Philosophy of Literary Form*, 3rd ed., revised. (Berkeley & Los Angeles: Univ. of California Press, 1973), 23.
129. Steven Knapp and Walter Benn Michaels, "Against Theory," *Critical Inquiry*, 8:4 (Summer, 1982), 723–4.
130. Ibid., 21.
131. Ironically, by making this particular distinction between language and a simulacrum of language, Michaels and Knapp go wrong in just the way they had hoped to avoid, the way that, in their account, "theory" repeatedly goes wrong: by creating a distinction where none is justified.
132. This is Knapp and Michaels' paraphrase of P. D. Juhl, in their essay "Against Theory," *Critical Inquiry* 8:4 (summer 1982), 733. They refer to P. D. Juhl, *Interpretation: An Essay in the Philosophy of Literary Criticism* (Princeton: Princeton Univ. Press, 1986), Ch. IV.
133. Let me add what is not, strictly speaking, an "argument" for formalism but a mere drawing out of consequences. If all of *The Faerie Queene* had entered the world demonstrably and unmistakably by chance rather than by the agency of Edmund Spenser or any other intending figure, Michaels and Knapp would be forced to refuse it literary or indeed linguistic status. It would just *look like* a poem in a little more than six books. It could not be interpreted or, indeed, treated as a piece of literature or language at all. As I say, this is not an argument, but it does point to some of the more bizarre consequences of their account of intention.
134. Alexander Nehamas, "What An Author Is," *Journal of Philosophy*, 83 (January 1986), 688, 689.
135. In the light of recent theorizing about intention, it is no denigration of Nehamas' lucid and terse exposition to say that much of his argument is a subtle, revisionist unpacking of the account of intention that the New Critics offered.
136. For the purposes of this example, the announced intention is both knowable and exactly what the intender says it is.
137. Interview with Barbara Johnson, in *Criticism in Society*, ed. Imre Salusinszky (New York and London: Methuen, 1987), 159–60.
138. "In etymology, the process of back-formation is the creation of a neologism by reinterpreting an earlier word as a derivation and removing apparent affixes, or more generally, by reconstructing an 'original' form from any kind of derived form (including abbreviations or inflected forms). The resulting new word is called a back-formation. The simplest

case is when a longer form of a word pair predates what would usually be the basic form. For example, the noun *resurrection* was borrowed
from Latin, and the verb *resurrect* was then derived from it. We expect
the suffix *-ion* to be added to a verb to create a noun; when as in this
case the suffix is removed from the noun to create the verb, this is a
back-formation." http://en.wikipedia.org/wiki/Back-formation

139. Pavol Štekauer, *English Word-Formation* (Tübingen: Gunter Narr, 2000), 74.
Thus, "what is removed in back-formation is the 'supposed' or 'fake' suffix –
not a genuine suffix" (Štekauer, 81). A common example is "-copter," redefined as a suffix by splitting "helicopter" not into its correct components,
"helico-" and "pter," but into "heli" and "copter," leaving the latter available for new coinages: the abbreviated form "copter," for example, or more
exotic instances such as the air transport of the superhero, Batman: the
Batcopter. See also Peter Meijes Tiersma, "Local and General Markedness,"
Language, 58:4 (Dec., 1982), 832–84. For Tiersma and other references, and
for helpful discussion of back-formation and related phenomena, I am
grateful to Jay Jasanoff of Harvard (formerly of Cornell) and Michael Weiss
of Cornell.

140. Esko V. Pennanen, (1966). *Contributions to the Study of Back-formation in
English* (*Acta Academiae Socialis* ser. A vol. 4 Julkaisija Yhteiskunnallinen
Korkeakoulu Tampere, 1966), 3.2.1. Cited in Štekauer, 72.

141. Stephen Gill, ed., *William Wordsworth* (Oxford and New York: Oxford Univ.
Press, 1990), 260, 705n.

142. J. R. R. Tolkien, *The Return of the King* (New York: Ballantine Books,
1965), 115.

143. It would be possible to distinguish between "reference," the actual designation of objects by linguistic structures, and "referentiality," a linguistic
mimesis of reference or a "reference effect" (like the one described in these
pages) that operates by back-formation rather than actual designation. In
ordinary usage, however, the two terms are virtually synonymous. On the
idea that what literary ("fictive") texts imitate are various sorts of "natural" or non-literary texts, see Barbara Herrnstein Smith's penetrating *On the
Margins of Discourse: The Relation of Literature to Language* (Chicago: University of Chicago Press, 1978). Also pertinent, of course, is Roland Barthes'
"L'Effet de Réel," *Communications* 11 (1968), 84–9.

144. It is possible to reach a similar if not identical conclusion by other routes.
Culler's paraphrase of the Saussurian notion that "language is not a nomen-
clature: it articulates the world rather than simply representing what is
already given" suggests one alternative path (Culler, *Literary in Theory*, 11).
Another is suggested by Derrida's positing of "an infinite chain, ineluctably
multiplying the supplementary mediations that produce the sense of the
very thing they defer: the mirage of the thing itself, of immediate presence, of originary perception. Immediacy is derived." Jacques Derrida, *Of
Grammatology*, trans. Gayatri Chakravorty Spivak (Baltimore and London:
The Johns Hopkins University Press, 1976), 157.

145. Wallace Stevens, "The Idea of Order at Key West," in *The Norton Anthology
of Poetry*, shorter 4th edition, ed. Margaret Ferguson, Mary Jo Salter, Jon
Stallworthy (New York and London: W. W. Norton, 1997), 725–6 (lines 12–
15, 36–42).

146. Ludwig Wittgenstein, *Zettel*, eds. G. E. M. Anscombe and G. H. von Wright, trans. G. E. M. Anscombe (Berkeley and Los Angeles: Univ. of California Press, 1970), entry No. 160, p. 28e.

147. On this question, which he terms (in language that I find problematic) "the word's generative duplications of itself rather than of the world," see Garrett Stewart's review essay, "Staying Powers," *MLQ* 54:2, 296. See also Veronica Forrest-Thomson's remark in her *Poetic Artifice: A Theory of Twentieth-Century Poetry* (Manchester: Manchester University Press, 1978), x:

    Every reader of poetry knows that statements are changed by their insertion in a poem, that they no longer mean what they would mean in ordinary speech because of the form in which they appear. To state the relationship between poetry and the external world, however – to show precisely how poetic form and poetic context affect the sentences they include and the non-verbal worlds which the sentences imply – is difficult.

148. William H. Galperin, *The Historical Austen* (Philadelphia: University of Pennsylvania Press, 2003), 1.

149. Lodge, *Language of Fiction*, 62.

150. Ted Hughes, *The Collected Poems*, ed. Paul Keegan (New York: Farrar, Straus & Giroux, 2003), 68.

151. This procedure of reading is a good deal like the operations of metaphor, which is at once an assertion of identity and, since one thing can never be another thing, a tacit presupposing of difference and thus a pretending that one thing is another; the first perspective is rhetorical, the second referential.

152. Keats, "Bright Star," in *The Norton Anthology of Poetry*, shorter 4th edition, ed. Margaret Ferguson, Mary Jo Salter, Jon Stallworthy (New York and London: W. W. Norton, 1997), 514.

153. The phonetic similarity is of course between "soft-fallen" and "soft fall and."

154. The conventional use of the terms "formalist" and "deconstructive" here should not obscure the extent to which deconstructive criticism is, at base, a modality of formalism.

155. 'We must bear in mind that the "third person" is the form of the verbal (or pronominal) paradigm that does *not* refer to a person because it refers to an object located outside direct address. But it exists and is characterized only by its opposition to the person *I* of the speaker who, in uttering it, situates it as "non-person." ' Emile Benveniste, *Problems in General Linguistics*, trans. Mary Elizabeth Meek, 2 vols. (Coral Gables, Fla.: University of Miami Press,1971), I:229. Cf. "Two's company, three's a crowd."

156. John Keats, *Selected Letters*, ed. Robert Gittings (Oxford and New York: Oxford Univ. Press, 2002), 95.

157. See Keats' "This Living Hand" for a poem which plays on just this ambiguity, and see also Jonathan Culler's discussion of the poem in

his illuminating essay, "Apostrophe," in *The Pursuit of Signs* (London: Routledge, 1981), 149–71.

158. The echo in "hung" of the last lines of the "Ode on Melancholy" may suggest a parallel to the gift of double aspect that the empirical poet's translation into textuality bestows: "His soul shall taste the sadness of her might,/And be among her cloudy trophies hung." It is worth recalling that "sadness" in Keats' time still means "seriousness" as well as melancholy, and – beyond that – that the word has origins in terms for fullness, satiety, thus enabling a kind of pun capturing both the deprivation and the plenitude of poetic existence. *OED*, s.v. "sad," offers this etymological note:

> Cognate with Old Dutch *sat* (Middle Dutch sat, zat, Dutch zat), Old Saxon *sad* (Middle Low German sat), Old High German *sat* (Middle High German *sat*, German *satt*), Old Icelandic *saðr* (rare; superseded by *saddr*, past participle of the derived verb *seðja* to satiate), Gothic *sas* (all in sense A. 1) < the same Indo-European base as classical Latin *sat*, *satis* enough, *satur* satisfied, full, Old Irish *sáith* (noun) sufficiency, Lithuanian *sotus* filling, full, also (with prefixation in – A- prefix6) ancient Greek insatiate, all showing a derivative formation (apparently originally a participial formation corresponding to ancient Greek forms in -*tos*, classical Latin -*tus*; compare OLD adj., COLD adj.) of an Indo-European base meaning 'to satisfy' also represented by ancient Greek (aorist) *asai* to satiate.

159. Abrams, "Transformation," 108–9; Brooks, *Urn*, 203.

3 New Formalist Interpretation

1. Charles Altieri, "Presence and Reference in a Literary Text: The Example of Williams' 'This Is Just to Say,'" *Critical Inquiry*, 5:3 (Spring, 1979), pp. 489–510. See especially pp. 497–8, 500 (and n. 11), 509. A slightly fuller excerpt (509, my emphasis) will do more justice to the way Altieri conceives of reference: "Literary actions, then, can be described as synthetic images which connect to experience as possible predicates or ways of picturing experience but do not themselves denote specific states of affairs. *These actions refer not to a world but to a grammar for describing actions in the world.*"

2. Similarly, the entire text concludes without any punctuation, even though the two parallel descriptive phrases, "so sweet/and so cold," intimate a conclusive-sounding cadence. The text undeniably ends, yet it is also not conventionally demarcated from other texts, or from the discourse and the world that are its contexts. Like Frost's "And miles to go before I sleep,/And miles to go before I sleep," Williams' concluding lines might be fancifully thought of as a Modernist nod to the closing couplet of the Shakespearean sonnet, e.g., No. 30: "But if the while I think on thee, dear friend,/All losses are restored and sorrows end."

3. Berryman, "Prufrock's Dilemma," in John Berryman, *The Freedom of the Poet* (New York: Farrar Straus & Giroux, 1976), 270.

4. http://www.dartmouth.edu/~milton/reading_room/sonnets/sonnet_19/index.shtml

5. Compare, to take just one instance, the final stanza of Matthew Arnold's "Dover Beach":

> Ah, love, let us be true
> To one another! for the world, which seems
> To lie before us like a land of dreams,
> So various, so beautiful, so new,
> Hath really neither joy, nor love, nor light,
> Nor certitude, nor peace, nor help for pain;
> And we are here as on a darkling plain
> Swept with confused alarms of struggle and flight,
> Where ignorant armies clash by night.

Admittedly, if we take Milton's line 7 to recall John 9:4 – and it is by no means inevitable that we should do so – then literal blindness becomes part of the poem's range of reference (at least, of allusion). But that is no argument against taking the reference to physical blindness metaphorically. Jesus himself says, in that very text, metaphorically, "I am the light of the world."

6. Though this last does not preclude the possibility of any number of similarities or shared traits between monologuist and actual poet.

7. Robert Browning, "My Last Duchess," in M. H. Abrams *et al.*, eds., *The Norton Anthology of English Literature*, 7th ed. (New York and London: Norton, 2000), II: 1352–3, line 5.

8. Ibid., ll. 11–13.

9. Ibid., ll. 53–4.

10. The real pertinence of the second definition of dramatic monologue is thus not that the poem is not in its author's voice but that the voice in the poem has a source other than its ostensible speaker. From a formalist point of view, saying that a poem is not in its author's voice is not a literary critical statement at all, though saying that a dramatic monologue has a speaker and a silent audience imagined as occupying the same portion of spacetime is.

11. William Keach, " 'Words Are Things': Romantic Ideology and the Matter of Poetic Language," in ed. George Levine, *Aesthetics and Ideology* (New Brunswick, NJ: Rutgers University Press, 1994), 221.

12. Ibid., 234.

13. I have silently corrected "Grave" to "Graven" in line 6.

14. Brooks, *Urn*, 3.

15. Barbara Johnson, "Teaching Deconstructively," in *Writing and Reading Differently*, ed. G. Douglas Atkins and Michael L. Johnson (Lawrence, Kansas: University Press of Kansas, 1985), 140.

16. The revolutionary reading is Stuart Curran's in *Poetic Form and British Romanticism* (New York: Oxford UP, 1986), 55, quoted in Susan Wolfson, *Formal Charges*, 205. The "self-arousal" remark is Wolfson's on the preceding page of *Formal Charges* (204).

17. *The Complete Poetry of Ben Jonson*, ed. William B. Hunter, Jr. (New York: W. W. Norton & Co., 1968), 95.

18. William Empson, *Seven Types of Ambiguity*, 1930 (New York: New Directions, 1966), 242. On 242–3, Empson has more to say of these lines, chiefly in the mode of biographical speculation.
19. The "drinke divine" is presumably nectar which, along with ambrosia, with which it was sometimes confounded, was taken to be a source of immortality.
20. See OED s.v. "but, prep., adv., conj," A.II.8.
21. Admittedly, Empson concedes that "you may take the matter more seriously, so as to regard these lines as a true statement of two opposites" (*Seven Types*, 242). But he then turns to speculations concerning Jonson's biography and psychology that do not so much read the lines differently as root their inadvertence in something besides sheer randomness.
22. Such "provisional closure" or revisable finality has much in common with the scientific assumption that what we currently know is both true and potentially revisable. For thinkers like many fundamentalist "Creationists," in contrast, the only choice is between unquestionable dogmatism and "a [mere] theory" such as evolution.
23. Henry James, Preface to *Roderick Hudson*, in *The Art of the Novel: Critical Prefaces by Henry James*, ed. R. P. Blackmur (New York and London: Charles Scribner's Sons, 1934), 5.
24. *Shelley's Poetry and Prose*, 2nd edition, ed. Donald H. Reiman and Neil Fraistat (New York: W. W. Norton & Co., 2002), 326–7.
25. Shelley to Leigh Hunt, 23 December 1819, *The Letters of Percy Bysshe Shelley*, ed. Frederick L. Jones (Oxford: Clarendon Press, 1964), 2:167. I allude, of course, to Matthew Arnold's notorious description of Shelley as "a beautiful and ineffectual angel, beating in the void his luminous wings in vain." Matthew Arnold, "Shelley," *Essays in Criticism: Second Series*, *Works* (London: Macmillan, 1903), 14:185.
26. See Wolfson, *Formal Charges*, 204–6.
27. Ibid., 205.
28. James Chandler, *England in 1819: The Politics of Literary Culture and the Case of Romantic Historicism* (Chicago: University of Chicago Press, 1998), 24.
29. Ibid., 24–5.
30. Ibid., 27.
31. Ibid., 27, 31.
32. The idea of temporal progress is underscored not just by the rhetorical prophecy of the lines, and the structure of expectation created by the periodic sentence, but also by the startling enjambment of "may/Burst" and by the etymological link between "tempestuous" and temporal duration. See the etymology in OED, s.v. "tempest": "OF. tempeste, fem. (11th c. in Roland) = It., Prov. tempesta:pop. L. *tempesta-m, for cl. L. tempests, -tem season, weather, storm, f. tempus a time, a season," my emphasis. On "tempest," syntax, rhyme, Shelley's intertextual relationship with Burke, and much else, see Susan Wolfson's closely argued "Popular Songs and Ballads: Writing the 'Unwritten Story in 1819,'" in *The Oxford Handbook of Percy Bysshe Shelley*, ed. Michael O'Neill and Anthony Howe, with the assistance of Madeleine Callaghan (Oxford: Oxford University Press, 2012), 341–59.

33. John 8:32 (KJV).
34. In my view, the phantom is not quite "the meaning of the terms that come before" but the possibility of our understanding that meaning correctly: a revelatory force that first shows princes to be dregs and mud, and rulers to be leeches, but then shows both to be graves.
35. Alexander Pope, "The First Satire of the Second Book of Horace Imitated" ll. 106–7, 115, in ed. John Butt, *The Poems of Alexander Pope* (New Haven & London: Yale Univ. Press, 1963), 613–18.
36. William Keach, *Arbitrary Power: Romanticism, Language, Politics* (Princeton: Princeton University Press, 2004), 21.
37. Percy Bysshe Shelley, *A Defence of Poetry*, in *Shelley's Poetry and Prose*, p. 535. My emphasis. Also available at: http://www.thomaslovepeacock.net/defence.html
38. W. H. Auden, lines 36–7 of "In Memory of W. B. Yeats," in *The Collected Poetry of W. H. Auden* (New York: Random House, 1945), p. 50.
39. William Shakespeare, *I Henry IV*, III.i.52–4, in *The Riverside Shakespeare*, 2nd. ed. G. Blakemore Evans and J. J. M. Tobin (New York: Houghton Mifflin, 1997), p. 906.
40. George Levine, "Introduction: Reclaiming the Aesthetic," in ed. George Levine, *Aesthetics and Ideology* (New Brunswick, NJ: Rutgers University Press, 1994), 20.
41. Ibid., 18.
42. I borrow Jonathan Culler's laconic definition of hegemony: "an arrangement of domination accepted by those who are dominated." Jonathan Culler, *Literary Theory: A Very Short Introduction* (Oxford and New York: Oxford UP, 1997), p. 48.
43. Antony Easthope, *Poetry as Discourse* (London and New York: Methuen, 1983), p. 119.
44. Terry Eagleton, *How to Read a Poem* (Oxford: Blackwell, 2007), p. 162. In one sense, Eagleton is undeniably correct. From the couplets as he reads them, we do indeed get "a whole social ideology," but it is Eagleton's, not Pope's.
45. Not to mention that Eagleton's primary point of reference is *The Dunciad*, the least likely text of Pope's to conform to these notions of social rigidity and order. Eagleton gets around this difficulty by viewing the verse-form of *The Dunciad* as a "riposte" to the "carnival of unreason" it portrays. Ibid., p. 88.
46. J. Paul Hunter, "Formalism and History: Binarism and the Anglophone Couplet," *MLQ* 61:1 (March 2000), 115.
47. Ibid., 119.
48. Ibid., 120. Virtually all modern discussions of Pope's couplet rhetoric, mine not least, owe a significant debt to two essays by Wimsatt: "One Relation of Rhyme to Reason," and "Rhetoric and Poems: Alexander Pope," both *in The Verbal Icon* (Lexington: The University Press of Kentucky, 1954), 152–66, 168–85. Another extremely influential early study is Maynard Mack, " 'Wit and Poetry and Pope': Some Observations on His Imagery," in *Pope and His Contemporaries: Essays Presented to George Sherburn*, ed. James L. Clifford and Louis A. Landa (Oxford, 1949), 20–40.

49. Alexander Pope, *The Rape of the Lock*, II. 20–21, IV. 53–4, in ed. John Butt, *The Poems of Alexander Pope* (New Haven & London: Yale Univ. Press, 1963), 217–42.
50. "Wit in the *Essay on Criticism*," in William Empson, *The Structure of Complex Words* (Ann Arbor: Univ. of Michigan Press, 1967), 92. The essay first appeared in *Hudson Review* 2 (1950): 559–77. On mock-forms, see also Fredric V. Bogel, *The Difference Satire Makes: Rhetoric and Reading from Jonson to Byron* (Ithaca and London: Cornell UP, 2001), 22–3.
51. Pope, *Rape*, IV.87, 100.
52. Ibid., III. 25–8, my emphasis.
53. Ibid., III. 95–100, my emphasis. My interpretation of the poem's gender politics is indebted to stimulating conversations with Wendy S. Jones.
54. Ibid., I.7–12.
55. Hunter, 121.
56. Particularly since the essay was reprinted in the significant New Formalist collection *Reading for Form*, Susan J. Wolfson and Marshall Brown, eds. (Seattle and London: Univ. of Washington Press, 2006), it is somewhat puzzling that Hunter's useful study offers so little in the way of detailed analysis – close reading – of the couplets that serve as the essay's central focus.
57. In the following paragraphs, I summarize and adapt some passages from my "Dulness Unbound: Rhetoric and Pope's *Dunciad*," *PMLA* 97 (No. 5), Oct. 1982, 844–55, esp. pp. 846 and 852–4.
58. At several points in his prose, Pope makes a similar argument. In *The Prose Works of Alexander Pope, 1711–1720*, ed. Norman Ault (Oxford: Blackwell, 1936), 47, he says that the passions must be regulated but not extinguished, for extinguishing them would put out "the light of the Soul." It is the nature of the passions that they be so regulated, for they were "designed for Subjection" and, like prefixes or suffixes, they properly exist only in bound form (*Prose Works*, 45). They are, so to speak, intrinsically *combinanda*. And like the passions, which in free form can destroy us, our very faults, when mastered, prove to be fortunate faults:

> It is not so much the being exempt from faults, as the having overcome them, that is an advantage to us; it being with the follies of the mind as with the weeds of a field, which, if destroyed and consumed upon the place of their birth, enrich and improve it more than if none had ever sprung there.

The Works of Alexander Pope, W. Elwin and W. J. Courthope, eds., Vol. 10 (London, 1886), 551, my emphasis.
59. C. J. Rawson, "Order and Cruelty: A Reading of Swift (with Some Comments on Pope and Johnson)," *Essays in Criticism* 20 (1970), 50.
60. Denis Donoghue, *Walter Pater: Lover of Strange Souls* (N.Y.: Knopf, 1995), 288, my emphasis. Donoghue, *Speaking of Beauty* (New Haven & London Yale UP, 2003), 121. Both cited in Leighton, *On Form*, 23.
61. Phillis Wheatley, "On Being Brought from AFRICA to AMERICA," in *Phillis Wheatley: Complete Writings*, ed. Vincent Carretta (New York: Penguin, 2001), 13.

62. Henry Louis Gates, Jr., *The Trials of Phillis Wheatley* (N.Y.: Basic Books, 2003), 70.
63. Ibid., 76–7. The quotations are, respectively, from Seymour Gross and Stephen Henderson.
64. Ibid., 77–8.
65. Ibid., 87, 89.
66. Ibid., 89.
67. In Wheatley, p. 11 (ll. 3–6).
68. Ibid., p. 41 (ll. 21–31, my emphasis). See also the variant versions of the poem on pp. 128–31.
69. See Revelation 7:14 (KJV).
70. I am pleased to note that a fine recent decent discussion of Wheatley agrees with this syntactic possibility, and finds a similar wavering in the meaning of "black." See Suvir Kaul, *Eighteenth-century British Literature and Postcolonial Studies* (Edinburgh: Edinburgh UP, 2009), 136–7:

    The penultimate line holds a similar tension in place – it appeals to, even exhorts, Christians to remember that "*Negroes*," who are "black as *Cain*," may still be redeemed. And yet readers of the Bible will know that Cain is "black" because of his sin, not by his color. That being the case, might the phrase "black as *Cain*" modify erring "*Christians*" as well as "*Negroes*," the comma between the two words not separating these communities as much as linking them into a commonality of sin and redemption?

71. Gates, *Trials*, 70, 71.
72. Carretta, xx–xxi.
73. Stephen Cohen, ed., *Shakespeare and Historical Formalism* (Aldershot, England: Ashgate, 2007), 14.
74. Richard Strier, "Afterword: How Formalism Became a Dirty Word, and Why We Can't Do Without It," *Renaissance Literature and Its Formal Engagements*, ed. Mark David Rasmussen (New York: Palgrave, 2002), 210. Brooks of course took up this challenge late in his career with *Historical Evidence and the Reading of Seventeenth-Century Poetry* (Columbia, MO, and London: University of Missouri Press, 1991).
75. John McIntyre and Miranda Hickman, eds., *Rereading the New Criticism* (Columbus: Ohio State University Press, 2012), 231.
76. Fredric Jameson, "The Ideology of the Text," in *The Ideologies of Theory* (Minneapolis: Univ. of Minnesota press1987), 18. Cited in Culler, *The Literary in Theory*, 245.
77. Garrett Stewart, "Staying Powers," 306.
78. Ellen Rooney, "Form and Contentment," in *Reading for Form*, ed. Susan J. Wolfson and Marshall Brown (Seattle and London: Univ. of Washington Press, 2006), 35. Rooney's essay was first published in 2000.
79. Gallop, "Ethics of Reading," 8.
80. Anthony Pollock, "Formalist Cultural Criticism and the Post-Restoration Periodical," *PQ* 86:3 (2007) 229.
81. Ibid., 235, 238.
82. http://www.americanrhetoric.com/speeches/mariocuomo1984dnc.htm
83. Jonathan Miller, *The Body in Question* (New York: Random House, 1978), 42.

84. Of course, "direct sensory experience" is itself an illusion, since sensory perception is powerfully mediated by conceptual activity. As Derrida says, "There never was any 'perception.'" Jacques Derrida, *Speech and Phenomena and Other Essays on Husserl's Theory of Signs*, trans. David Allison (Evanston: Nothwestern Univ. Press, 1973), 103.

85. Notice, as well, the intense nesting of interpretive frames that stretches from Voltaire himself to Houdon's bust, to the reproduction of Houdon's bust in Dali's painting (when it is not concealed by the slavemarket details), to the reproduction of Dali's painting in Miller's text, to the account of Dali's painting that Miller's caption to the illustration supplies, to the textual and argumentative frame of Miller's main text, to the apprehension and processing of that text by any reader of *The Body in Question*. Could there be a better object lesson in the non-immediacy of knowing?

86. Barbara W. Tuchman, *A Distant Mirror: The Calamitous 14th Century* (New York: Ballantine Books, 1978). For a particularly scathing review, see Bernard S. Bachrach in *The American Historical Review*, 84:3 (June 1979), 724–5.

87. Tuchman, xiv.

88. Tuchman, 88–9.

89. Ibid., 582.

90. The italics in the last two quoted passages are mine.

91. Charles Dickens, *Great Expectations*, ed. Jill Kriegel (San Francisco: Ignatius Press, 2010), 60.

92. Cohen, *Shakespeare and Historical Formalism*, 15.

93. Thorstein Veblen, *The Theory of the Leisure Class* (New York: Modern Library, 1961), 32–4. In this discussion of Veblen, I adapt a few pages (205–11) from my chapter "Understanding Prose" in *Teaching Prose: A Guide for Writing Instructors*, ed. Fredric V. Bogel and Katherine K. Gottschalk (New York and London: Norton, 1984), pp. 155–215.

94. Robert L. Heilbroner, *The Worldly Philosophers: The Lives, Times, and Ideas of the Great Economic Thinkers*, 7th ed. (New York: Simon and Schuster, 1999), 219, 247.

95. I borrow the at/through distinction from Richard A. Lanham, who formulates and discusses it brilliantly in a number of writings, including "*At* and *Through*: The Opaque Style and Its Uses," in *Literacy and the Survival of Humanism* (New Haven and London: Yale UP, 1983), 58–86.

96. Michael Barany, "Mathematical Ideality and the Practice of Translation," unpublished paper, used by kind permission of the author, p. 16.

97. Ibid., 6. Barany quotes from Ludwig Wittgenstein, *Remarks on the Foundations of Mathematics* (Oxford: Basil Blackwell, 1956), I:167.

98. Ibid., 20.

99. Ibid., 16. Cf. Barany's later remarks: "Strikingly often, theorists make exceptions in their arguments for mathematical and logical thought, and strikingly often the false edifice of mathematical ideality is allowed to stand unassailed and even unregarded" (25).

100. Ibid., 16, 18.

101. Ibid., 17.

102. "Logic's atemporality is constructed in large part through the structure of mathematical narratives," Ibid., 19.

103. Ibid., 19–20, my emphasis.
104. Ibid., 11.
105. Barany makes this point from a different angle in another essay, "The Proof is in the Putting: Testimony, Belief, and Why Mathematicians Make Bad Witnesses" (p. 11, my emphasis):

> The testimony of the mathematician aspires to be universal, to defy and efface the singularity upon which all witnessing is founded. In short, it tries to make the exterior into the interior. It is not a relation with the other, because to the mathematical proposition there is no other. The mathematician's testimony must be structured against belief. It is a proof, structured to create so many witnesses as to forbid perjury. It is put in such a way that witnesses come to number as the stars in the sky. *The proof, in the final analysis, is in the putting.*

Used by kind permission of the author. See also Michael Barany and Donald MacKenzie, "Chalk: Materials and Concepts in Mathematics Research," under revision for *New Representation in Scientific Practice*, eds. Catelijne Coopmans, Michael Lynch, Janet Vertesi, and Steve Woolgar (forthcoming, MIT Press).

4 Textual Infatuation, True Infatuation

1. Theodor Adorno, *Minima Moralia: Reflections From Damaged Life*, trans. E. F. N. Jephcott (London & New York: Verso, 2005), 74.
2. Aristotle, *Metaphysics*, trans. W. D. Ross, *The Internet Classics Archive*, http://classics.mit.edu/Aristotle/metaphysics.7.vii.html
3. See James Benziger, "Organic Unity: Leibniz to Coleridge," *PMLA* 66:2 (March 1951), 24:

> Yet even Socrates himself sometimes shows a bias in favor of seeing things only under the aspect of unity: for instance, of seeing the good, the true, and the beautiful as one, but of failing to see them as also different. A whole history of human thought might be compiled to show how in many ages and places philosophers of a certain sort, and perhaps ordinary men in certain moods, have derived great satisfaction from telling us that things generally regarded as distinct from one another are, in reality, one and the same. In such a history a chapter of some length would have to be devoted to the idea of organic unity in art.

4. Philip E. Lewis, "Review: Athletic Criticism," *Diacritics*, 1:2 (Winter, 1971), 5.
5. Geoffrey H. Hartman, "The Voice of the Shuttle: Language from the Point of View of Literature," in *Beyond Formalism* (New Haven: Yale Univ. Press, 1970), 337–55. Jonathan Culler, "Apostrophe," in *The Pursuit of Signs* (London: Routledge, 1981), 149–71.
6. Brooks, *Urn*, 203; Brooks and Warren, *Understanding Poetry*, 695.
7. T. S. Eliot, "Tradition and the Individual Talent," in Frank Kermode, ed., *Selected Prose of T. S. Eliot* (San Diego, New York, London: Harvest Books, 1975), 38–9.
8. Brooks and Warren, *Understanding Poetry* (1938), 562.

9. Brooks, *Urn*, 213.
10. As Douglas Mao notes in "The New Critics and the Text-Object," *ELH* 63.1 (1996), 233, both Geoffrey Hartman and John Guillory have also remarked on the convergence of New Criticism, Southern Agrarianism, and Frankfurt School critical theory.
11. Allen Tate, "Remarks on the Southern Religion," in *I'll Take My Stand: The South and the Agrarian Tradition*, by 12 Southerners (N.Y. & London: Harper & Row, 1930), 156–7.
12. These terms are part of the vocabulary of critique that pervades Adorno's *Minima Moralia: Reflections from Damaged Life*, trans. E. F. N. Jephcott (London & New York: Verso, 2005).
13. Max Horkheimer and Theodor W. Adorno, *Dialectic of Enlightenment: Philosophical Fragments*, ed. Gunzelin Schmid Noerr, trans. Edmund Jephcott (Stanford: Stanford UP, 2002), 29. See also p. 9, on enlightenment, abstraction, and the "herd."
14. Ibid., 175.
15. Ibid., 21. On the links between New Criticism and the Frankfurt School (the latter never explicitly mentioned in her essay), compare this shrewdly historical passage from Catherine Gallagher's "The History of Literary Criticism," *Daedalus* 126:1 (Winter 1997), 134:

> The New Critics of the 1930s identified themselves with an international, aesthetic modernist reaction against certain aspects of modernization. Against the homogenizing tendencies of the marketplace, the merely formal individualism of democratic politics, and the standardized consciousness produced by industrial work places and urban living, they counterposed a deeper, truer, and more qualitative selfhood. Their subjects were not interchangeable units with identical rights, but unique entities, substantive persons, whose very existence was threatened by marketplace exchange and mass culture. Their sentiments about modern society were translated into a critical practice by letting the 'integrity' of the literary work stand in for the 'integrity' of all forms of endangered specificity. In this regard, they did not depart from the standard aesthetic doctrines of the nineteenth century. Rather, the founding New Critics placed a new, Modernist emphasis on 'particularity,' on meanings that were inextricable from their expression. For example, they stressed ambiguity because they disapproved of language that was a medium of exchange. Fungibility and translatability were the enemy; an adequate paraphrase would be the sign of a bad poem. Hence, they made a new kind of problem out of meaning, one that was not amenable to the historical-philological methods then dominating the discipline.

16. Mao, 231.
17. Ibid.
18. John Crowe Ransom, *The World's Body* (New York and London: Charles Scribner's Sons, 1938), 45.
19. Ibid.
20. Ibid., 348.
21. Ibid., x.

22. John Crowe Ransom, *The New Criticism* (Norfolk, CT.: New Directions, 1941), 281; Ransom, *The World's Body*, 142. For Adorno's more skeptical contention that the lyric speaking voice, or "I," merely "creates the illusion of nature emerging from alienation," see his "On Lyric Poetry and Society," in Theodor W. Adorno, *Notes to Literature*, vol. 1, trans. Sherry Weber Nicholsen, ed. Rolf Tiedemann (N.Y.: Columbia, UP, 1991), 41.

23. W. K. Wimsatt, *The Verbal Icon: Studies in the Meaning of Poetry* (Lexington: The University Press of Kentucky, 1954), x. Ransom asserts, following Charles W. Morris, that "art deals essentially, though not exclusively, in iconic signs" (Ransom, *The New Criticism*, 287). In *A History of Modern Criticism: 1750–1950* (New Haven and London: Yale UP, 1986), 286, René Wellek links Wimsatt's conception of the way poetic tension, and particularly metaphor, offer "a fresh vision of reality, a fullness, completeness, concreteness of experience" with Ransom's idea of "The World's Body."

24. Mao, 235.

25. Ransom, *The World's Body*, 349.

26. Ibid., 127.

27. On meter, see (among many passages), Ransom's discussion in *The New Criticism*, 259–61, which includes this telling remark:

> Doubtless the meaning of the poem is more important than the meter, and so...we do not have so much a coincidence of two structures accomplished in the same set of words, as we have a logical structure manifesting a musical character which is adventitious, and amounts to a texture for it. (261)

28. Ransom *The New Criticism*, 219–20.

29. Ibid., 281.

30. Ransom, *The World's Body*, 349.

31. Ransom, *The New Criticism*, 167.

32. Ibid., 167, 169.

33. Brooks, *Urn*, 9.

34. Ibid., 3, 18. On unity, see also 212–14.

35. Ibid., 9–10.

36. Wolfson, *Formal Charges*, 16. Brooks's *Modern Poetry and the Tradition* (Chapel Hill: Univ. of North Carolina Press, 1939) is another source of such "alertly tortured" sentences moving between unity and disruption.

37. Benedetto Croce, *Aesthetic as Science of Expression and General Linguistic*, trans. Douglas Ainslie, 2d. ed. (London: Macmillan, 1922), Ch. II, p. 20.

38. William K. Wimsatt, Jr., and Cleanth Brooks, *Literary Criticism: A Short History* (New York: Knopf, 1957), p. 507.

39. Adorno, *Minima Moralia*, 74. On the general and the particular, as well as the objective and the subjective in Adorno, see Rei Terada's interesting discussion in Chapter 4 of *Looking Away: Phenomenality and Dissatisfaction, Kant to Adorno* (Cambridge, MA, and London: Harvard UP, 2009), esp. 191–95.

40. Alexander Pope, *An Essay on Criticism*, 245–6.

41. Alexander Pope, *An Essay on Man*, I.60.

42. Lacan's remark is cited in Shoshana Felman, *Jacques Lacan and the Adventure of Insight: Psychoanalysis in Contemporary Culture* (Cambridge, MA: Harvard UP, 1987), 12.
43. Cf. Ransom, *The World's Body*, 327–8: "But the philosopher is apt to see a lot of wood and no trees." Whether we take "a lot" to mean "much" or to mean "a woodlot," the point is clear.
44. Pope, *Essay on Man*, I. 292. Walter Benjamin examines the close-up and slow-motion photography as revelatory, not simply scale-altering, techniques in "The Work of Art in the Age of Mechanical Reproduction," in *Illuminations: Essays and Reflections*, ed. Hannah Arendt (N.Y.: Schocken Books, 1969), 217–52. See also Marjorie Garber, "Shakespeare in Slow Motion," *Profession* 2010, pp. 151–64.
45. Gallop, "Ethics of Reading," 11.
46. John Berryman, *Collected Poems, 1937–1971*, ed. Charles Thornbury (New York: Faber & Faber, 1991), 154.
47. Berryman was, incidentally, a close student of English Renaissance drama.
48. John Milton, *Paradise Lost*, V. 853–61, my emphasis. If we allow a pun on "-raised" and "-razed," Milton's "self-begot, self-raised" becomes a verbal precursor of Berryman's "suisired."
49. And the work of composing a whole book or concerto or painting, or coming to know a whole person, and so on.
50. See also Jacques Derrida, "The Law of Genre," trans. Avitall Ronell, *Critical Inquiry*, 7:1 (Autumn, 1980), 65: "Every text participates in one or several genres, there is no genreless text; there is always a genre and genres, yet such participation never amounts to belonging." See also Ralph Cohen, "History and Genre," *New Literary History* 17 (1986), 203–18. Finally, there is Kenneth Burke's much earlier (1945) and in certain ways more satisfactory discussion in Appendix B, "The Problem of the Intrinsic," in Kenneth Burke, *A Grammar of Motives and A Rhetoric of Motives* (Cleveland and New York: World Publishing Company, 1962), 465–84.
51. Here is Loesberg announcing a related embrace of partiality:

> If one positions the anti-formalism of the various genres of historicism and cultural studies now current in the study of Victorian literature as current versions of that Victorian anxiety at being hermetically enclosed in beautiful but empty forms, then surely an aestheticist and formalist backlash is more than overdue. And, rather than taking an analytical or neutrally critical response to this flux and reflux, I intend to espouse just such a backlash. If backlash implies partialness, *the potential partiality of formalism is, I think, one of its less recognized values.*

Jonathan Loesberg, "Cultural Studies, Victorian Studies, and Formalism," *Victorian Literature and Culture*, 27:2 (1999), 537, my emphasis.
52. Jonathan Culler, "In Defence of Overinterpretation," in Umberto Eco, with Richard Rorty, Jonathan Culler, Christine Brooke-Rose, ed. Stefan Collini, *Interpretation and Overinterpretation* (Cambridge: Cambridge Univ. Press, 1992), 113.
53. J. Hillis Miller, "The Critic as Host," *Critical Inquiry*, 3:3, (Spring, 1977), pp. 439–47, esp. 441–4. The phrase "inexorable law" appears on 447.

54. Richard Strier, *Resistant Structures: Particularity, Radicalism, and Renaissance Texts* (Berkeley, Los Angeles, London: University of California Press, 1995), 51.
55. See above, n. 10.
56. Adorno, *Minima Moralia*, 72.
57. Ibid.
58. Ibid.
59. Ibid., 80. Notice that Adorno does not say "the *truth* of a thought" but its "*value*" – that is, its power to generate further conceptual productivity.
60. Ibid., 73.
61. Simon Jarvis, *Adorno: A Critical Introduction* (Cambridge: Polity Press, 1998), 1.
62. Ibid., 91.
63. Mao, 235.
64. Adorno, *Minima Moralia*, 79.
65. Ibid.
66. Ibid., 72.
67. Adorno, *Minima Moralia*, 69.
68. Strier, *Resistant Structures* 4.
69. *Hart Crane's "The Bridge": An Annotated Edition*, ed. Lawrence Kramer (New York: Fordham Univ. Press, 2011), 1–2.
70. Of course, even the semantic import of words is not wholly given – exhausted – prior to particular instances, though dictionary definitions may implicitly suggest that it is. Cf. Cathy Caruth, "Introduction: The Insistence of Reference," in *Critical Encounters: Reference and Responsibility in Deconstructive Writing*, ed. Cathy Caruth and Deborah Esch (New Brunswick: Rutgers Univ. Press, 1995), pp. 1–3.
71. Jarvis, *Adorno*, 105. Cf. Rooney, "Form and Contentment," 45: "Form understood as a product of reading entails a revaluation of value whose results can never be known in advance."
72. T. S. Eliot, to Stephen Spender (May 1935), quoted in *Selected Prose of T. S. Eliot*, ed. Frank Kermode (San Diego, New York, London: Harvest Books, 1975), 13.
73. Ibid., 206.
74. Kevin Davies, *Comp.* (Washington, D.C.: Edge Books, 2000), 67.
75. Discussion, Neoformalism Conference, Univ. of Ghent (Belgium), Sept. 2010.
76. Ellen Rooney, "Form and Contentment," in *Reading for Form*, ed. Susan J. Wolfson and Marshall Brown (Seattle and London: Univ. of Washington Press, 2006), 45. Compare Adorno, *Minima Moralia*, 69, cited above, p. 31. And, substituting "materials" for "form," consider Robert Rauschenberg's declaration: "I don't really trust ideas, especially good ones. Rather I put my trust in the materials that confront me, because they put me in touch with the unknown" (Cited in commentary on Rauschenberg's "Migration," *Johnson Museum of Art*, Cornell University, 2011: *http://museum.cornell.edu/collections/view/migration.html*).
77. Vaihinger, xlvi–xlvii.
78. Jarvis, 91.
79. Adorno, *Minima Moralia*, p. 69.

80. Compare the lyric by Sting, "If you love somebody, set them free," which can be seen not only as an awkward effort to avoid a sexist pronoun by leaping into the ungrammaticality of the plural but also as a suggestion that a single person, understood adequately, unfolds as a plurality of personhood. http://www.azlyrics.com/lyrics/sting/ifyoulovesomebodysetthemfree.html
81. Adorno, *Minima Moralia*, p.77, my emphasis.
82. Ibid., 74. Cf. Maria DiBattista, " 'Sabbath Eyes': Ideology and the Writer's Gaze," in *Aesthetics and Ideology*, ed. George Levine (New Brunswick, NJ: Rutgers Univ. Press, 1994), p. 175:

> In Adorno's formulation, we observe not a desperate paradox, but a dialectical reversal in which the aesthetic may be seen to rejoin and redeem its ideological components and counterparts. It is the aesthetic that makes Injustice its own, acknowledges it, and so attains to that self-awareness that distinguishes the false consciousness from the true, the 'just overall view' from the partial, self-indemnifying one.

83. Adorno, *Minima Moralia*, §48, p. 76.
84. Roger Foster, "Lingering with the Particular: *Minima Moralia*'s Critical Modernism," *Telos* 155 (summer, 2011), 88. Adorno, *Minima Moralia*, 38 (my emphasis). Recall Ransom's distinction between illustrations and images.
85. Adorno, *Minima Moralia*, p. 75.
86. Ibid.
87. Theodor W. Adorno, *Aesthetic Theory*, trans. Robert Hullot-Kentor (Minneapolis: Univ. of Minnesota Press, 1997), 35. See also the important discussion later in *Aesthetic Theory*, and employing a different vocabulary, of the artwork as a "monad" and of proper and improper modes of "subsumption" (179–80).
88. OED, s.v. "agon": "Etymology: < Greek ἀγών, originally 'a gathering or assembly' (< ἄ γ-ειν to lead, bring with one), esp. for the public games; hence 'the contest for the prize at the games,' and by extension, 'any contest or struggle.' "
89. Walter J. Ong, S. J., "The Jinnee in the Well-Wrought Urn," *Essays in Criticism* IV (July 1954), 319.
90. Troy A. Jollimore, *Love's Vision* (Princeton: Princeton Univ. Press, 2011), 26. On p. 86, Jollimore cites Alexander Nehamas, *Only a Promise of Happiness: The Place of Beauty in a World of Art* (Princeton: Princeton Univ. Press, 2010), pp. 43–4:

> We don't read the critics of *Hamlet*, or *Hamlet* itself, in order to determine how good the play is but in order to grasp what it has to offer us, which requires us to understand what it says; what it says may be truly magnificent, but making *that* judgment is never the purpose of reading.

Not approval or evaluation, then, but explorations of ontology and signification.
91. Ibid., 57.
92. Adorno, *Minima Moralia*, §48 (p. 76)
93. An odd phrase (mine), but Adorno's use of "versöhnen" is also odd, since the construction would normally require something for the one-sidedness

to be reconciled (versöhnt) *to* (mit). Adorno seems to be coining a usage that insists on the particular but elides the universal that, in his view, always threatens to swallow it up. My wrestling with this passage has been considerably aided by the generous assistance of Professor Peter Gilgen, German Studies, Cornell University.

94. Harold Schweizer, "With Sabbath Eyes: The Particular and the Claims of History in Elizabeth Bishop's 'Poem,'" *Journal of Modern Literature*, 28:2 (winter 2005), 55.

95. Adorno, *Minima Moralia*, §48, p. 76.

96. The celebrity "roast" – an ironic variant of the purely laudatory "toast" – works in a related fashion. The stature and good humor of the chosen figure are presumed adequate to survive the innumerable slights, most of them comical and exaggerated but many also woundingly accurate, affectionately offered by the "celebrants" of the event.

97. Ibid., 75.

98. Jollimore, 44.

99. Ibid., 72.

100. Theodor W. Adorno, *Minima Moralia: Reflexionen aus dem beschädigten Leben*, http://offene-uni.de/archiv/textz/textz_phil/minima_moral.pdf, p. 41, my emphasis.

101. Adorno, *Minima Moralia*, trans. Jephcott, §29, p. 50.

102. Jollimore, 4, xiv, 26, 56.

103. J. Hillis Miller, "The Ethics of Reading," in *The J. Hillis Miller Reader*, ed. Julian Wolfreys (Stanford: Stanford Univ. Press, 2005), p. 58.

104. The phrase "true infatuation" was a gift from Susan Sandman, Professor Emerita of Music, Wells College, who produced it in response to the author's early attempt to describe in conversation what has become part of the argument of this chapter. Here, as at many points in this study, it is possible to wonder whether the philosophical overtones of "true" clash with the largely constructivist character of much New Formalism. But to surrender the notion that truth is intrinsic in the object, "out there," simply empirically discoverable, is not to surrender the idea of truth itself. What is being revised in such a refusal of the intrinsic is our understanding of how knowledge is produced, not our belief that knowledge exists or can be reliable. New and incontrovertible scientific evidence that human vision is enabled not by the optic nerve but by specialized cells in the Achilles tendon would have no bearing on an archer's actual behavior in a target-shooting contest – or on the difference between hitting the bull's eye and missing it.

105. Compare John M. Ellis' much more general attempt to effect a *rapprochement* between science and literary criticism in *The Theory of Literary Criticism: A Logical Analysis* (Berkeley & Los Angeles: Univ. of California, Press, 1974), 210: "My conclusion ... is that a general notion of critical procedure is possible and useful, and it does not differ significantly from the more general logic of inquiry."

106. Roland Barthes, *The Responsibility of Forms: Critical Essays on Music, Art, and Representation*, trans. Richard Howard (Berkeley and Los Angeles: University of California Press, 1991), 234.

107. Angela Leighton, "About About: On Poetry and Paraphrase," *Midwest Studies in Philosophy*, XXXIII (2009), 175.
108. Derek Attridge, "Literary Form and the Demands of Politics: Otherness in J. M. Coetzee's *Age of Iron*," in George Levine, ed., *Aesthetics and Ideology* (New Brunswick, NJ: Rutgers University Press, 1994), 245. Theodor Adorno, *Negative Dialectics*, trans. E. B. Ashton (New York: Continuum, 1973), 33. And compare Karen Simecek, "Hearing Meaning and Poetry: An Interview with Angela Leighton," *Postgraduate Journal of Aesthetics* 9:3 (Summer 2012), 4–5:

> We've got this word "meaning," which is a noun, an abstract thing, and therefore we use terms like "grasp the meaning," as if with one's hand, getting hold of something and there it is, you've got it! As if meaning were a tactile object to be caught. But if we change the question, we might get closer to what poetry is up to. So rather than asking, *what is the meaning that I can grasp?* we might ask: *how does this poem try to make meaning?* where the emphasis falls on *trying to make*. The meaning is not a given, the end of a process, an object we might seize and hold; it's something that is being constructed as we search for it.

109. Immanuel Kant, *Critique of Pure Reason*, trans. F. Max Müller (Garden City, N.Y.: Doubleday, 1966), pp. 44–5.
110. See Wimsatt's interesting discussion of parts and wholes in his 1952 essay, "Explication as Criticism" – in particular, his remarks on the rival claims of part and whole, and his comment that "Extreme holism is obviously contrary to our experience of literature." The essay is reprinted in W. K. Wimsatt, *The Verbal Icon: Studies in the Meaning of Poetry* (Lexington: The University Press of Kentucky, 1954); the passages I allude to are on pp. 236–38.
111. See above, pp. 85–7.
112. Adorno, Minima Moralia, p. 77.

Coda: New Formalisms

1. Susan Wolfson, "Reading for Form without Formalism," *Literary Matters* 3:2 (2010), 14.
2. Geoffrey Hartman, *Beyond Formalism: Literary Essays 1958–1970* (New Haven and London: Yale UP, 1970), 42.
3. Heather Dubrow, "Guess Who's Coming to Dinner," in Wolfson and Brown, eds., *Reading for Form*, 98.
4. Garrett Stewart, "Foreign Offices," in Wolfson and Brown, eds., *Reading for Form*, 256.
5. Michael P. Clark, "Introduction," Michael P. Clark, ed., *The Revenge of the Aesthetic: The Place of Literature in Theory Today* (Berkeley & Los Angeles: University of California Press, 2000), 4.
6. Peter Brooks, "Aesthetics and Ideology – What Happened to Poetics?" in George Levine, ed., *Aesthetics and Ideology*, 165.
7. Northrop Frye, *The Educated Imagination* (Bloomington & London: Indiana University Press, 1964), 22, 78.

8. Clark, 13, my emphasis.
9. St. Augustine, *Soliloquies*, Book II, ¶18, trans. C. C. Starbuck, in *Basic Writings of Saint Augustine, Volume One: The Confessions and Twelve Treatises*, Whitney J. Oates, ed. (New York: Random House, 1948), 286. Available online at: http://www.newadvent.org/fathers/170302.htm
10. Paul Valéry to Philip Guston, quoted in Dore Ashton, *A Critical Study of Philip Guston* (Berkeley and Los Angeles: University of California Press, 1976), 132.

Bibliography

Abrams, M. H. "Art-as-Such: The Sociology of Modern Aesthetics." in M. H. Abrams and Michael Fischer, eds., *Doing Things with Texts: Essays in Criticism and Critical Theory*. New York and London: W. W. Norton, 1989, 135–58.

——. "The Transformation of English Studies: 1930–1995." *Daedalus*, 126:1 (Winter 1997), 105–31.

Adorno, Theodor W. *Aesthetic Theory*, trans. Robert Hullot-Kentor. Minneapolis: University of Minnesota Press, 1997.

——. *Minima Moralia: Reflections from Damaged Life*, trans. E. F. N. Jephcott. London New York: Verso, 2005.

——. *Minima Moralia: Reflexionen aus dem beschädigten Leben*, http://offene-uni.de/archiv/textz/textz_phil/minima_moral.pdf

——. *Negative Dialectics*, trans. E. B. Ashton. New York: Continuum, 1973.

——. "On Lyric Poetry and Society." Trans. Sherry Weber Nicholsen, ed. Rolf Tiedemann, *Notes to Literature*, vol. 1. New York: Columbia UP, 1991, 31–54.

Altieri, Charles. "Presence and Reference in a Literary Text: The Example of Williams' 'This Is Just to Say.'" *Critical Inquiry* 5:3 (Spring 1979), 489–510.

——. "Taking Lyrics Literally: Teaching Poetry in a Prose Culture." *New Literary History* 32:2 (Spring 2001), 259–81.

——. *The Particulars of Rapture: An Aesthetic of the Affects*. Ithaca and London: Cornell UP, 2003.

——. "What Theory Can Learn from New Directions in Contemporary American Poetry." *New Literary History*, 43:1 (Winter 2012), 65–87.

Aristotle. *Metaphysics*, trans. W. D. Ross. *The Internet Classics Archive*, http://classics.mit.edu/Aristotle/metaphysics.7.vii.html

Arnold, Matthew. "Shelley." *Essays in Criticism: Second Series*, *Works*. London: Macmillan, 1903, 14:185.

Ashton, Dore. *A Critical Study of Philip Guston*. Berkeley and Los Angeles: University of California Press, 1976.

Attridge, Derek. "Literary Form and the Demands of Politics: Otherness in J. M. Coetzee's *Age of Iron*." in George Levine, ed., *Aesthetics and Ideology*. New Brunswick, NJ: Rutgers University Press, 1994, 243–63.

Auden, W. H. "Squares and Oblongs." in Charles Feidelson, Jr. and Richard Ellmann, eds., *The Modern Tradition: Backgrounds of Modern Literature*. New York: Oxford UP, 1965, 209–14.

——. *The Collected Poetry of W. H. Auden*. New York: Random House, 1945.

Augustine. *Basic Writings of Saint Augustine, Volume One: The Confessions and Twelve Treatises*, Whitney J. Oates, ed., New York: Random House, 1948.

Bachrach, Bernard S. "Medieval." *The American Historical Review*, 84:3 (June 1979), 724–5.

Barany, Michael. "Mathematical Ideality and the Practice of Translation." Unpublished. Used by kind permission of the author.

——. "The Proof is in the Putting: Testimony, Belief, and Why Mathematicians Make Bad Witnesses." Unpublished. Used by kind permission of the author.

Barany, Michael and Donald MacKenzie. "Chalk: Materials and Concepts in Mathematics Research." in Catelijne Coopmans, Michael Lynch, Janet Vertesi, and Steve Woolgar, eds., under revision for *New Representation in Scientific Practice*, Forthcoming, MIT Press.

Barthes, Roland. "L'Effet de Réel," *Communications* 11 (1968), 84–9.

——. *The Responsibility of Forms: Critical Essays on Music, Art, and Representation*, trans. Richard Howard. Berkeley and Los Angeles: University of California Press, 1991.

Benjamin, Walter. "The Work of Art in the Age of Mechanical Reproduction." in Hannah Arendt, ed., *Illuminations: Essays and Reflections*. New York: Schocken Books, 1969, 217–52.

Benveniste, Emile. *Problems in General Linguistics*, trans. Mary Elizabeth Meek, 2 vols. Coral Gables, Fla.: University of Miami Press,1971.

Benziger, James. "Organic Unity: Leibniz to Coleridge." *PMLA* 66:2 (March 1951), 24–48.

Berryman, John. *Collected Poems, 1937–1971*, Charles Thornbury, ed., New York: Faber and Faber, 1991.

——. "Prufrock's Dilemma." John Berryman, *The Freedom of the Poet*. New York: Farrar Straus Giroux, 1976, 270–78.

Best, Stephen and Sharon Marcus. "Surface Reading: An Introduction." *Representations*, 108:1 (Fall 2009), 1–21.

Blackmur, R. P. Rev. of Norman Macleod, "Horizons of Death." *Poetry* 46:2 (May 1935), 108–12.

Bogel, Fredric V. "Dulness Unbound: Rhetoric and Pope's *Dunciad.* " *PMLA* 97:5 (October 1982), 844–55.

——. *The Difference Satire Makes: Rhetoric and Reading from Jonson to Byron*. Ithaca and London: Cornell UP, 2001.

——. "Understanding Prose." in Fredric V. Bogel and Katherine K. Gottschalk, eds., *Teaching Prose: A Guide for Writing Instructors*. New York and London: Norton, 1984, 155–215.

Boswell, James. *Boswell's Life of Johnson, Together with Boswell's Journal of a Tour to the Hebrides and Johnson's Diary of a Journey into North Wales*, ed. George Birkbeck Hill and rev. L. F. Powell. 2nd ed. Oxford: Clarendon Press, 1964–1971.

Brooks, Cleanth. "Empson's Criticism." *Accent* 4 (Summer 1944), 208–16.

——. *Historical Evidence and the Reading of Seventeenth-Century Poetry*. Columbia, MO and London: University of Missouri Press, 1991.

——. *Modern Poetry and the Tradition*. Chapel Hill: University of North Carolina Press, 1939.

——. "My Credo – The Formalist Critics." *Kenyon Review* 13 (Winter 1951), 72–81.

——. *The Well Wrought Urn: Studies in the Structure of Poetry*. New York: Harcourt, 1947.

Brooks, Cleanth and Robert Penn Warren. *Understanding Poetry: An Anthology for College Students*, rev. ed. New York: Henry Holt and Co., 1953.

Brooks, Peter, "Aesthetics and Ideology – What Happened to Poetics?" in George Levine, ed., *Aesthetics and Ideology*. New Brunswick, NJ: Rutgers UP, 1994, 153–67.

Bruster, Douglas. "Shakespeare and the Composite Text." in Mark David Rasmussen, ed., *Renaissance Literature and its Formal Engagements*. New York: Palgrave, 2002, 43–66.

——. "The Materiality of Shakespearean Form." in Stephen Cohen, ed., *Shakespeare and Historical Formalism*. Aldershot, England: Ashgate, 2007, 31–48.

Burke, Kenneth. *A Grammar of Motives and A Rhetoric of Motives*. Cleveland and New York. World Publishing Company, 1962.

Burke, Kenneth. *The Philosophy of Literary Form: Studies in Symbolic Action*, rev. ed. New York: Random House, 1957.

Butt, John, ed. *The Poems of Alexander Pope*. New Haven and London: Yale UP, 1963.

Cain, William E. *The Crisis in Criticism: Theory, Literature, and Reform in English Studies*. Baltimore: Johns Hopkins UP, 1984.

Carretta, Vincent, ed. *Phillis Wheatley: Complete Writings*. New York: Penguin, 2001.

Caruth, Cathy. "Introduction: The Insistence of Reference" in Cathy Caruth and Deborah Esch, eds., *Critical Encounters: Reference and Responsibility in Deconstructive Writing*. New Brunswick: Rutgers UP, 1995, 1–8.

Cassirer, Ernst. *Language and Myth*, trans. Susanne K. Langer. New York: Harper and Brothers, 1946.

——. *The Philosophy of Symbolic Forms, Volume Two: Mythical Thought*, trans. Ralph Manheim. New Haven and London: Yale UP, 1955.

Caudwell, Christopher. *Illusion and Reality: A Study of the Sources of Poetry*. New York: International Publishers, 1937.

Chandler, James. *England in 1819: The Politics of Literary Culture and the Case of Romantic Historicism*. Chicago: University of Chicago Press, 1998.

Clark, Michael P. "Introduction" in Michael P. Clark, ed., *The Revenge of the Aesthetic: The Place of Literature in Theory Today*. Berkeley and Los Angeles: University of California Press, 2000, 1–24.

Cohen, Ralph. "History and Genre." *New Literary History* 17 (1986), 203–18.

Cohen, Stephen. "Between Form and Culture: New Historicism and the Promise of a Historical Formalism." in Mark David Rasmussen, ed., *Renaissance Literature and its Formal Engagements*. New York: Palgrave, 2002, 17–41.

Cohen, Stephen, ed. *Shakespeare and Historical Formalism*. Aldershot, England: Ashgate, 2007.

Coleridge, Samuel Taylor, James Engell, and W. Jackson Bate, eds., *Biographia Literaria*. Princeton: Princeton UP, 1983.

Croce, Benedetto. *Aesthetic as Science of Expression and General Linguistic*, trans. Douglas Ainslie, 2nd. ed. London: Macmillan, 1922.

Culler, Jonathan. "Apostrophe" in Jonathan Culler, ed., *The Pursuit of Signs*. London: Routledge, 1981, 149–71.

——. "In Defence of Overinterpretation." in Umberto Eco, with Richard Rorty, Jonathan Culler, Christine Brooke-Rose, Stefan Collini, eds., *Interpretation and Overinterpretation*. Cambridge: Cambridge UP, 1992, 109–23.

——. *Literary Theory: A Very Short Introduction*. Oxford and New York: Oxford UP, 1997.

——. "The Closeness of Close Reading." *ADFL Bulletin* 41:3 (2011), 8–13.

——. *The Literary in Theory*. Stanford: Stanford UP, 2007.

Cuomo, Mario. "1984 Democratic National Convention Keynote Address." http://www.americanrhetoric.com/speeches/mariocuomo1984dnc.htm

Curran, Stuart. *Poetic Form and British Romanticism*. New York and Oxford: Oxford UP, 1986.

Daniel, Stephen H. "Notes for PHIL 251: Intro to Philosophy – Epistemology: Kant and Theories of Truth." http://philosophy.tamu.edu/~sdaniel/Notes/epi-kant.html

Davies, Kevin. *Comp*. Washington, DC: Edge Books, 2000.

Davis, Colin. *Critical Excess: Overreading in Derrida, Deleuze, Levinas, Žižek and Cavell*. Stanford: Stanford UP, 2010.

de Man, Paul. *Allegories of Reading: Figural Language in Rousseau, Nietzsche, Rilke and Proust*. New Haven and London: Yale UP, 1979.

——. "Semiology and Rhetoric." *Diacritics*, 3:3 (Autumn 1973), 27–33.

——. *The Resistance to Theory*. Minneapolis: University of Minnesota Press, 1986.

Derrida, Jacques. *Of Grammatology*, trans. Gayatri Chakravorty Spivak. Baltimore and London: The Johns Hopkins UP, 1976.

——. *Speech and Phenomena and Other Essays on Husserl's Theory of Signs*, trans. David Allison. Evanston: Northwestern UP, 1973.

——. "The Law of Genre," trans. Avitall Ronell. *Critical Inquiry*, 7:1 (Autumn 1980), 55–81.

DiBattista, Maria. "'Sabbath Eyes': Ideology and the Writer's Gaze." George Levine, ed., *Aesthetics and Ideology*. New Brunswick, NJ: Rutgers UP, 1994, 168–87.

Dickens, Charles. *Great Expectations*. Jill Kriegel, ed., San Francisco: Ignatius Press, 2010.

Donoghue, Denis. *Speaking of Beauty*. New Haven and London: Yale UP, 2003.

——. *Walter Pater: Lover of Strange Souls*. New York: Knopf, 1995.

Dryden, John and George R. Noyes, ed., *The Poetical Works of John Dryden*. Boston: Houghton Mifflin, 1909.

Dubrow, Heather. "Foreword." in Verena Theile and Linda Tredennick, eds., *New Formalisms and Literary Theory*. Basingstoke, England: Palgrave Macmillan, 2013, vii–xviii.

——. "Guess Who's Coming to Dinner: Reinterpreting Formalism and the Country House Poem." in Susan J. Wolfson and Marshall Brown, eds., *Reading for Form*. Seattle and London: University of Washington press, 2006, 80–98.

——. "The Politics of Aesthetics: Recuperating Formalism and the Country House Poem." in Mark David Rasmussen, ed., *Renaissance Literature and its Formal Engagements*. New York: Palgrave, 2002, 67–88.

Dutton, Denis. "Mad About Flowers: Elaine Scarry on Beauty." *Philosophy and Literature* 24 (2000), 249–60, http://denisdutton.com/scarry_review.htm

Eagleton, Terry. *How to Read a Poem*. Oxford: Blackwell, 2007.

Easthope, Antony. *Poetry as Discourse*. London and New York: Methuen, 1983.

Eliot, T. S. and Frank Kermode, ed., *Selected Prose of T. S. Eliot*. San Diego, New York, London: Harvest Books, 1975.

Ellis, John M. *The Theory of Literary Criticism: A Logical Analysis*. Berkeley and Los Angeles: University of California Press, 1974.

Empson, William. *Seven Types of Ambiguity*. New York: New Directions, 1966.

——. "Wit in the *Essay on Criticism*." in William Empson, ed., *The Structure of Complex Words* Ann Arbor: University of Michigan Press, 1967, 84–100. First published in *Hudson Review* 2 (1950): 559–77.

Ensor, Sarah. "Spinster Ecology: Rachel Carson, Sarah Orne Jewett, and Nonreproductive Futurity." *American Literature*, 84:2 (2012), 409–35.

Felman, Shoshana. *Jacques Lacan and the Adventure of Insight: Psychoanalysis in Contemporary Culture*. Cambridge, MA: Harvard UP, 1987.

Finneran, Richard J., ed., *W. B. Yeats: The Poems. A New Edition*. NY: Macmillan, 1983.

Fish, Stanley. *Is There a Text in This Class? The Authority of Interpretive Communities*. Cambridge, MA, and London: Harvard UP, 1980.

Focillon, Henri. *The Life of Forms in Art*, trans. Charles B. Hogan and George Kubler. New York: Zone Books, 1992.

——. *Vie des Formes*. Paris: Ernst Leroux, 1934.

Forrest-Thomson, Veronica. *Poetic Artifice: A Theory of Twentieth-Century Poetry*. Manchester: Manchester UP, 1978.

Foster, Roger. "Lingering with the Particular: *Minima Moralia*'s Critical Modernism." *Telos* 155 (Summer 2011), 83–103.

Freud, Sigmund Freud. *New Introductory Lectures on Psycho-analysis*, trans. James Strachey. New York and London: Norton, 1990.

Fried, Debra. "Andromeda Unbound: Gender and Genre in Millay's Sonnets." *Twentieth-Century Literature* 32:1 (Spring 1986), 1–22.

——. "The Stanza: Echo Chambers" in Erik Martiny, ed., *A Companion to Poetic Genre*. Oxford: Wiley-Blackwell, 2012, 53–63.

Fried, Michael. *Roger Fry's Formalism*. http://www.tannerlectures.utah.edu/lectures/documents/volume24/fried_2001.pdf

Frost, Robert. "Education by Poetry." in Hyde Cox and Edward Connery Lathem, eds., *Selected Prose of Robert Frost*, New York: Collier Books, 1968, 33–46.

Frye, Northrop. *Anatomy of Criticism: Four Essays*. Princeton: Princeton UP, 1957.

——. "On Value-Judgements." in Northrop Frye, *The Stubborn Structure: Essays on Criticism and Society*. Ithaca, N.Y.: Cornell UP, 1970.

——. *The Educated Imagination*. Bloomington and London: Indiana UP, 1964.

Gallagher, Catherine. "The History of Literary Criticism." *Daedalus* 126:1 (Winter 1997), 133–53.

Gallop, Jane. "The Ethics of Reading: Close Encounters." *Journal of Curriculum Theorizing*, 16:3 (2000), 7–17.

Galperin, William H. *The Historical Austen*. Philadelphia: University of Pennsylvania Press, 2003.

Garber, Marjorie. "Shakespeare in Slow Motion." *Profession* 2010, 151–64.

Gates, Henry Louis, Jr. *The Trials of Phillis Wheatley*. New York: Basic Books, 2003.

Gill, Stephen, ed. *William Wordsworth*. Oxford and New York: Oxford UP, 1990.

Ginsborg, Hanna. "Kant's Aesthetics and Teleology." *Stanford Encyclopedia of Philosophy*, §2. http://plato.stanford.edu/entries/kant-aesthetics/

Goodman, Nelson. *Ways of Worldmaking*. Indianapolis: Hackett, 1978.

Greene, Roland, ed. *The Princeton Encyclopedia of Poetry and Poetics*, 4th ed. Princeton and Oxford: Princeton UP, 2012.

Haffenden, John. *William Empson: Among the Mandarins*. Oxford and New York: Oxford UP, 2005.

Hartman, Geoffrey H. "Beyond Formalism." *MLN*, 81:5 (December 1966), 542–56.

——. *Beyond Formalism: Literary Essays 1958–1970*. New Haven and London: Yale UP, 1970.

——. *Criticism in the Wilderness: The Study of Literature Today*. New Haven and London: Yale UP, 1980.

——. "The Voice of the Shuttle: Language from the Point of View of Literature." in *Beyond Formalism*, 337–55.

——. Heilbroner, Robert L. *The Worldly Philosophers: The Lives, Times, and Ideas of the Great Economic Thinkers*, 7th ed., New York: Simon and Schuster, 1999.

Horace. *Ars Poetica*. D. A. Russell, trans. *The Norton Anthology of Theory and Criticism*, Vincent B. Leitch, general editor. New York and London: Norton, 2001, 121–35.

Horkheimer, Max, and Theodor W. Adorno. *Dialectic of Enlightenment: Philosophical Fragments*, ed. Gunzelin Schmid Noerr, trans. Edmund Jephcott. Stanford: Stanford UP, 2002. http://www.dartmouth.edu/~milton/reading_room/sonnets/sonnet_19/index.shtml

Hughes, Ted. *The Collected Poems*. Paul Keegan, ed., New York: Farrar, Straus and Giroux, 2003.

Hunter, J. Paul. "Formalism and History: Binarism and the Anglophone Couplet." *MLQ* 61:1 (March 2000), 109–29.

Hunter, William B., Jr., ed. *The Complete Poetry of Ben Jonson*. New York: W. W. Norton and Co., 1968.

Jakobson, Roman. "Closing Statement: Linguistics and Poetics" in Thomas A. Sebeok, ed., *Style in Language*. Cambridge, MA: MIT Press, 1960, 350–77.

James, Henry. "Preface to *Roderick Hudson*" in R. P. Blackmur, ed., *The Art of the Novel: Critical Prefaces by Henry James*. New York and London: Charles Scribner's Sons, 1934, 3–19.

Jameson, Fredric. "The Ideology of the Text." *The Ideologies of Theory*. Minneapolis: University of Minnesota Press1987, 17–71.

——. *The Political Unconscious*. Ithaca, N.Y.: Cornell, UP, 1981.

Jarvis, Simon. *Adorno: A Critical Introduction*. Cambridge: Polity Press, 1998.

Johnson, Barbara. *A World of Difference*. Baltimore and London: Johns Hopkins UP, 1987.

——. "Teaching Deconstructively" in G. Douglas Atkins and Michael L. Johnson, eds., *Writing and Reading Differently*. Lawrence, Kansas: University Press of Kansas, 1985, 140–48.

——. *The Critical Difference: Essays in the Contemporary Rhetoric of Reading*. Baltimore: Johns Hopkins UP, 1980.

Johnson, Samuel. "Life of Cowley" in M. H. Abrams *et al.*, eds., *The Norton Anthology of English Literature*, 7th ed. New York and London: Norton, 2000, I:2737.

——. "Preface to The Plays of William Shakespeare" in Frank Brady and W. K. Wimsatt, eds., *Samuel Johnson: Selected Poetry and Prose*. Berkeley and Los Angeles, London: University of California Press, 1977, 299–335.

Jollimore, Troy A. *Love's Vision*. Princeton: Princeton UP, 2011.

Jones, Frederick L., ed. *The Letters of Percy Bysshe Shelley*. Oxford: Clarendon Press, 1964.

Juhl, P. D. *Interpretation: An Essay in the Philosophy of Literary Criticism*. Princeton: Princeton UP, 1986.

Kant, Immanuel. *Critique of Pure Reason*, F. Max Müller, trans. Garden City, N.Y.: Doubleday, 1966.

Kaufman, Robert. "Everybody Hates Kant: Blakean Formalism and the Symmetries of Laura Moriarty." *MLQ* 61:1 (March 2000), 131–55.

——. "On Susan J. Wolfson's *Formal Charges: The Shaping of Poetry in British Romanticism.*" *Romantic Circles Reviews* 4:1 (2001), 25 pars. 15 January http:/www.rc.umd.edu/reviews/wolfson.html

Keach, William. *Arbitrary Power: Romanticism, Language, Politics.* Princeton: Princeton UP, 2004.

——. " 'Words Are Things': Romantic Ideology and the Matter of Poetic Language" in George Levine, ed., *Aesthetics and Ideology.* New Brunswick, NJ: Rutgers UP, 1994, 219–39.

Keats, John. "Bright Star" in Margaret Ferguson, Mary Jo Salter, Jon Stallworthy, eds., *The Norton Anthology of Poetry*, shorter 4th ed. New York and London: W. W. Norton, 1997, 514.

——. *Selected Letters*, Robert Gittings, ed., Oxford and New York: Oxford UP, 2002.

Kermode, Frank. *The Sense of an Ending: Studies in the Theory of Fiction.* New York: Oxford UP, 1967.

——. *The Genesis of Secrecy: On the Interpretation of Narrative.* Cambridge: Harvard UP, 1979.

Kernan, Alvin. *In Plato's Cave.* New Haven and London: Yale UP, 1999.

Knapp, Steven. *Literary Interest: The Limits of Anti-Formalism.* Cambridge, MA, and London: Harvard UP, 1993.

Knapp, Steven and Walter Benn Michaels. "Against Theory." *Critical Inquiry*, 8:4 (Summer 1982), 723–42.

Kramer, Lawrence, ed. *Hart Crane's "The Bridge": An Annotated Edition.* New York: Fordham UP, 2011.

Kuhn, Thomas S. *The Structure of Scientific Revolutions.* Chicago: University of Chicago Press, 1962.

Lanham, Richard A. "*At* and *Through*: The Opaque Style and Its Uses" in Richard A. Lanham, ed., *Literacy and the Survival of Humanism.* New Haven and London: Yale UP, 1983, 58–86.

Leighton, Angela. "About About: On Poetry and Paraphrase." *Midwest Studies in Philosophy*, 33 (2009), 167–76.

——. *On Form: Poetry, Aestheticism, and the Legacy of a Word.* Oxford and New York: Oxford UP, 2007.

Lentricchia, Frank and Andrew Dubois, eds., *Close Reading: The Reader.* Durham, NC: Duke UP, 2003.

Levine, Caroline Levine. "Scaled Up, Writ Small: A Response to Carolyn Dever and Herbert F. Tucker." *Victorian Studies*, 49:1 (Autumn 2006), 100–05.

——. "Strategic Formalism: Toward a New Method in Cultural Studies." *Victorian Studies*, 48:4 (Summer 2006), 625–57.

Levine, George. "Introduction: Reclaiming the Aesthetic" in George Levine, ed., *Aesthetics and Ideology.* New Brunswick, NJ: Rutgers UP, 1994, 1–28.

Levinson, Marjorie. Unpublished Talk, School of Criticism and Theory, Cornell University. August 2007.

——. "What is New Formalism? Long Version." Available online at http://sitemaker.umich.edu/pmla_article

——. "What is New Formalism?" *PMLA*, 122 (2007): 558–69.

——. Unpublished talk, School of Criticism and Theory, Cornell University, Summer 2012.

Lewis, Philip E. "Review: Athletic Criticism," *Diacritics*, 1:2 (Winter 1971), 2–6.

Liu, Alan. "The Power of Formalism: The New Historicism." *ELH* 56:4 (1989), 721–71.

Lodge, David. *Language of Fiction: Essays in Criticism and Verbal Analysis of the English Novel*. New York: Columbia UP, 1966.

Loesberg, Jonathan. "Cultural Studies, Victorian Studies, and Formalism." *Victorian Literature and Culture*, 27:2 (1999), 537–44.

Macé, Marielle. "Ways of Reading, Modes of Being." *New Literary History*, 2013, 44: 213–229.

Mack, Maynard. " 'Wit and Poetry and Pope': Some Observations on His Imagery" in James L. Clifford and Louis A. Landa, eds., *Pope and His Contemporaries: Essays Presented to George Sherburn*. Oxford: Clarendon Press, 1949, 20–40.

MacLeish, Archibald. "Ars Poetica." Archibald MacLeish, *Collected Poems 1917–1982*. Boston: Houghton Mifflin, 1985, 106–7.

Mao, Douglas. "The New Critics and the Text-Object." *ELH* 63.1 (1996), 227–54.

McIntyre, John and Miranda Hickman, eds., *Rereading the New Criticism*. Columbus: Ohio State UP, 2012.

Merleau-Ponty, Maurice and Richard C. McCleary, trans., *Signs*. Evanston: Northwestern UP, 1964.

Metzger, Mary Janell. "Teaching Shakespeare and the Uses of Historical Formalism." Stephen Cohen, ed., *Shakespeare and Historical Formalism*. Aldershot, England: Ashgate, 2007, 195–208.

Michaels, Walter Benn. "Saving the Text: Reference and Belief." *MLN*, 93:5 (December 1978), 771–93.

Mill, John Stuart. "What is Poetry?" M. H. Abrams and Stephen Greenblatt, eds., *The Norton Anthology of English Literature*, 7th edition, vol. 2. New York: W. W. Norton and Co. 1143.

Miller, J. Hillis. "The Critic as Host." *Critical Inquiry*, 3:3 (Spring 1977), 439–47.

——. "The Ethics of Reading." Julian Wolfreys, ed., *The J. Hillis Miller Reader*. Stanford: Stanford UP, 2005, 17–76.

——. *The Linguistic Moment: From Wordsworth to Stevens*. Princeton: Princeton UP, 1985.

Miller, Jonathan. *The Body in Question*. New York: Random House, 1978.

Mitchell, W. J. T. "The Commitment to Form; Or, Still Crazy after All These Years." *PMLA* 118:2 (March 2003), 321–5.

Mukarovsky, Jan. "Poetic Designation and the Aesthetic Function of Language." John Burbank and Peter Steiner, eds., *The Word and Verbal Art*. New Haven and London: Yale UP, 1977.

Nehamas, Alexander. *Only a Promise of Happiness: The Place of Beauty in a World of Art*. Princeton: Princeton UP, 2010.

——. "What An Author Is." *Journal of Philosophy*, 83 (January 1986), 685–91.

Newman, John Henry, Cardinal and Svaglic, Martin J., ed., *The Idea of a University*. New York: Holt, Rinehart, Winston, 1964.

Ogden, C. K., I. A. Richards, James Wood. *The Foundations of Aesthetics*, 2nd ed. New York: International Publishers, 1925.

Ong, Walter, S. J., "The Jinnee in the Well-Wrought Urn." *Essays in Criticism* IV (July 1954), 309–20.

——. "Wit and Mystery: A Revaluation in Mediaeval Hymnody." *Speculum* XXI (July 1947), 310–41.

Otter, Samuel. "An Aesthetics in All Things." *Representations*, 104:1 (Fall 2008), 116–25.

Pennanen, Esko V. *Contributions to the Study of Back-formation in English*. *Acta Academiae Socialis ser. A* vol. 4 Julkaisija Yhteiskunnallinen Korkeakoulu Tampere, 1966.

Phillips, Dana. "Ecocriticism, Literary Theory, and the Truth of Ecology." *New Literary History*, 30:3 (Summer 1999), 577–602.

——. *The Truth of Ecology: Nature, Culture, and Literature in America*. Oxford: Oxford UP, 2003.

Plotinus. *Ennead* I.vi.8, Stephen MacKenna, trans. London: Faber and Faber, 1917–30.

Pollock, Anthony. "Formalist Cultural Criticism and the Post-Restoration Periodical." *PQ* 86:3 (2007), 227–250.

Poovey, Mary. "The Model System of Contemporary Literary Criticism." *Critical Inquiry* 27 (Spring 2001), 410, 432.

Pope, Alexander and Norman Ault, ed., *The Prose Works of Alexander Pope, 1711–1720*. Oxford: Blackwell, 1936.

——. W. Elwin and W. J. Courthope, eds., *The Works of Alexander Pope*. Vol. 10. London, 1886.

Ransom, John Crowe. *The New Criticism*. Norfolk, CT: New Directions, 1941.

——. *The World's Body*. New York and London: Charles Scribner's Sons, 1938.

Rasmussen, Mark David, ed. *Renaissance Literature and its Formal Engagements*. New York: Palgrave, 2002.

Rauschenberg, Robert. "Migration." *Johnson Museum of Art*. Cornell University, 2011. http://museum.cornell.edu/collections/view/migration.html

Rawson, C. J. "Order and Cruelty: A Reading of Swift (with Some Comments on Pope and Johnson)." *Essays in Criticism* 20 (1970), 24–56.

Reiman, Donald H. and Neil Fraistat, eds., *Shelley's Poetry and Prose*, 2nd edition. New York: W. W. Norton and Co., 2002.

Richards, I. A. *Practical Criticism: A Study of Literary Judgment*. San Diego, New York, London: Harcourt Brace, n.d.

Rooney Ellen. "Form and Contentment." Susan J. Wolfson and Marshall Brown, eds., *Reading for Form*. Seattle and London: University of Washington Press, 2006.

Russo, John Paul. *I. A. Richards: His Life and Work*. Baltimore: Johns Hopkins UP, 1989.

Sahlins, Marshall. *Culture and Practical Reason*. Chicago: University of Chicago Press, 1976.

Salusinszky, Imre, ed. *Criticism in Society*. New York and London: Methuen, 1987.

Savoy, Eric. "Restraining Order." *ECS: English Studies in Canada*, 29:1–2 (March/June 2003), 77–84.

——. "Subjunctive Biography." *The Henry James Review*, 27:3 (Fall 2006), 248–55.

Scarry, Elaine. *On Beauty and Being Just*. Princeton: Princeton UP, 1999.

Schweizer, Harold. "With Sabbath Eyes: The Particular and the Claims of History in Elizabeth Bishop's 'Poem.'" *Journal of Modern Literature*, 28:2 (Winter 2005), 49–60.

Shakespeare, William. *The Riverside Shakespeare*, 2nd. ed. G. Blakemore Evans and J. J. M. Tobin, New York: Houghton Mifflin, 1997.

Sharratt, Bernard. *Reading Relations*. Brighton: Harvester Press, 1982.

Simecek, Karen. "Hearing Meaning and Poetry: An Interview with Angela Leighton." *Postgraduate Journal of Aesthetics* 9:3 (Summer 2012), 3–14.

Smith, Barbara Herrnstein. *On the Margins of Discourse: The Relation of Literature to Language*. Chicago: University of Chicago Press, 1978.

Sontag, Susan. *Against Interpretation and Other Essays*. New York: Farrar, Straus, and Giroux, 1966.

Spurlin, William J. "Afterword: An Interview with Cleanth Brooks." William J. Spurlin and Michael Fischer, eds., *The New Criticism and Contemporary Literary Theory*. New York: Garland, 1995, 365–83.

Stampfel, Barry. "Hans Vaihinger's Ghostly Presence in Contemporary Literary Studies." *Criticism*, 40 (Summer 1998), 437–54. http://findarticles.com/p/articles/mi_m2220/is_n3_v40/ai_21182132

Štekauer, Pavol. *English Word-Formation*. Tübingen: Gunter Narr, 2000.

Stevens, Wallace. "The Idea of Order at Key West." Margaret Ferguson, Mary Jo Salter, Jon Stallworthy, eds., *The Norton Anthology of Poetry*, shorter 4th edition. New York and London: W. W. Norton, 1997, 725–6.

Stewart, Garrett. "The Foreign Offices of British Fiction." Susan J. Wolfson and Marshall Brown, eds., *Reading for Form*. Seattle and London: University of Washington Press, 2006, 256–82.

——. "Staying Powers" *MLQ* 54:2, 295–306.

Sting (Gordon Sumner). "If You Love Somebody, Set Them Free." *AZLyrics*. http://www.azlyrics.com/lyrics/sting/ifyoulovesomebodysetthemfree.html

Strier, Richard. "How Formalism Became a Dirty Word, and Why We Can't Do Without It." Mark David Rasmussen, ed., *Renaissance Literature and Its Formal Engagements*. New York: Palgrave, 2002, 207–15.

——. *Resistant Structures: Particularity, Radicalism, and Renaissance Texts*. Berkeley, Los Angeles, London: University of California Press, 1995.

Tate, Allen. "Remarks on the Southern Religion." Twelve Southerners, *I'll Take My Stand: The South and the Agrarian Tradition*. New York and London: Harper and Row, 1930, 155–75.

Terada, Rae. *Looking Away: Phenomenality and Dissatisfaction, Kant to Adorno*. Cambridge, MA, and London: Harvard UP, 2009.

Theile, Verena and Linda Tredennick, eds., *New Formalisms and Literary Theory*. Hampshire, England: Palgrave Macmillan, 2013.

Tiersma, Peter Meijes. "Local and General Markedness." *Language*, 58:4 (December 1982), 832–84.

Tolkien, J. R. R. *The Return of the King*. New York: Ballantine Books, 1965.

Tuchman, Barbara W. *A Distant Mirror: The Calamitous 14th Century*. New York: Ballantine Books, 1978.

Tucker, Herbert F. "Tactical Formalism: A Response to Caroline Levine." *Victorian Studies*, 49:1 (Autumn 2006), 85–93.

Urban, Willard Marshall. *Language and Reality: The Philosophy of Language and the Principles of Symbolism*. New York: Macmillan, 1939.

Vaihinger, Hans. C. K. Ogden, trans., *The Philosophy of "As If,"* 2nd ed. London: Routledge and Kegan Paul, 1935.

Valéry, Paul. "Léonard et les Philosophes." *Morceaux Choisis*. Paris: Gallimard, 1930, 98–111.

Veblen, Thorstein. *The Theory of the Leisure Class*. New York: Modern Library, 1961.

Wade, Allan, ed. *The Letters of W. B. Yeats*. London: Rupert Hart-Davis, 1954.

Weinsheimer, Joel. *Philosophical Hermeneutics and Literary Theory*. New Haven and London: Yale UP, 1991.

Wellek, René. *A History of Modern Criticism: 1750–1950*. New Haven and London: Yale UP, 1986.

Wellek, René and Austin Warren. *Theory of Literature*, 3rd edition. New York: Harcourt Brace, 1956.

Wimsatt, W. K., and two preliminary essays written in collaboration with Monroe C. Beardsley. *The Verbal Icon: Studies in the Meaning of Poetry*. Lexington: The University Press of Kentucky, 1954.

Wimsatt, William K. and Cleanth Brooks. *Literary Criticism: A Short History*. New York: Knopf, 1957.

Wittgenstein, Ludwig, G. E. M. Anscombe, and G. H. von Wright, eds., *Zettel*. G. E. M. Anscombe, trans., Berkeley and Los Angeles: University of California Press, 1970.

——. G. H. von Wright, R. Rhees, G. E. M. Anscombe, eds., *Remarks on the Foundations of Mathematics*. G. E. M. Anscombe, trans., Oxford: Basil Blackwell, 1956.

Wolfson, Susan. *Formal Charges: The Shaping of Poetry in British Romanticism* Stanford: Stanford UP, 1997.

——. "Popular Songs and Ballads: Writing the 'Unwritten Story' in 1819." Michael O'Neill and Anthony Howen, eds., with the assistance of Madeleine Callaghan, *The Oxford Handbook of Percy Bysshe Shelley*. Oxford: Oxford UP, 2012, 341–59.

——. "Reading for Form without Formalism." *Literary Matters* 3:2 (2010), 2–15.

Wolfson, Susan J. and Marshall Brown, eds., *Reading for Form*. Seattle and London: University of Washington Press, 2006.

Index

Note: The letters 'n' following locators refer to notes respectively

Printed and bound in the United States of America